More Praise for *Shame*

"Dr. Burgo wants us to stop being ashamed of feeling shame! His new book illuminates the concept of shame as a normal part of life that can be instructive, instead of toxic. Shame is an ubiquitous emotion that must be recognized and understood, not denied and buried. Dr. Burgo shares personal experiences and his work with his patients to describe how shame can crush self-esteem and intensify anxiety. This book describes exercises that can help you overcome the harmful manifestations of experiencing shame and can provide ways to use the emotion to build and share self-pride."

—Jerold J. Kreisman, M.D., author of *I Hate You—Don't Leave Me*

"Dr. Joseph Burgo has written a powerful book which will be a boon to readers everywhere. Drawing on cutting-edge research and thirty-five years of experience as a therapist, he carefully builds a case for why we need to move away from seeing shame as a single and toxic emotion and, instead, understand it as a complex of emotions which, counterintuitively, can help us embrace our true selves and experience greater joy in living. Burgo is a fine storyteller with great empathy, and the stories of patients (and, yes, his own) vividly demonstrate how facing shame is the well-spring of true respect and pride in the self. His argument is by the far the most cogent in explaining why the notion of self-esteem being founded in constant praise and lack of criticism is both wrong-headed and ultimately destructive. Step by step, Burgo shows us both how to give voice to the feelings of shame that have been holding us back and to bolster our ability to identify what we're feeling with precision. On every page, but especially in the unique exercises at the end, *Shame* encourages us again and again to look not just at what shames us but why it does and to face both squarely. It's a book I will recommend to my readers without a single reservation."

—Peg Streep, author of *Daughter Detox*

"*Shame* delivers on an unanswered prayer for so many who suffer silently. The distinctions and layers of discovery about human identity is a godsend. This book takes you deeper to understanding not only yourself, but the makeup of family and workplace dynamics where shame is dispensed and consumed to a fault. Read this to shed the burden of shame and be free!"

—Laura Berman Fortgang, author of
Now What?: 90 Days to a New Life Direction

SHAME

FREE YOURSELF, FIND JOY, AND BUILD TRUE SELF-ESTEEM

JOSEPH BURGO, PH.D.

ST. MARTIN'S PRESS ☙ NEW YORK

www.stmartins.com

Designed by Steven Seighman

Library of Congress Cataloging-in-Publication Data is available upon request.

ISBN 978-1-250-15130-8 (hardcover)
ISBN 978-1-250-15131-5 (ebook)

Our books may be purchased in bulk for promotional, educational, or business use. Please contact your local bookseller or the Macmillan Corporate and Premium Sales Department at 1-800-221-7945, extension 5442, or by email at MacmillanSpecialMarkets@macmillan.com.

First Edition: November 2018

10 9 8 7 6 5 4 3 2 1

For my beautiful sons

CONTENTS

INTRODUCTION

IMAGINE YOURSELF AT A SOCIAL gathering with people you recently met and whose company you enjoy. Conversation is lively; everybody appears to be having a good time. When another guest makes a comment that reminds you of a funny story you once heard, you take advantage of the natural opening and begin to recount it. Because you remember how much you laughed when you first heard the story, you look forward to sharing your enjoyment with these new friends.

As you glance from face to face, anticipating their laughter, you finally reach the conclusion of your story.

Silence.

After a moment somebody says, "Oh, I see—that's funny." Still, no one laughs.

You suddenly feel yourself blushing as your face goes hot. You glance down and avoid making eye contact with any of the other guests. You feel briefly confused, your thoughts unfocused and disorderly. You wish you'd never told the story and that you could disappear. When another guest changes the subject and conversation moves on, you feel relieved that group attention has shifted, and you soon recover. No more than seven or eight seconds have passed since you finished your story.

What is the name of the emotion you felt when that story fell flat?

If I tell you that you felt a type of shame, you'll probably object by say-ing, "That's not shame, that's embarrassment." Most people react this way when I use the word *shame* to describe such an experience. They might insist there's no reason to feel shame about something so minor. Everyone occasionally tells a joke that turns out to be a dud. Embarrassing, of course, but nothing to feel ashamed about.

Yet, from Darwin onward, researchers who study the biology of emo-tion widely agree that the mental and physiological symptoms you experi-enced during those awkward seconds unambiguously denote the emotion of shame. Human beings everywhere, in every culture and on every con-tinent the world over, experience shame in exactly the same way: gaze aversion, brief mental confusion, and a longing to disappear, usually ac-companied by blushing of the face, neck, or chest.

What scientists understand and believe about shame differs broadly from the way a layperson conceives of it. Most people tend to view shame as something big and bad, a toxic emotion we hope never to feel—SHAME written in scary capital letters.

SHAME lays waste to a person's sense of well-being.

SHAME is inflicted on children by abusive parents.

SHAME strikes when society rejects those who cannot help being dif-ferent.

In contrast, researchers who study the emotions, including me, conceive of shame as more varied in nature and not always so imposing—an entire family of emotions, as Léon Wurmser describes it in *The Mask of Shame*. To feel shame can be agonizing or just slightly unpleasant; it might be transient or enduring.

I'll be using the word *shame* in this larger sense—as an overarching category that includes a variety of specific emotions. It might help to think of this latter experience as *shame* written in benign lowercase letters, in contrast to SHAME.

Most preeminent books in the field of popular psychology, some of which you may have read, focus on SHAME as a largely destructive force. This book will introduce you to the entire shame family of emotions (including embarrassment, guilt, and self-consciousness), which are unavoidable aspects of everyday life and not always toxic. You will learn to recognize the ways we typically speak of shame without ever using the word itself. When we say that we feel bad about some aspect of ourselves, for example—our bodies, our behavior, or our failures—we're usually alluding to some member of the shame family of emotions.

People react to shame in varying ways, influenced by how they were socialized as children and the methods they learned for managing their pain. Our different responses also depend upon the degree of confidence we feel in our personal worth: those of us who grew up in an atmosphere that was far from optimal and who struggle to feel good about ourselves may experience the telling of a failed joke—what might have caused mild embarrassment for someone else—as a source of SHAME.

However we respond to it, each and every one of us deals with the shame family of emotions on a daily basis. Without always realizing it, we regularly anticipate potential shame in our interactions with other people and try to avoid it whenever possible. *How dressed up will the other guests be and what should I wear to the party? What will my boss say during my performance review? If I invite Sandra out for a drink after work, will she say no?* As the psychoanalyst and shame expert Donald Nathanson has described it, shame in all its varieties "is the hidden power behind much of what occupies us in everyday life."[1]

To help you enter more fully into this perspective, I invite you to consider and eventually shed a few preconceptions about shame that most of us share. Or perhaps you might reserve those preconceived views for SHAME and make room for a new concept: everyday, ordinary, and inevitable shame.

PRECONCEPTION I: SHAME IS BAD

Most of us find it difficult to acknowledge, even to ourselves, that we feel shame. The very word makes most people uncomfortable, as John Bradshaw, among many other researchers, has noted: "There is shame about shame. People will readily admit guilt, hurt or fear before they will admit shame."[2] Especially today, in our narcissistic age, when so many people feel compelled to come across as social media winners, if you admit to feeling shame, you run the risk of becoming a contemptible loser. In my experience most people feel uneasy about acknowledging their own feelings of shame and prefer to keep them at a distance, by denying their existence or referring to them with a word that doesn't carry such a strong negative charge. As the shame researcher Michael Lewis has noted, "We often use the term 'embarrassing' to avoid acknowledging shame."[3]

For this reason you may find yourself resisting the central message of this book—that shame is a pervasive and common experience in daily life. You might readily admit to feeling embarrassed about making a mistake in public, but you'll object when I describe it as a type of shame. *Everybody makes mistakes so what's the big deal? There's nothing to feel ashamed about.* At those moments try to remember the distinction between SHAME as a toxic, largely destructive, experience and shame as an entire family of emotions, many of them mild and fleeting, an unavoidable part of everyday life.

PRECONCEPTION 2: SHAME IS THE ENEMY

Since John Bradshaw published his groundbreaking work in 1988, the psychologically minded public has come to view shame as virtually synonymous with his concept of *toxic shame*—destructive messaging inflicted by parents, educators, and other significant adults in a child's life that leaves the youth with a sense of being defective and unworthy of love. Brené Brown's writings on unattainable (and ultimately shaming) ideals that society imposes on women, largely through advertising and conflicting role expectations, have contributed to this view of shame as the product of noxious external influences.

If you, like most people, have adopted this view, you may see shame as the enemy. You might believe that shame is a uniformly negative experience imposed from without—by society, by hurtful parents, or by advertisers who want to make you doubt yourself so you'll buy their product. If you believe that resisting shame and throwing off its shackles are necessary, you will find it difficult to accept my view that shame is an unavoidable aspect of everyday life. While some forms of shame are undoubtedly toxic (and I'll be discussing those, too, in the pages that follow), try to open your mind to the possibility that other varieties don't pose such a threat and might even be useful or instructive.

I believe that a shame experience sometimes contains an important lesson about who we are or the person we'd like to become; if we dismiss or resist it, we lose an opportunity to grow.

PRECONCEPTION 3: SHAME IS THE OPPOSITE OF SELF-ESTEEM

If you view shame as synonymous with toxic shame, then of course you'll see it as inimical to strong feelings of self-worth. How can people who feel defective and unworthy of love simultaneously feel good about themselves? Most popular titles in the field of self-esteem share this view, offering techniques for developing self-love through affirmations, radical self-acceptance, and resistance to the shame-based messaging that pervades our society.

Once you understand shame as an inevitable part of daily life, not necessarily a toxic experience imposed from outside, shame and self-esteem don't seem like such clear opposites. In fact, as I'll show, the emergence of shame (not SHAME) during the second year of life plays a crucial role in the development of authentic self-esteem. In my view self-esteem and shame are not opposites but rather are interrelated experiences that depend upon and influence each other.

Because my ultimate goal in writing this book is to explain how we grow to feel good about ourselves—that is, how we develop authentic and lasting self-esteem at every stage of life—I ask you to consider one more preconception.

PRECONCEPTION 4: SELF-ESTEEM IS ALL ABOUT THE SELF

The very term implies a kind of self-contained experience without reference to the outside world. How you feel about yourself seems unrelated to other people; self-esteem embodies an internal relationship you have with the person you feel yourself to be. High self-esteem implies a positive relationship: I love and respect the person that is me. In our narcissistic, all-about-me age, this view of self-esteem has become even more dominant.

But human beings are social animals who define their identities to a significant degree in relation to other people, the members of their tribe. We are sons and daughters, mothers and fathers, related and bound to a circle of significant others whose feelings and opinions about us invariably influence how we feel about ourselves, even when we possess a strong self-concept. The view of an isolated self that exists and can be understood without reference to those others is untenable because we develop our sense of self, as the psychiatrist Francis Broucek says, "in the interpersonal field. The concept of the atomistic isolated self is a delusion."[4]

The development of authentic and lasting self-esteem ultimately depends upon those interpersonal relationships and, in particular, those that are infused with reciprocal joy.

These four preconceptions pervade our society and run deep. I don't expect your own assumptions to suddenly vanish because of this brief discussion, so I'll occasionally remind you of the distinction between SHAME and shame. If you open yourself to my point of view and fully grasp the unexpected role of shame in your life, I promise you'll ultimately find it a rewarding experience, especially if you struggle with self-esteem issues.

In my thirty-five years of practicing psychotherapy, the most important lesson I have learned is this: the road to authentic self-esteem inevitably passes through the land of shame and never entirely leaves it. Along the way, joy and pride in achievement, especially when shared with the people who matter most to us, will often transform our encounters with shame from painful defeats into opportunities for growth and self-fulfillment.

SHAME AWARENESS SURVEY

The goal of this survey is to awaken your memories and sensitize you to common experiences in daily life with the potential to stir up some member of the shame family of emotions. Before reading on, take this brief survey and then read appendix 1, where I discuss the results of my study sample. An online version of this survey is also available at www.shametoself esteem.com, with free automatic scoring and a discussion of survey results more detailed in nature.

During your lifetime, how often have you encountered the following experiences?

1. **HEARING THAT YOU HAVE BEEN THE SUBJECT OF UNKIND GOSSIP**

   ☐ Never   ☐ Rarely   ☐ Occasionally   ☐ Frequently   ☐ Very Frequently

2. **GIVING THE WRONG ANSWER ALOUD, AT SCHOOL OR AT WORK**

   ☐ Never   ☐ Rarely   ☐ Occasionally   ☐ Frequently   ☐ Very Frequently

3. **APPLYING TO JOIN A GROUP OR ORGANIZATION AND BEING TURNED DOWN**

   ☐ Never   ☐ Rarely   ☐ Occasionally   ☐ Frequently   ☐ Very Frequently

4. **HEARING FROM A FRIEND OR LOVED ONE THAT YOU HAVE DISAPPOINTED THEM**

   ☐ Never   ☐ Rarely   ☐ Occasionally   ☐ Frequently   ☐ Very Frequently

5. **LEARNING THAT YOUR SIGNIFICANT OTHER HAS BEEN UNFAITHFUL TO YOU**

   ☐ Never   ☐ Rarely   ☐ Occasionally   ☐ Frequently   ☐ Very Frequently

6. **FEELING THAT YOUR BOSS HAS A GROUP OF FAVORITES THAT DOESN'T INCLUDE YOU**

   ☐ Never   ☐ Rarely   ☐ Occasionally   ☐ Frequently   ☐ Very Frequently

7. **BUYING A HOLIDAY GIFT FOR SOMEONE WHO DIDN'T RECIPROCATE**

   ☐ Never   ☐ Rarely   ☐ Occasionally   ☐ Frequently   ☐ Very Frequently

8. BEING "GHOSTED" BY SOMEONE YOU THOUGHT OF AS A FRIEND

☐ Never   ☐ Rarely   ☐ Occasionally   ☐ Frequently   ☐ Very Frequently

9. FEELING ALONE AMONG PEOPLE WHOSE OPINIONS STRONGLY DIFFER FROM YOURS

☐ Never   ☐ Rarely   ☐ Occasionally   ☐ Frequently   ☐ Very Frequently

10. DOING SOMETHING CLUMSY IN PUBLIC

☐ Never   ☐ Rarely   ☐ Occasionally   ☐ Frequently   ☐ Very Frequently

11. FAILING IN A PUBLIC COMPETITION

☐ Never   ☐ Rarely   ☐ Occasionally   ☐ Frequently   ☐ Very Frequently

12. LOSING OUT ON A PROMOTION YOU WERE HOPING FOR

☐ Never   ☐ Rarely   ☐ Occasionally   ☐ Frequently   ☐ Very Frequently

13. FAILING TO KEEP YOUR NEW YEAR'S RESOLUTIONS

☐ Never   ☐ Rarely   ☐ Occasionally   ☐ Frequently   ☐ Very Frequently

14. DRINKING TOO MUCH AT A PARTY AND FEELING BAD ABOUT YOURSELF THE NEXT DAY

☐ Never   ☐ Rarely   ☐ Occasionally   ☐ Frequently   ☐ Very Frequently

15. LEARNING THAT A GROUP OF YOUR CLOSE FRIENDS GOT TOGETHER WITHOUT YOU

☐ Never   ☐ Rarely   ☐ Occasionally   ☐ Frequently   ☐ Very Frequently

16. LEARNING THAT SOMEONE YOU THINK OF ROMANTICALLY HAS NO INTEREST IN YOU THAT WAY

☐ Never   ☐ Rarely   ☐ Occasionally   ☐ Frequently   ☐ Very Frequently

Now total the number of answers for each frequency category and compare them with the results from my sample study in appendix 1, pages 257–259.

Part I

THE SHAME SPECTRUM

one

THE SHAME FAMILY OF EMOTIONS

WE TEND TO OVERLOOK the central role of shame in our everyday lives because we code it in diverse ways, naming the experience with a variety of words other than *shame* itself. Consider the following scenario, an account of emotions felt by one woman during a single day, emotions that most of us feel regularly.

OLIVIA

Although Olivia and Kevin had separated on (mostly) amicable terms, she often felt vaguely humiliated every time she talked about the divorce with friends . . . as if she were a failure, although she knew better. When she heard that he had already become involved with someone new, she felt even worse. How had he managed to find a partner so quickly when she seemed to be striking out online? Most of the men were inappropriate and easily forgotten. Yet weeks later she still felt bad about Josh, an attractive lawyer from the public defender's office whom she couldn't quite forget. He'd ghosted her after their second date.

She knew it to be irrational (she had wanted out of the marriage as much as Kevin did), but she saw her ex-husband as winning, which made her feel like a loser.

And so, at the age of thirty-six, she'd accepted a transfer when the company offered it—new title, greater responsibility, and a raise in pay. She figured she might do better in a different city surrounded by new people, on the other side of the country, without those frequent reminders of disappointed love and failed marriage. This move would undoubtedly be good for her career.

On the morning of her first day on the new job, Olivia awoke to the sound of her alarm clock, with vague worries that she might have made the wrong decision. She felt unexpectedly anxious as she imagined what lay ahead. When she tried on the new blouse she'd bought for that day, she felt doubtful about her choice, wondering whether the low neckline drew too much attention to her prominent collarbones. She'd always felt self-conscious about the way they protruded. She opted instead for a white cotton blouse that buttoned higher.

After making coffee with her new coffee machine, she checked her email and felt guilty that she hadn't responded to Molly's last message, which was still sitting in her in-box. With the complicated cross-country move, Olivia had understandably fallen behind on correspondence, but she nonetheless felt disappointed in herself. Over the years she'd made repeated resolutions to be a better correspondent but kept dropping the ball. And Molly had always been such a good friend, utterly reliable, forever there when Olivia needed her. She dashed off a quick reply and asked if Molly would be free to Skype that evening after work. They could discuss her first day at the new job.

As she left her apartment, Olivia heard the sharp ping announcing the elevator and hurried down the corridor toward it. Just as the stainless steel doors opened, she caught a heel on the carpet and stumbled, nearly falling to her knees, while two other tenants inside the elevator looked on. A middle-aged man. A woman about her own age she'd noticed in the lobby just the day before.

Olivia's face went hot and she felt foolish. How embarrassing! She felt better when the woman touched her arm and smiled. "That happened to me once," she said. "Did a face-plant in front of a whole elevator full of people!"

By the time she reached the office Olivia was feeling calmer and more confident that she possessed the skills and experience to master this new position. The smiling receptionist made her feel welcome and phoned Human Resources to announce her arrival. The vice president in charge of Olivia's new department had scheduled a series of appointments for her to meet the rest of the team; the morning flew by. As the last of those meetings concluded near lunchtime, Olivia's boss smiled uncomfortably.

"This is a little awkward," she said. "I was planning to take you out to lunch today, but I didn't realize—the thing is, there's a conflict. A baby shower for Celia in Accounting. It's her last day before taking leave. Dan has a client lunch he can't miss, and David's out in the field. Just really unfortunate timing. I'm sorry."

"Not a problem," Olivia said. "I'll manage on my own."

"Tomorrow," the woman said. "I promise. And thanks for understanding."

Olivia did understand. All the same, as she was eating alone, she felt a little hurt. She knew there was no reason to take it personally, no reason they should have invited her to a baby shower honoring a woman she'd never met, but even so she felt left out. She also disliked eating by herself in public. Even here at the fast-casual restaurant, where a few other people also were dining alone, she felt vulnerable and exposed. Did those other people, alone at their tables, worry about being viewed as friendless, as an outsider unworthy of companionship? Olivia fished in her briefcase for several memos she had received during her morning meetings. For the rest of her lunch she kept her gaze fixed on the papers and made sure to avoid eye contact with the other diners.

That night Olivia told Molly the whole story—about her grueling drive cross-country and the flat tire in Kansas, the two boxes that were missing when the movers unloaded the van, and her first day on the new job. As she recounted the challenges she'd faced, she felt a rising sense of pride in what she'd done. She could have stayed back home, mired in her routines and a sense of failure after the divorce; instead she'd accepted a transfer and opened herself to an entirely new life.

"I think you're incredibly brave," Molly said. "I don't know if I could've done it."

When Olivia saw the smile of love and admiration on her friend's face, the sense of pride she felt ran deeper.

THE SHAME SPECTRUM

According to many researchers in the area of affect theory, shame is actually a family of emotions ranging from mild embarrassment to deep humiliation. Olivia was feeling (or anticipating feeling) many of these emotions. During her day, however transient the experience, she felt

- vaguely humiliated
- bad about herself
- like a loser
- insecure about her appearance
- foolish and embarrassed
- self-conscious
- guilty
- hurt and left out
- vulnerable and exposed
- unworthy

Some of these emotions are mild, others more intense. All describe a painful experience related to Olivia—her appearance, her connections with other people, expectations for how she ought to behave or what she'd like to accomplish. Some relate to specific features or acts (her collarbones, stumbling in front of the elevator), while others are global (feeling like a loser or unworthy of friendship).

The shame family of emotions varies along two spectrums: from mild to intense and from specific to global.

As psychiatrist and shame researcher Michael Lewis notes, "Embarrassment and shame are, in fact, related and . . . only vary in intensity."[1] Other emotions that human beings typically experience also occur along a spectrum of intensity, some related to specific areas and others more global. This diagram, for example, needs no explanation:

$$\rightarrow \text{Annoyance} \rightarrow \text{Anger} \rightarrow \text{Outrage}$$

You might have experienced movement along this spectrum while squabbling with a loved one. What began as mild irritation about some oversight might have intensified to anger as your disagreements mounted and finally erupted in explosive rage, which made you feel, perhaps temporarily, that the relationship was at an end.

Like shame, what we refer to as anger is in fact a family of emotions that occur along a spectrum; the English language assigns specific names to various points along that spectrum, and we then make further distinctions based on whether each is mild, moderate, or intense. The same could be said of the sadness family of emotions or those feelings that reflect degrees and intensities of fear.

Throughout this book I'll approach and discuss shame as a family of emotions—painful feelings that invariably draw attention to oneself. Sadness and fear are also painful to experience, but the pain of shame uniquely draws attention to who one is and how one appears, to oneself and to others. For this reason shame, guilt, embarrassment, and other emotions in this family are often referred to as "self-conscious emotions."[2]

Emotions in the family of shame share a painful awareness of self.

GUILT VERSUS SHAME

Many writers on the topic of shame make efforts to distinguish it from guilt, as if they are entirely separate emotions. The psychoanalyst Helen B. Lewis first put this distinction forward in the early 1970s: "The experience of shame is directly about the *self*, which is the focus of evaluation. In guilt, the self is not the central object of negative evaluation, but rather the *thing* done or undone is the focus."[3] More succinctly (paraphrasing John Bradshaw): Guilt is about what you've done, and shame is about who you are.

Theorists in this camp usually offer examples such as the following to illustrate the distinction.

Guilt: "I feel awful because I forgot your birthday." Here *guilt* refers to an act "done or undone" and says nothing about one's overall worth as a person; it often leads the guilty party to apologize or try to make up for the hurt.

Shame: "I feel like I'm worthless and nobody likes me." Here shame pervades and defines the person's sense of self. This person may feel that nothing can be done to ameliorate it.

A professional orthodoxy may have consolidated around the view that guilt and shame are entirely separate emotions, but most laypeople remain unaware of this distinction; the average person uses *guilt* and *shame* more or less interchangeably. The dictionary definition of *shame* offered by *Merriam-Webster's Collegiate Dictionary* captures what most people mean when they use the word: "A painful emotion caused by consciousness of guilt, shortcoming, or impropriety." Defining shame as the awareness of guilt merges two emotions that, in theory, ought to be entirely separate and distinct.

This blurring of conceptual boundaries persists because the painful self-awareness we call *guilt* and the painful self-awareness we call *shame* feel similar in our bodies. We may consciously distinguish guilt from shame, but both involve the same physiological responses. Whether we label those responses as guilt or shame will depend upon their intensity, the event that caused them, and the specific action we might undertake to relieve our pain.[4] Shame makes you want to hide, for example, while guilt might lead you to make amends; on a physiological level both feel bad in a similar way.

Meticulous researchers have produced many compelling studies that distinguish shame from guilt, embarrassment, humiliation, and the other emotions in the shame family. But in focusing on the undeniable distinctions between them, we risk losing sight of the painful self-consciousness they share. This book views all these emotions as part of a single family with a common physiological basis. As I noted earlier, these emotions vary along two spectrums, from mild to intense and from specific to global. From this perspective guilt belongs to the shame family of emotions and relates to something specific, an act or a failure to act; it may be mild or intense.

Throughout this book I'll use the word *shame* as an umbrella term to include the entire family of emotions that involve a *painful awareness of self.* As you read along, bear in mind the distinction between SHAME and *shame.* Remember: all emotions occur along a spectrum of intensity, and all members of the shame family of emotions make the person who feels them painfully self-aware.

POPULAR CONCEPTIONS OF SHAME

Thanks to John Bradshaw's classic book, *Healing the Shame That Binds You,* many people have become familiar with a particular type of shame—toxic shame, or the residue of emotional and physical abuse of a child by parents and other significant adults; it leaves behind a feeling of being damaged and unworthy of love.

More recently Brené Brown's work has made readers aware of a different type of shame, what I refer to as "social shame," instilled by the perfectionism and unattainable ideals that permeate our society and conveyed in particular by advertising and pervasive stereotypes. According to Brown, a research professor of social work, social shame promotes a sense, especially for women, that they are "never enough."

In this book I take a more expansive view of shame. While Bradshaw and Brown have made important contributions to our understanding of the nature of shame, both tend to view it as a largely destructive force (SHAME) imposed from outside by hurtful parents or a perfectionistic society. In contrast, I believe we also experience shame even when nobody intends for us to feel that way, even when we're alone. I believe the shame family of emotions is an inevitable part of everyday life and not merely a painful experience inflicted on us by other people.

Let's return to the account of Olivia's day at work. While some of her body image issues might be the result of perfectionistic messages she absorbed from advertising, external forces or the intentional acts of other people did not cause much of what she was feeling.

She felt vaguely humiliated because she was divorced and "like a loser" in comparison with her ex-husband, who was in a relationship while she remained single. Being ghosted by a man she was dating only deepened those feelings. She felt bad about herself for failing to answer Molly's email and embarrassed when she tripped in front of the elevator. Although her colleagues did not deliberately exclude her from the baby shower, she felt left out and later wondered whether she appeared friendless to the other diners at lunch.

Nobody intended that Olivia would feel any of these emotions. She felt shame for one or more of several reasons: that she (1) had disappointed herself, (2) felt exposed in an unwanted way, (3) found her interest in other people to be unreciprocated, or (4) felt disconnected from her social environment.

In chapters 3 and 4, I will examine each of these situations, what I refer to as the "Shame Paradigms," to help you understand how and why all human beings regularly feel shame.

THE MASKS OF SHAME

Shame not only occurs more often in everyday life than most people realize; it also plays a largely unrecognized part in the suffering that leads people to seek therapy. During the several decades that I've been practicing, few clients have entered treatment consciously aware that they were struggling with shame. Sometimes they will mention that they have low self-esteem, but more often they tell me about the crippling anxiety they feel in social situations, an eating disorder, or recurrent depressions. During our work together it often turns out that these clients struggle with profound shame, although they had not realized it previously.

When shame walks into my consulting room, it nearly always shows up in disguise: to shield themselves from their pain, these clients have masked the shame they feel, hiding it from themselves and from other people. Allow me to introduce you to three of those clients, each of whom used one of the three key strategies that most people use to shield themselves from the pain of shame.

Jeremy—Avoiding Shame

An attractive and successful man in his late twenties, Jeremy found it hard to articulate his reasons for starting therapy. He worked at a high-paying, prestigious job that many of his friends envied, although he described it as "only okay." He was dating a beautiful, successful woman he found extremely attractive, but the relationship lacked passion. "It's only okay," he told me. In fact most aspects of his life seemed to be only okay. He never seemed excited about anything that happened or enthusiastic about anyone he met. He rarely smiled.

Jeremy once told me that optimism is foolish because it only sets you up for disappointment. If you expect the worst, he explained, then you'll be pleasantly surprised if things turn out much better. Except that he never was pleasantly surprised. He found little joy in life and rarely felt happy about anything good that came his way. Through our work together we learned that Jeremy deprived himself of potential joy because he didn't want to risk disappointment. He longed for contact but what he feared most was taking joy in another person's presence, only to find that the person did not reciprocate his joy. He could imagine no experience more shaming.

Later in this book you'll meet other clients like Jeremy who warded off encounters with shame by avoiding situations that might stir it up. In related ways, states of indifference, social anxiety, perfectionism, procrastination, and promiscuity all serve the same purpose.

Serena—Denying Shame

When I called Serena after receiving her voice message asking about treatment, her first words were "I'm glad you called back so quickly. One thing I can't stand is people who think they're so important they take days getting back to you." This remark set the tone for our work together; it also had a bearing on her workplace and social relationships.

Serena described herself as a radical feminist and refused to tolerate any sign of masculine entitlement. "I have too much self-respect," she told me. I heard her say those words many times during our work together. It often felt to me as if Serena, like the character in Shakespeare's *Hamlet*, did "protest too much," and I suspected that profound shame lurked behind her strident pride. Our work together later confirmed this view.

Although I could not be certain how Serena behaved outside my office, I had the impression that she took offense easily and imagined slights where none was intended. At work she apparently treated her coworkers in a high-handed, often condescending, manner. A performance review had prompted her to seek treatment. A supervisor had told her she needed to work on her "empathy skills" so she could understand how and why she had alienated many of her colleagues.

In later chapters you'll meet other clients like Serena who have dealt with profound shame by denying that they felt it while causing other people around them to feel bad. Pretentiousness, arrogance, blame, and self-righteousness are all strategies for offloading (projecting) unconscious shame and forcing other people to feel it.

James—Controlling Shame

For months after we began treatment, I couldn't understand why James remained with his girlfriend. Although she was young and beautiful, more than twenty years his junior, she was so emotionally unstable and abusive that she made his life a misery. From his descriptions it quickly became clear that she suffered from borderline personality disorder, most obviously in the way she saw James as a Prince Charming one day and as a "fucked-up loser" the next.

James was a highly successful professional and universally respected in his field, although he had no real friends. A good-natured jokester on the surface, he kept everyone at arm's length with his humor. While he acknowledged feeling shame, it took us many months to understand the self-protective way he warded off the most unexpected, excruciating encounters with shame by living with someone whose attacks were cyclical, predictable even, and whom he could dismiss as mentally ill. It eventually became clear that James also knew exactly how to provoke his girlfriend to attack him and did so intentionally from time to time.

In these pages you'll get to know James better and meet other clients like him who tried to cope with unbearable and unpredictable shame by controlling when and how they experienced it. Self-pity, self-hatred, masochism, and various types of self-deprecation all represent strategies for submitting to shame while making it a known and predictable experience rather than a surprising one.

Avoid, deny, and control—these are the primary strategies people use to mask and mitigate exposure to the pain of shame. In part 2, I present nine psychotherapy case histories that bring these strategies to life, linking them to the ordinary, nonpathological ways all of us try to avoid, deny, or control our daily encounters with shame.

two

THE VALUE OF SHAME

ALL HUMAN BEINGS INHERIT the same emotional repertoire encoded in their DNA. Beginning with Darwin, many scientists writing on this topic have demonstrated that "certain emotions . . . have the same expressions and experiential qualities in widely different cultures from virtually every continent of the globe, including isolated preliterate cultures having had virtually no contact with Western Civilization." These inherited emotions are encoded in "innate neural programs" that involve the muscles in the face as well as the circulatory and respiratory systems.[1]

Theorists in this area refer to these inherited programs as "innate affect"—the purely physiological and automatic component of emotion, something akin to a reflex. While researchers have minor disagreements about the exact affective repertoire we inherit, most of their theories agree that anger, joy, excitement, fear, and distress are universal human experiences. Shame also shows up on that list.

Darwin long ago observed that people from every culture around the world physically express shame with the same set of physiological signs: lowering of the eyes and gaze aversion, a slumping posture, and usually blushing of the face or other body parts. A century later the painstaking observations of the neuropsychologist Silvan Tomkins confirmed the biological basis of shame, identifying it as one of nine primary affects encoded in our DNA; the others include enjoyment-joy, interest-excitement, fear-terror, and anger-rage.[2]

Affect theory holds that emotions evolved to promote pair bonding between infant and caregiver as well as to facilitate communication among all members of a tribe, thereby promoting survival.[3] But if affects promote pair bonding and communication, why should shame be a part of our genetic inheritance? Why should our history have encoded such a painful and apparently destructive affect into our genes? From an evolutionary perspective, for shame to be a part of our makeup it must serve some useful purpose for human beings.

Recent studies suggest that the capacity to experience shame evolved during the millennia when human beings lived primarily in small social units or tribes. Survival depended heavily upon cooperation among members of the tribe. Members who violated the norms of their tribe, or who behaved in ways that damaged the collective interest, would find themselves shunned or ostracized by others within the group. The tribe might withdraw protection, stop sharing food, and exclude the individual, thus lowering the odds of that person's survival.

According to this view, shame evolved as a way to enforce group cohesion and thereby promote survival of both the individual and the tribe; the capacity to experience shame thus has survival value. According to the lead researcher in one of these studies, "People who can't feel physical pain often die young because they don't have a mechanism to tell them when their tissue is being damaged. Shame is the same as physical pain—it protects us from social devaluation," which might ultimately lead to isolation and death.[4]

Shame also was a civilizing influence and defined the boundaries between public and private. While our ancestors might long ago have urinated, defecated, and even copulated in full view of others, over time those bodily functions gradually became invisible within polite society.[5] As a civilizing influence, shame drove those bodily functions into hiding, where they remain to this day: just about anyone would feel humiliated if a stranger suddenly found them on the toilet. In part this capacity to feel shame about our basic animal nature makes us civilized.

In differing ways all cultures use our built-in capacity to feel shame as a means of enforcing their particular norms and values, presumably to build social cohesion, discourage behaviors that operate against society's collective interest, and thereby promote survival. In this sense all humans share a built-in capacity to experience shame, but societies activate and make use of it in varying ways.

It helps to use the personal computer as a metaphor: shame affect is part of our body's hardware, analogous to a computer's fixed components and firmware; differing social values represent the software that can activate it, just as identical computers might behave differently depending upon the software installed in them.[6] The specifics of physiological shame affect do not vary, but from culture to culture the software that sets it in motion differs widely.

That software, or set of cultural values, also changes over time within each culture—that is, it is constantly being updated. In the immortal words of Cole Porter, though "in olden days a glimpse of stocking/was looked on as something shocking," now just about "Anything goes!" Here in the West, for example, we're in the process of reevaluating the shame attached to homosexual behavior; what formerly led to contempt and social stigma may now be consecrated with marriage vows, although a large portion of our society still endorses the former view. It once was shameful for unmarried couples to live together and for women to give birth out of wedlock. Not so today.

In fact for the last century Western civilization has been engaged in a major update to its shame software, attempting to dramatically reduce the experience of shame for a huge number of people. Our age is characterized by what I describe as an "antishame zeitgeist": diverse groups and political movements have vigorously rejected the strictures of social shame that attach to those who differ widely from the typical, giving rise to a broad spectrum of advocacy movements.

In his monumental and bestselling book *Far from the Tree* (2012), Andrew Solomon details the often-heroic efforts parents make to relieve their children of the social stigma associated with dwarfism, deafness, growing up with a transgender identity, or struggling with an autism spectrum disorder. Most people would agree that this type of stigma is toxic to individuals who cannot help being different; in a liberal society we should support them in their efforts to resist and reject the shame imposed on them.

But we must not make shame the enemy. We must not lose sight of the potential value of shame in discouraging antisocial behavior, even today in our apparently shameless world. Readers often ask me whether shame has any value—that is, are there circumstances when it might be appropriate to feel shame? People who ask this question appear to believe the answer must be an unqualified no. I usually answer with a question of my own: Do we really want sexual harassers to feel no shame? While the scope of shame may have narrowed, it still has a role to play in enforcing our values and discouraging behavior destructive to the social fabric.[7]

In the public arena shame also has its toxic forms, of course. The anonymity afforded by social media has made it possible to use shame for character assassination, as the journalist Jon Ronson vividly describes in his 2015 bestseller, *So You've Been Publicly Shamed*. Ronson details several cases in which the misunderstanding of people's tweets or public remarks led to public outrage that fueled social media shaming campaigns and destroyed these people's reputations and careers. Ronson sees public shaming as a largely destructive force in our world.

In contrast Jennifer Jacquet of New York University argues that "the right amount of shame has helped [our species] to get along, to the extent that we have, and has coordinated social life to make it a little less painful, a little more dignified."[8] In other words "the right amount of shame" allows us to enforce an ideal of civilized behavior governing social relations.

Chris Cillizza, then a columnist for *The Washington Post*, made a similar point regarding the behavior of politicians:

Shame has long been the tool of choice in politics. As in: A president says something that fact-checkers rule is totally false. The president, concerned—even if he won't acknowledge it—

about how he is perceived by the political class, either apologizes for the remark or just stops saying it. [Whether you] like the political class or hate them, that shaming was a way of regulating political rhetoric.[9]

Because most politicians care about their public reputation, shame (or the threat of it) encourages them to abide by an ideal we hold for our elected representatives—in this case, honesty and truthfulness. But if a politician such as Donald Trump is unable, or refuses, to feel shame, Cillizza writes, "there's almost nothing to be done to change his behavior." In short, politicians without shame cannot learn from their experience and modify their actions accordingly; a disapproving public cannot influence them.

Whenever we describe someone as shameless, we also implicitly say something about ourselves and the values we hold for acceptable behavior. On the day I wrote those words, a Google search for "shameless self-promotion" returned more than one million results. A great many people apparently feel that someone who constantly grabs the spotlight to trumpet their accomplishments *ought* to feel ashamed. Even today, in our culture of narcissism, we expect people to display some degree of humility.

On the personal level our sense of shame may hold us accountable, encouraging us to behave in ways that conform to our own ideals and those of society. Shame sometimes tells us who we are and who we expect ourselves to be. The sociologist and social philosopher Helen Merrell Lynd says that it "is possible that experiences of shame if confronted full in the face may throw an unexpected light on who one is and point the way toward who one may become. Fully faced, shame may become not primarily something to be covered, but a positive experience of revelation."[10]

In rejecting shame or making it the enemy, we risk ignoring the lessons it sometimes has to teach us—about ourselves and the social world we inhabit. Once again, I'm not referring to shame as a harsh and destructive force (SHAME) but its larger sense, as a family of emotions that share a painful awareness of self. The chagrin that Olivia felt for being a poor correspondent and not following through on her intentions (see chapter 1) is also a type of shame, one that may deliver to Olivia a useful reminder of her own standards.

If she can pay attention and not try to brush off the feeling of shame, it might help her respond to emails in a timely fashion. She doesn't need to heal from this type of shame, as Bradshaw suggests, or to become more resilient in the face of its destructive message, as the noted sociologist Brené Brown teaches her readers; rather, for Olivia, achieving her goals and consequently feeling good about herself depends upon *listening to her shame and learning from it.*

Unlike most other psychologists who write self-help books, I believe that the shame family of emotions often has value and plays a crucial role in the development of our sense of self. As I'll show, the seeds of self-esteem take root during early childhood within the fertile soil of parental joy and adulation. But if self-esteem is to continue growing, it needs healthy shame at age-appropriate times and in manageable amounts.

In surprising ways, which I describe in the chapters that follow, both joy and shame serve as midwives at the birth of self-esteem. Even for adults, healthy self-respect does not mean being without shame; rather, it means being able to tolerate and endure the experience—to be "shame resilient," as Brown describes it—but also to learn from it when necessary.

PRIDE VERSUS SELF-ESTEEM

Self-esteem is an unfortunate but unavoidable term in my field. Usually described as being either low or high, self-esteem sounds as if it is a quantifiable amount that might be "topped up" with enough external praise or self-affirmations. Since the late 1980s, theories advocating such praise and affirmations have influenced child-rearing practices: psychologists, child development experts, and parenting guides have been teaching us to shield our children from shame and nurture healthy self-esteem with unstinting praise and encouragement. They say this will guarantee children's happiness and success.

One trenchant study of the self-esteem movement and its results in the United States has described ours as an "age of entitlement" defined by a pervasive culture of narcissism.[11] Years of parental praise and encouragement, teachers who constantly tell their students that they're special, and self-help books that promote "self-love" as the answer to all your problems have not led to a generation of young adults who possess healthy self-esteem. Instead, those men and women tend to have an inflated sense of self that is out of touch with the reality of their true strengths and achievements; they often feel entitled to have what they want without doing the work necessary to achieve it, and they place an undue emphasis on image and appearance rather than true substance.

The cultural influences that gave rise to this new parenting style are complex, but one important factor was a reaction against the harsh and often shaming practices of earlier generations of parents. Shaming a child for misbehavior was standard practice a hundred years ago; throughout the more permissive 1960s and 1970s, the use of shame as a parenting tool became less and less acceptable. Today you almost never hear a parent use the words "Shame on you!" or tell children that they are bad. Instead, parents have learned to lavish praise upon their children and, if correction is absolutely necessary, to deliver it as gently as possible.

No sensitive, psychologically minded person would advocate a return to the days of harsh shaming, but, as I'll show, shame (in its broader sense) is an inevitable part of growing up, even when parents try to shield their children from it. Just as Olivia experienced mild shame throughout her day, even when nobody intended that she feel that way, children will constantly encounter the shame family of emotions as they strive toward their goals and interact with people who matter to them.

Like Olivia, they will encounter shame when they (1) find their interest in or affection for another person to be unreciprocated; (2) are excluded from their significant peer group and isolated from other people; (3) feel exposed in an unwanted way; or (4) fall short of fulfilling their own expectations or those of other important people in their lives. Once again, these are the Shame Paradigms, and I'll examine them more closely in the next two chapters.

Children do not develop healthy self-esteem when they are shielded from every experience of shame; rather, they must sometimes learn to take responsibility for the shame they feel and to learn from it. In the process they learn to appreciate the role of joyful achievement in nurturing self-esteem and the importance of sharing their joy with the other important people around them.

Let's return one last time to Olivia and her encounters with the shame family of emotions in chapter 1. At the very end of the day, while Skyping with her best friend, Olivia began to feel a sense of pride—for bravery in the face of the unknown and for successfully mastering so many challenges, one after the other, as she moved to an unfamiliar city. Her feeling of pride deepened when she shared a joyful smile with Molly.

Although the word *pride* sometimes carries a negative connotation when it refers to arrogance, I prefer it to *self-esteem*. I use *pride* throughout this book to mean "a feeling of deep pleasure or satisfaction derived from one's own achievements or reaching one's goals." Researchers in affect theory usually include pride as one of the self-conscious emotions.[12] Whereas embarrassment, guilt, and shame involve a painful awareness of self, pride involves a pleasurable one, usually resulting from personal competency and achievement.

I also find the concept of self-respect to be useful. You develop self-respect by living up to your own values and expectations. As I often say to my clients, self-respect (like all forms of respect) must be earned.

I don't mean goals and expectations in a grandiose or exacting sense; aspiring to be a wealthy celebrity or expecting that you will be perfect at everything you do can be destructive goals. But all human beings are purposeful by nature: each of us has intentions and makes plans to do things every day of our lives—smaller ones like responding to emails in a timely fashion or bigger ones such as advancing in our careers through excellence. When we fulfill our goals, even small ones, we usually feel good about ourselves. Olivia felt disappointed in herself when she forgot about Molly's email, but she felt proud of her courage in embracing major change. Through her bravery she earned her self-respect.

Pride and self-respect are the foundations of enduring self-esteem and an antidote to feelings of shame. It isn't enough for your parents to tell you that you're special, although feeling beautiful and loved by those around you will sow the seeds of self-esteem. For self-esteem to thrive you must also set and achieve goals that fill you with pride. You must develop a set of values and expectations for yourself and then live up to them. In this respect my views diverge from much that has been written on the topic of self-esteem.

Self-esteem is an accomplishment, something to be worked for and achieved, rather than a fuel tank within our psyche to be filled by external praise. It is not a condition that can be permanently attained but one that requires ongoing effort to nurture and sustain.

One final component of healthy self-esteem is this, and it's important: because human beings are social animals and "wired for connection," as Brown describes it, you need to share your joy and pride with the people who matter most to you—your friends, your family, your cohort at work. Just as our ability to feel shame developed within the context of our long tribal history, so did our ability to feel pride. Self-esteem goes deepest when we share our joy in achievement with others.

As paradoxical as it may sound, the development of self-esteem is an interpersonal experience.

For readers who would like to use this book to guide their personal development, I have included a set of ten sequential exercises in appendix 2. They are best undertaken at ends of chapters at specific points in the book. I'll flag each exercise for you at the appropriate point, as I do here:

SEE EXERCISE 1, PAGE 265

An interactive video course focused on these exercises can also be found online at www.shametoselfesteem.com/learning-from-shame.

three

UNLOVED AND LEFT OUT

SHAME IS A PARADOX. On the one hand shame can cause us to disconnect from other people—for example, if we discredit ourselves in some public way and then long to disappear or isolate ourselves. On the other hand shame arises as a result of feeling disconnected, insignificant, or left out. Shame arouses a wish to become invisible; shame often takes hold if we feel unseen and unimportant.

Shame evolved as a means to discourage antisocial behavior and promote survival of the tribe; the emotional cost of opposing group needs is a shame-ridden feeling of Exclusion. At the same time, and again paradoxically, we experience shame whenever we feel excluded, even when we have transgressed no standards or values. Shame is at heart the affect of disconnection—both its cause and a result of it.

In addition, shame is the affect of disappointment. In the last chapter I described pride as a feeling of deep pleasure or satisfaction derived from our own achievements or reaching our goals. Shame is the opposite of pride, a painful feeling that we have fallen short of expectations, either ours or those of other people who are important to us. Even when those expectations are neither harsh nor perfectionistic, we will inevitably feel a degree of shame when we disappoint.

In short, shame is the affect of disappointment and disconnection.

In this chapter and the next, I discuss shame through four different perspectives or lenses and explore the various ways that shame inevitably arises for all of us. These Shame Paradigms illustrate familiar situations that typically arouse one or more of the emotions in the shame family—self-consciousness, embarrassment, humiliation, guilt, and the like. In one way or another each of these paradigms reveals shame as an experience of disappointment and/or disconnection.

Each section concludes with a list of the words we typically use to name these emotions. As with the description of Olivia's day in chapter 1, my goal is to enlarge readers' "shame vocabulary" and show how the shame family of emotions plays a much larger role in daily life than we usually recognize.

PARADIGM 1—SHAME AS UNREQUITED LOVE

Our earliest need for connection is with our parents. The British psychoanalyst Donald Winnicott holds that infants are born into this world with a "blueprint for normality"—a genetic, built-in expectation concerning what caregivers will provide and how development should unfold when those caregivers are "good enough."[1] Children will thrive when their actual experience confirms and validates their hard-wired expectation for loving, attentive parents.

In two moving and painful books, *Daughter Detox* and *Mean Mothers*, Peg Streep describes the damage wrought by mothers who, because of their own narcissism or other psychological issues, were unable to love their daughters. As they grew, the daughters described by Streep constantly struggled to win the love that their genetic inheritance had led them to expect; they continued to love their mothers, making excuses for them, and usually blamed themselves when that love wasn't returned. The legacy of shame afflicting such women lasts a lifetime.

Unrequited Love is the fundamental and most painful of the Shame

Paradigms, and it may afflict us at any stage of life. This truth first came home to me many years ago when I read the following passage from Tolstoy's *Anna Karenina*. Kitty and Vronsky are dancing at a ball. Kitty is in love with Vronsky and until this moment has believed the feeling to be reciprocated: "Kitty looked into his face, which was so close to her own, and long afterwards—for several years after—that look, full of love, to which he made no response, cut her to the heart with an agony of shame."

Kitty's experience is one to which all of us can relate. Did you ever have a crush on someone in high school and later felt humiliated when you learned that your affections weren't returned? Perhaps you've suffered the particular pain of being told by someone you adored that they wanted to be only a friend. Even if we objectively believe there's no actual shame involved, it turns out that to love and feel unloved in return is a shaming experience. "At least in our culture, shame is probably a universal reaction to unrequited or thwarted love," Helen Lewis holds.[2] To gaze as Kitty does into a loved one's eyes and be met with indifference is the quintessential experience of shame and the easiest of the Shame Paradigms to understand.

Everyone who loves wants to be loved in return. All of us want to feel that we're a source of joy to the one who matters most to us, especially our romantic partner. Endless poems, pop songs, novels, and screenplays focus on the search for this kind of reciprocal love. When we get it, we feel completely fulfilled; we feel good about ourselves. When we're disappointed, it can crush us. Even if rebuff comes in a kindly way, softened to minimize our pain, it can feel devastating.

Sometimes we want to become the close friend of a person who doesn't reciprocate our feelings—that's also a kind of Unrequited Love. We're likely to experience one of the emotions in the shame family whenever our phone calls, texts, or emails go unreturned; when a friend cancels a social plan because something better came up or begs off at the last moment with some feeble excuse; when someone turns down our invitation or we're always the one to initiate social contact.

Extramarital affairs usually inflict feelings of shame or humiliation, even if the betrayed partner soon takes flight from those feelings into rage. Parents with a rebellious teenager may feel a type of shame because their child apparently has withdrawn the love they once felt for their parents and has bestowed it upon members of a peer group. Children who recognize that a sibling is the favorite child of a beloved parent often experience a kind of shame.

Unreciprocated affection or interest will always stir emotions in the shame family. As part of our genetic inheritance, we want to connect with a loved one who will love us in return; when our longing is disappointed, when we fail to connect, we inevitably experience shame, however we name the feeling.

Shame Vocabulary

While I refer to the experience of Unrequited Love as shame, we usually code it in other ways. Here are some of the words we typically use to describe our experience to ourselves. Rather than calling it shame, you might say to yourself *I feel . . .*

> *hurt, rejected, or spurned*
> *unlovable or unworthy of love*
> *ugly (not attractive or fit enough)*
> *not masculine (or feminine) enough*
> *humiliated*
> *unwanted (unvalued or uncared for)*
> *ignored or slighted*
> *unimportant, overlooked, or forgotten*

Each of these descriptions connotes the painful awareness of a self that has failed to secure affection from the loved one or that has failed to gain acceptance from a friend. When we love and take joy in another person, we naturally want that regard to be reciprocated; when it isn't, we will feel an emotion in the shame family.

PARADIGM 2—SHAME AS EXCLUSION

Throughout most of our evolutionary history, human beings have lived a tribal existence; one of our deepest needs, encoded in our genes, is to belong to some group larger than ourselves. Psychologists sometimes refer to this innate drive as the "need for affiliation."[3] As Brené Brown and many others have described it, we are "wired for connection," not only with romantic partners but also with our friends, relatives, and colleagues—all the members of our extended tribe. We need emotional involvement with others of our kind to complete our sense of self.

Because shame makes us want to hide, it causes us to "feel isolated, terribly alone, shorn from the herd," as Nathanson puts it.[4] Paradoxically, we also feel shame whenever we find ourselves excluded from some group to which we'd like to belong. In chapter 1 Olivia felt hurt when her new colleagues didn't invite her to join them at the baby shower. Most of us have felt this way at one time or another, although you may not have recognized your experience as belonging to the shame family of emotions. Like Olivia, you might have thought of it as feeling left out. In a darker moment you might have wondered what was wrong with you or why nobody liked you, or you might have worried that you were a loser.

In recent years the fear of missing out (FoMO) has become an Internet meme and inspired scientific studies to determine its roots. The research tends to focus on how social media platforms and our ever-widening web of connections now present us with more options for social engagement than we can possibly enjoy within any given day, overwhelming us with so many choices that we fear making the wrong one. Dig a little deeper, however, and it becomes clear that people who suffer from FoMO are afraid of being left out or excluded by their friends. FoMO is less about overwhelming choice than about the desire to be included.

One study by researchers at the University of Exeter devised a self-rating instrument to measure FoMO. Participants were asked to respond to each of ten statements according to a five-point scale, ranging from *not at all true of me* to *extremely true of me*. Here are the first five statements in that measure:

> I fear others have more rewarding experiences than me.
> I fear my friends have more rewarding experiences than me.
> I get worried when I find out my friends are having fun
>   without me.
> I get anxious when I don't know what my friends are up to.
> It is important that I understand my friends' in-jokes.

These statements clearly speak to the fear of being left out, of not being an insider or a member of the in-group. Social media have allowed us to become superficially connected with a much wider circle of people than would have been possible before the turn of the century but at the same time confront us with increasing evidence that some of our friends are getting together without us. Facebook, Twitter, Instagram, and the like thus confront us with a quandary: we now have greater opportunities to belong but at the same time a greater chance of finding ourselves excluded.

If you were one of the last kids in grade school picked for a team at recess, or if you felt like you didn't belong to one of the popular cliques in high school, you will understand the pain of Exclusion. Middle and high school students often suffer because they feel unpopular, not one of the cool kids, or like a loser. Finding yourself on the outside of a group to which you wish you belonged always stirs up a member of the shame family of emotions.

Having your college application turned down stirs up shame because you've been excluded from a community you longed to join. Being disqualified from military service might likewise cause shame if you've always dreamed of belonging to the marines. Rejection by a fraternity or sorority during pledge week, being denied membership in a social club, failing to secure a place in your church choir or a part in a play—these are but a few of the ways Exclusion can stimulate feelings of shame.

Opportunities to feel left out abound in adult life. Friendship groups often form within neighborhoods, just like cliques in high school, with the popular couples/families getting together for parties while excluding others. When parents are actively involved with their children's participation in sports, a group of popular moms often, intentionally or not, makes other mothers feel second tier. A group of men might form intramural teams or go to sporting events together without realizing that other men they know feel left out.

Colleagues at work regularly cluster together and exclude other people—at lunch, for happy hour, for outside socializing. The boss may favor a select group from within the full company roster. Just about any activity in which people connect makes it possible for someone on the outside to feel excluded or less important than those within.

Middle-aged people who find that they've suddenly become invisible—without currency in the youth-oriented sexual marketplace—often experience a kind of shame, as if they no longer matter and don't belong to the same world they used to inhabit. When the elderly live alone and isolated from the rest of their community, the shame they feel has a profound impact on their mental and physical health. Just about anyone who lives a life of isolation, without human connection, will struggle with shame.

The shame of Exclusion might also arise for internal reasons, even if you haven't actually been excluded. You might experience yourself as being on the outside if you feel different from other people you know or if your way of looking at things makes it difficult for others to understand you. You might feel like an outsider if nobody you know shares your passions and interests. Being a unique individual with idiosyncratic opinions and taste might be a source of pride, but sometimes it can feel lonely if it makes you feel disconnected from other people.

Because we are wired for connection, we have a strong need to belong that lasts all our lives; when that need goes unmet, we will feel an emotion in the shame family.

Shame Vocabulary

I feel . . .

like an outsider or a loner

lonely and misunderstood
like I don't belong
unpopular, uncool, or unwelcome
left out, shunned, or excluded
weird or strange
second tier, less important
that people are avoiding me
overlooked, forgotten, or invisible

Just as we feel shame when our love goes unrequited, so do we feel shame when we're excluded from a desirable group, for whatever reason. We may fear that an inferior or defective self is the cause of our Exclusion.

four

EXPOSED AND DISAPPOINTED

PARADIGM 3—SHAME AS UNWANTED EXPOSURE

- In public you try to unobtrusively ease pressure in your bowels and audibly pass gas instead.
- At home after an evening out, you check the mirror and realize you've had a piece of spinach stuck in your teeth since dinner.
- At work your period comes early, you're unprepared, and you spot your clothes.
- You've had a smelly bowel movement at your friend's apartment, can't find the air freshener or a match, and someone is waiting outside the bathroom door as you exit.
- You're talking at the dinner table and unintentionally spew a bit of food onto someone's arm.

Most of us have suffered through a variety of experiences that we usually code as embarrassment. Everyone wants to make a good impression in public; when we don't, when we feel unexpectedly and suddenly exposed in an unflattering way, or when something personal and private unintentionally becomes public, shame takes hold. "Shame often has to do with matters of exposure when one is not prepared for such exposure," Broucek writes.[1]

Our physiological shame response is unmistakable: our face goes hot, we blush, avert our gaze or close our eyes, and long to disappear, if only for a few seconds.

In the preceding examples, Unwanted Exposure derives from bodily functions. Western civilization has evolved a set of rules, what we call manners or etiquette, that encourage people to conceal their animal nature to some degree. Elimination of bodily waste should take place in private; so should sex. In Turkey, India, or Saudi Arabia burping after a meal is considered a compliment to the host, whereas here in the West we would consider it bad manners. Young children often find their own farts hilarious, but most adults consider them a source of embarrassment when overheard by others.

All societies make use of shame, or the threat of it, to uphold their code of manners, although different societies target different behaviors. Within any given society the shame software that enforces specific behaviors may also vary over time; the values of modesty and reticence in one generation may be considered prudish by the next.[2] While passing gas in public may not feel quite as mortifying as it once did, most people today would nonetheless find it embarrassing. Most people would find it humiliating if a stranger walked into their bedroom while they were having sex.

In 2005 I attended a party at my local psychoanalytic institute commemorating the hundredth anniversary of Freud's *Interpretation of Dreams*. Guests were invited to come in a costume that embodied one of their favorite or most significant dreams. One of my colleagues observed another woman, a stranger, emerging from the restroom with a long piece of toilet paper snagged on her skirt and trailing behind her. My colleague felt so mortified on the woman's behalf that she hurried over to alert her. The woman smiled, gave thanks for this act of kindness, and said, "This is my dream."

During the years I have been in practice, I have heard a great many clients relate shame-ridden dreams, often about appearing naked in public.

When the private body is unexpectedly exposed to public view, we usually feel shame. Middle-aged men vividly recall how humiliating it felt, decades earlier, to ride home from high school on the bus with the outline of an erection visible through their pants.

As I learned only late in my career, psychotherapy often involves the shame of Unwanted Exposure. To give a client an interpretation of unconscious material—that is, to tell her what you heard her saying that she didn't consciously intend to say—often inspires shame, although it may go unnoticed. In psychotherapy, Lynd writes, "shame is the outcome not only of exposing oneself to another person but of the exposure to oneself of parts of the self that one has not recognized and whose existence one is reluctant to admit."[3]

Sometimes we feel exposed in an unwanted or unexpected way when we make mistakes, when we do or say something unintended in a public setting, or when we compare unfavorably with those around us.

- During a group conversation you use a word that you've read but never heard spoken aloud, only to realize from the way another person later says the word that you probably mispronounced it.
- You've dressed up for a party and everyone else has dressed down.
- You're walking along a crowded sidewalk and unexpectedly trip on a crack in the concrete, nearly falling to your knees as others look on.
- When asked your opinion about a current event, you have to admit you have no idea what your friends are talking about.
- During a staff meeting your boss singles you out for criticism.
- You call someone by the wrong name and he corrects you.

We also feel the shame of Unwanted Exposure if personal information that we'd rather keep private goes public. You might feel an emotion in the shame family, for example, if you learned of rumors that your child struggles with a drug addiction and was admitted to rehab, that your spouse has been unfaithful to you, or that your company is downsizing and you were let go. Because we're social animals who belong to a community, we of course care deeply about our reputation and how we appear to others within our milieu.

Sudden Unwanted Exposure always stirs up one of the emotions in the shame family, however we name it. It can be mild or intense; it might be the result of a simple mistake we regret and soon forget, or it might haunt us for hours as we repeatedly relive the painful scene.

Shame Vocabulary

I feel . . .

self-conscious
embarrassed, shy, or bashful
vulnerable and exposed
foolish, ridiculous
like an idiot, a dope, or a jerk
mortified
as if I'm a laughingstock
stupid or uninformed
awkward, inept, or clumsy

PARADIGM 4—DISAPPOINTED EXPECTATION

If you ever studied hard for an exam and thought you'd done well, only to receive a middling grade, you might have felt keenly disappointed, embarrassed, or chagrined, especially if you told classmates beforehand that you expected to ace it. "Exposure of misplaced confidence can be shameful," Lynd observes. "The greater the expectation, the more acute the shame."[4] Had you earned top marks, you would have felt proud and welcomed public recognition of your success, but you probably didn't want your friends to know about the actual grade you received. It might have felt like a source of shame that you preferred to keep secret.

Whenever we set a goal, we open the door to potential shame. Every year millions of us make New Year's resolutions—to quit smoking, lose weight, or go to the gym; most years we fail to keep them. When we do, when we go for the pint of ice cream or buy another pack of cigarettes, we often feel guilty or bad about ourselves. Sometimes a feeling of self-loathing might take hold. New Year's resolutions represent a kind of expectation we too often fail to meet.

If you apply for an open position at your place of work, hoping for a promotion, but someone else gets the job, you might also feel the shame of Disappointed Expectation. Running for office and losing the election could also stir up feelings of shame; so can competing unsuccessfully in a sporting event. As much value as society appears to place on personal best, awarding an A for effort, most of us will feel one of the emotions in the shame family whenever we set goals and then fall short. We often code it as disappointment or regret.

We also feel the shame of Disappointed Expectation whenever we fall short of our own standards and values or those of people we respect. The discrepancy between what we expect of ourselves and what we actually do may lead to painful feelings of disappointment: "To be in a state of shame I must compare my action against some standard, either my own or someone else's," Michael Lewis explains. "My failure, relative to the standard, results in a state of shame."[5]

Whenever we compare ourselves unfavorably with other people, we identify an expectation we have failed to meet, a painful disappointment that may lead to feelings of shame and envy. In choosing our role models and striving to emulate them, we establish a kind of expectation about the person we'd like to be, and living up to the example of a role model can be a source of pride. If we idealize these role models, however—if we expect ourselves to be as perfect as we perceive them to be—we set ourselves up for inevitable disappointment and a pernicious form of shame (SHAME).

Holding reasonable expectations for ourselves is not the same as harboring harsh, perfectionistic, and self-defeating ones. As Brené Brown notes, "Shame is the voice of perfectionism."[6] Adopting reasonable standards that embody our core values and holding ourselves accountable will enable us to build pride and lead a life of integrity. Many self-help books recommend cognitive-behavioral techniques for modifying punitive self-talk. Sometimes this is an appropriate and helpful approach; at other times we need to listen to, and learn from, the shame of Disappointed Expectation so we may eventually earn self-respect.

When we fall short of a goal or behave in ways we don't respect, we usually don't like to talk about it or share our disappointment with others. Shame usually drives us into isolation. In contrast, when we plan ahead, work hard, and ultimately succeed, we want to share our pride in accomplishment with others. Achieving a goal contributes to our sense of self-worth; that pride runs deeper when the people who matter most to us, our tribe, acknowledge and celebrate our success. Healthy pride and recognition is different from boasting or bragging to make others feel bad about themselves, and it's also different from a slavish devotion to the opinions of others.

Competition of all kinds inevitably involves shame: when someone emerges as the winner, fulfilling their dreams of victory, others must fall short of their own goals. As the narcissism researchers Jean Twenge and Keith Campbell note in *The Narcissism Epidemic*, the self-esteem movement has tried to eliminate the shame involved in competition by turning everyone into a winner. Parents continually praise their children as special and unique; at school kids absorb similar messages from their teachers through "All About Me" and "I Am Special" projects. My children's elementary school used to host a Halloween costume competition each year, and every child won first prize.

I'm not suggesting that children (or adults) ought to feel shame if they compete and fall short; I'm saying that they inevitably do—not shame in the toxic, debilitating sense we usually use the word (SHAME), but rather an entire family of emotions that involve some painful feeling about ourselves. It might be a mild feeling of disappointment that quickly passes, or it might demoralize us for weeks. It might motivate us to try harder next time, or it might instill a crippling doubt that causes us to withdraw from further competition.

As much as we might wish it to be otherwise, we live in a highly competitive world. Competition to deliver the best product at the lowest price as quickly as possible lies at the heart of our system of free enterprise. Some companies will succeed and others will inevitably fail. In well-run companies employees who deliver excellent work product will receive raises and promotions while others will not advance. Although it is less obvious, competition also plays a role in social relations. "Keeping up with the Joneses" describes the widespread wish not to appear socially or economically inferior to our neighbors, like comparative losers.

In its most toxic and narcissistic form, competition turns the world into a battleground between enviable winners and contemptible losers. Within the narcissistic worldview, self-esteem is a zero-sum game: I feel better about myself by putting you down. Think of it as akin to a teeter-totter: I triumph whenever I send you plummeting down into shame but fear the reverse when you begin rising higher with success. As I'll discuss in greater detail in part 2, narcissistic defenses, which are a particular mask against shame, often drive people to humiliate others to shore up their own self-esteem and escape from unbearable shame.

Because even healthy competition invariably involves some degree of shame for those who don't prevail, we've developed rules and codes of behavior to help mitigate that shame. Good sportsmanship, for example, means not gloating in triumph or ridiculing your adversaries. Even if winning represents perhaps the highest good in our society, we also praise dignity in defeat. We dislike sore losers. And we try to reframe losing or failure as an opportunity to learn from Disappointed Expectation.

Why didn't we prevail in a specific case and what can we learn from our loss to compete more effectively next time?

This attitude toward the shame of failure or defeat lies at the heart of the American economic engine and occupies a central place within the Silicon Valley start-up culture. Failure is to be expected on the road to success, and the only real shame is not learning and growing from it. In later chapters I'll apply this perspective to the development of lasting self-esteem: I believe that the experience of shame in many cases presents us with an opportunity to grow and learn; if we listen to it, shame sometimes tells us who we are and who we expect ourselves to be. What largely stand in the way of personal growth are our defenses against and inability to tolerate shame.

So far, the examples I've provided to illustrate this paradigm—shame as Disappointed Expectation—should be clear and readily understandable. I'd like to conclude this section with another example of shame from this perspective, one that might at first seem puzzling. It comes from the stand-up comedy of Ellen DeGeneres.

Like many comedians, DeGeneres enacts familiar shame-inducing experiences in a way that makes them funny. Much of the pleasure we feel in watching her comes from seeing ourselves in her characters, identifying with the shame they feel, and then laughing with relief when that shame becomes both shared and funny, rather than acutely painful in a way that isolates us.

In a well-known segment from one of her stand-up routines, DeGeneres pretends to be walking down the street when she spots a friend of hers in the distance. *Oh, there's Nancy*, she says to herself. DeGeneres smiles and energetically waves, making clear how glad she feels to see her. She calls out Nancy's name and makes a vigorous effort to get her attention. Then her face abruptly freezes: she has realized that the person is not Nancy after all but a stranger who resembles her.

DeGeneres is a brilliant physical comedian; in the next seconds she vividly conveys her feelings of acute distress. She drops her head and averts her gaze. She looks miserable. She talks to herself in a tense, high-pitched voice full of agony and finally walks away at a fast clip. DeGeneres never uses the word, but she physically expresses the physiological signs of shame.

While most of us can relate to this experience, it's not immediately clear why misidentifying a stranger should produce such an acute feeling of discomfort. After all, it's a common error based on misperception. Why should that mistake distress us to such an intensely painful degree?

DeGeneres's vignette suggests that our discomfort arises whenever we demonstratively express joy, expecting it to be reciprocated, only to be disappointed. And that specific discomfort, however we choose to name it, belongs to the shame family of emotions. It's a kind of Disappointed Expectation—a wish for joyful connection that goes unmet.

Shame Vocabulary

Whenever you code the shame of Disappointed Expectation, you might tell yourself:

I feel . . .
> *let down, sad, or disappointed*
> *defeated or discouraged*
> *frustrated with myself*
> *like I can't make the grade*
> *like a wimp or a dud*
> *inept, feeble, or ineffective*
> *inadequate or incompetent*
> *like a failure or a loser*
> *weak, undisciplined, or lacking in resolve*
> *crestfallen, despondent*

In the next chapter I discuss our need for joyful connection beginning in early life and the role it plays in the development of self-esteem. Then I explore the inevitable emergence, during the second year of life, of shame in all its forms and the surprising ways that shame also contributes to feelings of pride, self-respect, and self-worth.

SEE EXERCISE 2, PAGES 266–268

five

JOY AND THE BIRTH OF SELF-ESTEEM

To PROMOTE HEALTHY SELF-ESTEEM IN their children, parents face two roughly sequential challenges. The initial task, which corresponds mostly to the first year, is to make their babies feel that almost everything they do is a source of joy and interest; caregivers must support a "stage-typical narcissistic state of grandiosity and omnipotence"—the felt belief that the babies are living at the center of their parents' emotional universe and are more important than anything or anyone else.[1] During this period babies don't yet understand parents as fully separate people but relate to them as if their sole purpose were tending the babies' needs and emotions—as comfort givers, feeders, suppliers of joy and stimulation.

Freud referred to this condition as "primary narcissism." For roughly the first year of their lives babies need to feel, at least most of the time, that it is all about them. Such an experience lays the foundation for healthy self-esteem.

During their second year of life toddlers gradually acquire the concept of parents as separate and distinct beings with an interior life of their own and not merely sources of gratification. To promote this crucial development, to socialize growing children into a larger world full of other people, parents must gradually and gently challenge that "grandiosity and omnipotence." They must now communicate to the toddler that "although she is indeed special, she is no more so than anyone else," including her parents.[2]

During the second year of life not everything a toddler does is a source of unqualified joy to his parents; now he must conform to their expectations if he is to elicit the reward of reciprocal joy and interest. This experience will build upon the foundation of self-esteem laid down during the first phase by curtailing grandiosity. In learning that he is not, in fact, the center of the universe, that he must adapt to parental expectation concerning acceptable behavior, a toddler continues to earn that reward of reciprocal joy that makes him feel good about himself.

Throughout both phases most of the emotional exchanges between parent and child occur face to face. Although preverbal sounds also play a part, in the first phase parents and babies talk to each other largely through eye contact and changing facial expressions. Caregivers rely upon these face-to-face exchanges to communicate their joy and interest; they also receive and mirror the joy and interest they read upon their babies' faces.

During the second year of life face-to-face exchanges play an equally important role, but parents dramatically change how they respond to their baby's bids for mutual joy and interest. Sometimes a caregiver looks away, frowns, or says no if a toddler's excited behavior is unacceptable. When toddlers expect a joyful exchange with caregivers but don't receive it, we might describe their experience as one of frustration, disappointment, or rejection. Neurobiologists refer to such states of misattunement or mismatch between parent and child as "interactive error."[3]

Whatever name we give to that experience, it is painful.

THE STILL FACE EXPERIMENT

Within an observation room at the University of Massachusetts, a researcher's camera records the scene: A young mother sits before her baby girl, who is in a car seat on a table. As the two make eye contact, joy immediately suffuses the baby's face. Mother coos to Baby with a look of joyful adoration; she takes both of Baby's hands into her own, and they greet each other, one using words, the other making happy preverbal sounds.

The baby then points to an object in the distance, drawing her mother's attention to it. With a delighted smile Mother looks in that direction, then back to Baby's face, crooning her acknowledgment. *Yes, I see! Isn't that fascinating?* Mother's voice is soft and high-pitched, the voice most parents instinctively use when talking to their babies. Mother smiles again and gives her baby a joyful laugh. Baby's face lights up with happiness.

These two are emotionally attuned. At this moment they are the joyful center of one another's universe.

Following the researcher's instruction from off-camera, Mother then breaks eye contact and briefly turns away. When she turns back, her face is an impassive mask, her body still and unexpressive. She no longer reaches out to Baby or responds in any way.

Baby immediately notices that something has changed; a look of confusion crosses her face. She gives her mother a smile meant to entice a joyful response; Mother's face remains a stony mask. Baby then points to a different object in the distance, trying to engage her mother's interest. Mother continues gazing at Baby with an unreadable expression on her face. She appears remote and completely detached.

Baby leans forward, with both hands raised toward Mother's face, then falls back into her car seat with a sound of dismay. Baby's face tightens up in distress. Clapping her hands, she directs a high-pitched screech of protest at her mother. The longer Mother remains detached and unresponsive, the greater Baby's distress. She begins to flail about in her car seat and finally bursts into tears.

Mother at last reengages, crooning and smiling at Baby. Within a few seconds the two are once again attuned, making eye contact and sharing the joy they feel in one another's presence.

Conducted by Dr. Edward Tronick of the University of Massachusetts at Boston, the 1980s study commonly referred to as the "Still Face Experiment" filmed many such encounters between parents and their babies, for the first time offering scientific support for the view that babies are profoundly affected by their parents' behavior and emotional states. Tronick showed that infants as young as two months actively seek face-to-face engagement with their parents.

The actual encounter can be viewed in a YouTube video. In the first part of this video the joy shared by the mother and baby makes the viewer want to smile too. When parents gaze into their babies' eyes with a look of infatuation, beaming joy, it feels entirely healthy and right. Every baby ought to begin life in the glow of parental adoration, feeling perfect and beautiful. Repeated reliably for many months, such an experience cannot help but make a growing child feel good about herself.

An infant-caregiver relationship suffused with reciprocal joy forms the bedrock of self-esteem.

RECIPROCAL JOY AND EARLY
BRAIN DEVELOPMENT

During the first year of life a surprisingly large number of the interactions between parents and their children involve shared joy and interest. By the end of their first ten months of life, babies interact with their caregivers in positive, joyful ways as much as 90 percent of the time. Recent neuroscience research shows that these joyful interactions release hormones that help an infant's brain to develop normally. In fact such normal development depends upon their release.

If you spend much time reading the professional literature in the burgeoning field of neonatal neuroscience, you'll come upon the phrase "experience-dependent maturation of the brain." The human brain is not fully formed at birth but continues to develop throughout the earliest months and years of life; whether it will develop optimally depends upon certain conditions being met. During the first year that means a relationship between infant and caregiver that is suffused with mutually attuned exchanges of joy and interest. Inevitable and frequent interactive error will produce frustration, distress, sadness, and the like; those mismatches must be reliably corrected in a timely fashion, returning mother and baby to a state of mutual joy and interest. Neurobiologists refer to this latter process as "interactive repair."

In both caregiver and baby joyful attunement and interactive repair release specific hormones known as endogenous opioids or opioid peptides. (An endogenous opioid is one produced by the body, as opposed to one that comes from outside and is ingested—like the illegal drug opium or the FDA-approved medication fentanyl.) Also known as endorphins, endogenous opioids make both members of the dyad feel good—about themselves and about each other, thereby building self-esteem for each and a healthy attachment relationship between them.

Endogenous opioids also promote neural growth in the infant's brain. During the first year of life they play a special role in the maturation of the orbitofrontal cortex—a part of the brain "intimately involved with the pleasurable qualities of social interaction."[4] In other words the degree to which a growing child experiences mutually attuned exchanges of joy and interest during her first year will influence not only the development of self-esteem but also her capacity to build satisfying relationships with other people throughout her life.

The love and passionate interest that parents feel toward their children resembles romantic infatuation—the way we feel as adults when we fall in love and believe the object of our affections to be perfect. For infants during the first year of life, the seeds of self-esteem take root when they feel themselves to be the center of their parents' universe, uncritically adored, and both the source and recipient of devoted interest. We might also describe this experience as one of unconditional love.

While the self-esteem movement did not evolve from this neuroscience, it has based its guidance on a basic understanding of the role of joy in building self-esteem. Researchers have advised parents and educators to lavish praise upon children, regardless of what they do: expressing unconditional love and approval, they are told, will build healthy self-esteem in a growing child.

As I discuss in the next chapter, however, joy is a necessary but not sufficient condition for healthy self-esteem to continue developing in the second and later years.

DISAPPOINTMENT AND FRUSTRATION

Busy parents cannot always respond to their baby's need for joyful interaction, of course; they must contend with the realities of their adult lives and the needs of people other than their baby. In short, even the child of well-attuned parents will confront pain, frustration, and moments of parental distraction or disengagement. Neuroscientists group these experiences of interactive error under the heading of stress. We need stress in order to grow: frustration is an inevitable part of life, and we must therefore learn to tolerate it if we're to thrive. It's a matter of proportion: Does the world deliver stress in tolerable amounts and under conditions that don't last too long before relief finally arrives?

When parents are "good enough" in Winnicott's terms, when their infants confront early frustration and disappointment in manageable amounts, when interactive error leads soon enough to interactive repair, their babies learn that they can survive those experiences and not be overwhelmed by them. The research of Tronick and others suggests that perfect attunement between parent and child is neither possible nor desirable and that optimal growth occurs when the dyad successfully moves from painful states of misattunement to joyful connection. During the first year of life infants depend heavily upon caregivers to help them recover from stress and return to joy. In the language of my profession they are not yet able to autoregulate their emotional states.

If pain, disappointment, and frustration arrive in manageable amounts, if infants repeatedly recover from stress through interactive repair, they develop a sense of confidence not only in the reliability of their caregivers but also in themselves. As Tronick writes, "With the accumulation and reiteration of success and reparation, the infant establishes a positive affective core"—the foundation of self-esteem.[5]

In Erik Erikson's classic formulation of the maturational challenges that confront human beings throughout life, he defines the challenge of the first year as one of basic trust versus mistrust. Successfully weathering stressful experiences during these early months instills in the babies confidence not only in their caregivers but in the babies' ability to cope with future adversity; such confidence contributes to the growth of self-esteem.

The mutual gaze between parent and baby, filled with joy, is the birthplace of self-esteem, leading the infant to feel beautiful and worthy of love. Successfully navigating experiences of frustration and disappointment with the help of reliable caregivers contributes to the growing child's feelings of self-confidence.

CORE SHAME

Sometimes parents are not good enough for a variety of reasons, and self-esteem fails to take root in their child. Perhaps a mother suffers from prolonged postpartum depression or is in despair because the father of her child has abandoned them. A young widower may feel overwhelmed, emotionally unequipped for single parenthood, and full of grief following the untimely death of his wife. Perhaps the household is the site of physical or emotional violence. Drug addiction, the stress of extreme poverty, severe mental illness, high-conflict divorce—these are some conditions that might make parents unable to fulfill their caregiving roles or to engage in joyful interaction with their child.

Recall the second half of the interaction in the Still Face Experiment, after the mother has assumed an impassive expression; it's painful to watch. As our bodies resonate with the baby's mounting distress, we want to avert our gaze. The mother's disengagement feels terribly wrong, not at all how a parent should respond to a baby reaching out to her. Repeated consistently for months and years, such an experience couldn't help but make that baby feel bad about herself—just the opposite of beautiful and worthy.

When the bad far outweighs the good—when a baby's encounters with pain, frustration, or disappointment profoundly overshadow his experiences of joyful connection, when reliable interactive repair does not follow states of misattunement—the infant's brain lacks the conditions it needs to develop normally. You may be familiar with the concept of critical periods—maturational stages during which our nervous system is especially dependent upon specific environmental stimuli for acquiring a skill or trait. If we don't receive the appropriate stimulus during a given critical period, we will find it difficult, and sometimes impossible, to develop those abilities later in life.

Critical periods for the human brain are the maturational stages when it is not yet fully formed and is continuing to grow. If an infant's experience does not involve enough mutually joyful exchanges with caregivers during the first year of life, his brain will not develop normally because optimal brain development is dependent upon the hormones released during such exchanges. Allan Schore of UCLA's Neuropsychiatric Institute has conducted MRI studies of infants brought up in grossly deficient environments; he has shown that, compared with infants brought up in healthy families, the brains of babies from deficient environments are smaller in size, with fewer neurons and fewer interconnections between them.

Despite the neuroplasticity that researchers have touted in recent years, such compromised brain development during the first months of life cannot be entirely overcome. In this respect insufficient joy and attunement in early life is analogous to the vitamin deficiency found in rickets. Children whose diets lack vitamin D during those critical years when their bones are immature will, in later life, have skeletons that differ from the norm, even if they eat more healthily as adults. Children whose brains develop under circumstances far less than optimal will forever be different from children brought up in healthy environments. This doesn't mean that growth is impossible, only that it has limits.

When brain development goes awry, the baby senses on the deepest level of his being that something is terribly wrong—with his world and with himself. As the psychoanalyst James Grotstein has described it, "These damaged children seem to sense that there is something neurodevelopmentally wrong with them, and they feel a deep sense of shame about themselves as a result."[6] Throughout my work I have referred to this experience as "core shame." It is both intense and global. Under conditions that depart widely from the norm, shame also becomes structural, an integral part of a developing child's felt self. Rather than feeling beautiful and worthy of love, these children come to feel defective, ugly, broken, and unlovable.

In terms of the Shame Paradigms, core shame embodies both Unrequited Love and Disappointed Expectation—profoundly so. If we're born into this world with a built-in expectation for reciprocal joy, if our deepest need is to love and be loved in return but our caretakers disastrously disappoint us, core shame will take hold. To get some idea of the agony that is core shame, think again of that baby from the Still Face Experiment when her mother didn't respond; imagine that distress occurring repeatedly throughout the first months of life, day after day. "With the reiteration and accumulation of failure and non-reparation, the infant develops a representation of himself or herself as ineffective," Tronick writes. Over time, he continues, "psychopathology is likely to arise in situations where there is persistent and chronic interactive failure."[7]

I have worked with many clients who struggled with core shame, although none of them realized it at the beginning of our work together. They revealed it to me in dreams they brought to session: a landscape blighted by war, a ghetto ravaged by poverty with buildings in advanced states of decay, a burned-out and abandoned car. From more than one client I have heard dreams featuring a disease-ridden or disfigured baby whom the dreamer is trying desperately to save. These dreams all convey the sense of a profoundly damaged self that the dreamer fears is beyond repair.

In *Stigma*, his classic work on social stigma, Erving Goffman describes the person burdened with major personal or physical defects as possessing a spoiled identity. The conviction that you are physically spoiled or ruined lies at the heart of core shame. We describe vegetable produce as spoiled after it has rotted and lost all nutritional value, fit only for the trash heap. To struggle with core shame is to fear, on the deepest level of your being, that you are so damaged that you have no value and no reason to exist. If it becomes intolerable, core shame may lead to suicide.

Core shame is so excruciatingly painful that people afflicted by it usually try to ward it off or run away from it. In ways that are mostly unconscious, they learn to hide from, or mask, their shame and thereby exclude pain from awareness. I discuss these various masks in part 2, where I link them to the ways all of us avoid, deny, and control experiences of shame. Although core shame leads to entrenched defenses against it, most of us intermittently rely on the very same defenses in our daily lives to shield us from the shame family of emotions.

JOY AND ACHIEVEMENT

At some point during the first year of life, usually in the second half, most babies develop enough muscular strength and coordination that they begin to crawl. Independent locomotion represents a huge achievement: being able to move from place to place without being carried by an adult brings a new sense of power and autonomy, contributing to a child's self-esteem. This milestone is so meaningful to parents, too, that hundreds of them have posted amateur videos on YouTube documenting their child's first successful attempt to crawl. Most of these videos have titles that end in more than one exclamation point.

These videos have a remarkable sameness. The majority show a baby on the floor with some desirable object out of reach, usually a brightly colored toy or stuffed animal. On all fours the baby wobbles and makes tentative efforts to move toward the object. Invisible behind the camera, parents excitedly call out their encouragement. "Come on! You can do it!" These babies may fall over or whimper in frustration; they may briefly give up and direct their attention to some other object already within reach. Eventually, with a focused look of determination, they will return to the effort and struggle awkwardly toward the toy.

As they begin to coordinate the motion of their legs and arms, some babies will spontaneously laugh with joy. In response the parents often cry out with excitement: "That's amazing! She actually crawled for the first time! What a big girl! You're such a big girl!" Many of these parents applaud or laugh with joy.

Throughout the first year of life babies strive to master a great many developmental challenges. They learn to sit up, to grasp and hold on to objects, to crawl, and eventually, near the end of that period, to walk. Observe babies as they struggle to master a new skill and you will notice that they are remarkably determined. When they succeed, they appear to experience feelings of pleasure.

Many developmental psychologists will argue that this emotion cannot accurately be called pride, because pride depends on a concept of a self that exists apart from the baby's parents. According to such theories, children do not develop this self-awareness until the end of the second year of life; what looks to the lay observer like pride is actually a kind of pleasure in function, or what one researcher has called "competence pleasure." Whether it is pride proper or only its precursor, successfully achieving what they want to do makes babies feel good and ultimately feel good about themselves. When the parents signal their own pride and joy in this achievement with smiles, cries of delight, and a special gleam in their eyes, the pride these babies feel goes deeper. As the clinical psychologist Gershen Kaufman notes, "When a child is admired, that child feels affirmed. To be admired by another is to be gazed upon with deepening enjoyment, to be openly smiled upon. It is the gleam in the parent's eyes along with the smile on the parent's face. Admiration from a parent also mirrors back to the self the self's own joy. Affirmation of self is a recurring need, observed in adulthood no less than in childhood."[8]

These experiences serve as a model for the development of self-esteem, beginning during infancy but lasting throughout our lives. It involves three elements:

- purposeful behavior
- pride in achievement
- shared joy

In part 3, I show how developing self-esteem at any stage of life depends upon these three elements. It's not enough to be told (or to tell ourselves through affirmations) that we are unique and special. To develop authentic self-esteem we must also set and achieve goals or live up to our own standards. Achievement leads to feelings of joy and pride that run even deeper when we share them with those who matter most to us.

Whenever we fall short of achievement or when our caregivers fail to join with us in our joy, we will feel shame rather than pride. Of the Shame Paradigms, such an experience corresponds to Disappointed Expectation. If we strive toward a goal but fail to achieve it, we will feel an emotion in the shame family, often coded as frustration or disappointment. We might feel hurt or rejected if our significant others remain indifferent to our joy or, worse, disparage it.

Two memories from my own childhood illustrate this latter situation, and it's still painfully vivid to me after many decades. When I was five or six years old, I unfurled a roll of beige butcher paper in my bedroom and, with my box of crayons, drew a long mural of cars driving along a freeway. Proud of my achievement, I carried the mural to my mother, whose only remark, delivered with a frown, was "They all look the same." She sounded dismissive as she handed the drawing back to me and turned away. I can still recall the feeling that I'd let her down in some important way, that she disliked me. I didn't yet have a word to capture her expression of contempt.

At Christmastime one year during my early teens, I sang "O Holy Night," my favorite carol, to her. I loved music but feared I couldn't carry a tune, so it took some courage to sing for my mother. I remember standing in the kitchen as I began, my confidence quickly waning and my voice growing shakier as her expression turned impatient, disapproving, possibly disgusted. Once I'd finished my performance, she smirked and said, "Nice." Then she turned away.

Parental sarcasm and contempt will poison a child's developing self-esteem, of course, but all children must confront failures of achievement in the form of temporary setbacks. They are inevitable, and so is the accompanying shame (not SHAME) of Disappointed Expectation. The ability to weather such shame and to continue working toward goals lies at the heart of authentic self-esteem, reflected in an old adage: "If at first you don't succeed, try try again."

Healthy self-esteem does not mean the absence of shame but rather the ability to recover from its inevitable occurrence in life, to learn from it when necessary, and to continue working toward goals.

six

SHAME AND THE GROWTH OF SELF-ESTEEM

A DECISIVE SHIFT IN THE NATURE of infant-caregiver interactions occurs during the second year of life. Growing children, accustomed to engaging in mutually attuned exchanges of joy and interest with caregivers, now find that their parents regularly frustrate, correct, ignore, and reprimand them. Consider these typical situations:

- Little Jenny's mother has been talking to another mother for what seems like an eternity. Jenny tugs on the leg of her mother's pants and raises her arms with a smile, asking for attention. With a firm expression on her face, her mother briefly looks down and says, "Mommy is talking to Adele's mommy right now. Don't interrupt."
- Dressed in his training pants, Dylan plays in the backyard while his mother looks on from a lawn chair. When Dylan finds an empty snail shell, intact and shiny, he wants to share the discovery with his mother. He approaches and places the shell in her hand; instead of smiling, Mom's face unexpectedly wrinkles up. "Did you have another accident?" she asks.
- At the park her attentive dad watches as little Alexa plays with her sandbox toys near the slide. Her father briefly glances down at his cell phone to check messages. When he looks up again, Alexa

has abandoned her pail and shovel and is toddling toward the slide. Dad abruptly jumps up and cries out in fear: "Alexa, no! Stop!" Alexa freezes. Dad hurries over and scoops her up, saying, "You're too little for the slide."

• While playing with other children, Miles grabs a shiny toy from Stephen and excitedly shows it to his mother, who frowns. "That's not nice. Give the toy back to Stephen," she tells Miles. One of the other children points at Miles and says, "Not nice." Stephen grabs his toy and makes an angry face at Miles.

For anyone who has reared children or spent much time around toddlers, these situations will seem familiar. As their children become toddlers, parents must curtail their youngsters' grandiosity to protect them from danger, as in the case of Alexa. Like Dylan's mother, they must eventually potty-train them. Whereas at ten months approximately 90 percent of infant-caregiver interactions are suffused with positive emotion, a decisive shift occurs during the second year of life. Mothers of twelve-month-old children express a prohibition approximately 5 percent of the time, but by the time their child is eighteen months old, mothers do so every nine minutes, or about 11 percent of the time.[1]

Parents of toddlers must also instill the social values and expectations governing relationships that are less exclusive than caregiver-infant. We refer to this as socialization:

• Urinating and defecating in clothing is no longer acceptable; the child must use the potty.
• Interrupting a parent when she's having a conversation with someone else is rude.
• Snatching toys away from other children is "not nice," especially when the toys don't belong to the snatcher.

You may be nodding with understanding at this point, but you'll probably stop nodding when I describe these typical communications as shame based.

That's not shame. Shame is when you tell your child he or she is bad. And shame has no place in parenting if you want to bring up children with healthy self-esteem.

These objections revert to the preconceptions I described in the introduction: Shame is bad. Shame is the enemy. Shame is the opposite of self-esteem. In a moment I'll return to experts in affect theory and neuroscience, who largely agree that shame (not SHAME) is the primary tool parents use to socialize their children during the second year of life. But first I want to review those typical toddler-parent encounters and apply the shame vocabulary I developed in the preceding chapters. The vocabulary is adult, unfamiliar to toddlers, of course, but it approximates the pain these children feel when their parents begin to socialize them.

Jenny wanted to connect with Mom but was rebuffed. Accustomed to life at the center of her mother's universe, Jenny might suddenly feel rejected or unwanted as a result of this demotion. She might feel let down, sad, or disappointed, too, but also second tier and less important than her mother's adult friend. The longer the two grown-ups talk together, the more Jenny is likely to feel excluded, overlooked, forgotten, or invisible.

Dylan expected to share his joyful discovery of the snail shell with his mother, only to be met with a look of mild disgust because she had smelled his bowel movement. As a result Dylan may feel disappointed, hurt, ignored, or rejected. Eventually, as he better understands what his parents expect, his mother's disapproval if he again soils his training pants might make Dylan feel embarrassed, inadequate, incompetent, or like a failure.

Alexa wanted to enjoy the slide like the big kids but her father intervened. Hearing what sounded to her like anger in Daddy's voice, Alexa suddenly stopped her excited movement toward the slide and probably felt defeated or discouraged. Confused about what she did to make her father unhappy, she might also feel vulnerable and exposed, as if she had done something foolish. When her father told her she was "too little," Alexa might have felt awkward, inferior, or inept.

Miles wanted his mother to share his excitement about that new toy but met with disapproval. When his mother reprimanded him, he might, like Dylan, have felt disappointed, hurt, or unworthy. The reactions of the other children might have made him feel lonely and misunderstood. As he grows older, feeling excluded by other children when he violates a social norm might make him feel left out, shunned, or rejected.

What about the Shame Paradigms—Unrequited Love, Exclusion, Unwanted Exposure, and Disappointed Expectation?

Recall that Kitty felt shame when Vronsky failed to reciprocate her look of joy (see chapter 3). When Jenny gazed joyfully at her mother, who then told her to wait, she was experiencing a kind of Unrequited Love. It's also a form of Exclusion that at the very least feels unpleasant. Each of these situations involves some type of Disappointed Expectation—for joyful connection with a caregiver or for an exciting new experience. Over time, having an accident and witnessing his mother's subtle expression of disgust will feel to Dylan like a kind of Unwanted Exposure.

Silvan Tomkins, the father of modern affect theory, describes shame as an affect that interrupts other positive affects such as enjoyment-joy or interest-excitement. Again, because all emotions occur along a spectrum of intensity, Tomkins uses two words to name the affects, one from each end of its spectrum. He therefore speaks of shame-humiliation, where shame represents a milder form that corresponds to the everyday experiences I'm attempting to describe and humiliation resembles what Bradshaw has called toxic shame.

Look again at the four typical situations. Although tone of voice plays a role in early socialization, most of the communication occurs face to face, through changes of facial expression. During the second year of life toddlers regularly approach their parents and expect to see a look of joy on their faces or a gleam in their eyes—the reaction to which they grew accustomed during their first year. Instead they see an entirely different and unfamiliar face—so different, in fact, that their mother suddenly appears to be a stranger.[2]

Now we're in a better position to understand the distress Ellen DeGeneres feels when she abruptly realizes that it's not her friend Nancy, after all (see chapter 4). To reach out in joy, hoping for connection with a familiar face, only to be met by a stranger, will induce a classic shame response—gaze aversion, a wish to disappear, a momentary confusion of thoughts. It resembles the way toddlers feel when their caregivers begin to respond to them in strange and unfamiliar ways. This type of Disappointed Expectation produces one or more feelings from the shame family of emotions, and parents use it to modify their children's behavior in the service of socialization.

As I discussed in chapter 5, neuroscientists who study early childhood development refer to these interactions as forms of interactive error between caregiver and child that produce painful feelings of stress in the toddler; neuroscientists also describe such stressful misattunement as an early form of shame. Without quite realizing they are doing so, caregivers make selective use of their facial expressions to induce shame, or stressful states of mismatch, to encourage a change in behavior. It's the facial equivalent of saying "No, don't do that."

The psychiatrist and shame researcher Michael Lewis has extensively studied the ways in which parents subtly express disgust to their children when they want to convey disapproval. "Most people," he writes, "would be surprised to learn that a disgusted face is widely used in the socialization of children. After all, the middle class is not supposed to be punitive toward their children." The facial expression to which Lewis alludes is a brief and subtle one—nostrils and upper lip raised, perhaps showing teeth; most parents are unaware they are making it. This transient look might be accompanied by a verbal prohibition such as "Oh, don't touch that."

Lewis has observed that this combination of a verbal prohibition with a disgusted/contemptuous look occupies "at least 40% of codable facial expression in parents' behavior."

Although the disgusted face appears only briefly, children do perceive it. "When they see a disgusted face they turn sharply away and seem inhibited for a moment," Lewis continues. "It is likely that such behavior reflects shame. The disgusted face is effective in socialization through shaming as well as informing the child not to repeat that action."[3] When parental disgust intensifies into contempt or rage, it will traumatize the child. But in strategic amounts it induces a mild shame experience in the children that helps them develop.

On a biological level these states of shame stress lead to the release of the hormones called corticosteroids, or cortisol. Excessive amounts of cortisol are associated with adverse effects on general health throughout the human life span and upon brain development during early child-hood. Cortisol reduces the production of nerve growth factor, for example, which helps nerves to expand and interconnect during critical periods. But small amounts of cortisol actually help the brain to develop normally.

Just as endorphins are crucial for optimal brain development during the first year of life, low amounts of corticosteroids are necessary for continued brain growth during the second year.

These hormones play an important role during a critical period involving the frontal cortex (the site of higher adaptive functions that regulate social interaction) and its connections to lower brain areas involved in emotions and impulsivity (the limbic system). Under the influence of optimal and nontraumatic levels of cortisol, the frontal cortex matures and exerts "hierarchical dominance" over the limbic circuits, thereby allowing "for the emergence of a number of adaptive functions" crucial for success within a larger social context: impulse control and emotional self-regulation.[4]

To avoid the stressful experience of everyday shame, toddlers will eventually modify their behavior to conform with parental expectations. They will internalize the no expressed on a caregiver's face and eventually learn to tell themselves no. In other words they will learn to control their bowel movements. They will learn how to wait for their mother to finish her conversation before asking to be picked up. They will learn to resist the impulse to snatch that toy, although they would dearly love to hold it. As a reward for learning, they reattune with caregivers (interactive repair) in a state of reciprocal joy and interest.

In summary, interactions of reciprocal joy were predominant during the first year of life, taken for granted as the norm (unconditional love). During the second year reciprocal joy becomes contingent upon meeting expectations (conditional approval). Toddlers earn the reward of joyful reconnection once they have learned the rules of socialization and obey them.

"Good boy! You used the potty this time."

"Thank you for letting Mommy finish what she was doing."

"I'm so proud of you for sharing with Stephen."

Caregivers convey those rules by instigating strategic interactive error, in part by displaying a subtly disgusted face that will produce shame stress for the toddler. These misattunements must be at the mild end of the shame-humiliation spectrum, and followed by the reward of joyful reconnection through reattunement.

This cycle of joy-shame-joy socializes children and at the same time encourages the seeds of self-esteem planted during the first year of life to continue growing.

When toddlers succeed in meeting expectations, they also feel proud of themselves. The process of weathering the shame stress experience, learning what is expected, and then managing their own feelings and impulses to finally meet expectation will build feelings of self-confidence and pride in achievement, a pride that runs deeper when they can share it with, and have it validated by, caregivers through joyful reconnection.

During the first year of life achievement and shared joy plant the seeds of self-esteem. During the second year shared joy involves a cycle of (a) shame stress, followed by (b) the meeting of parental expectations, and then (c) reconnection with caregivers who validate their child's achievement and rejoice in it.

In part 3, I show how building authentic self-esteem at any stage of life involves the same cycle. Setting goals or standards and then meeting our own expectations, as well as those of our community, will lead to feelings of pride that run deeper when shared with the people who matter most to us. Throughout our lives we will inevitably encounter the shame family of emotions whenever we fall short of expectation. Weathering those stressful experiences without defending against them, persevering despite disappointment or pain, will contribute to our feelings of self-worth.

As they grow older, one of the ways in which children learn to confront and master their inevitable encounters with shame is through team sports. Playing on a team with peers helps children learn to compete effectively and to cooperate with others in pursuing a shared goal—an important skill in later life, especially as they mature and enter the workplace. Competition is a fact of life, of course, and, as I said, the possibility of a shame experience arises whenever people compete. Someone wins and someone else must lose.

Learning to weather the shame of losing a game (Disappointed Expectation) without feeling utterly discouraged helps children to master the inevitable setbacks they will encounter throughout their lives and to continue pursuing their goals. At its best competition through team sports builds strength of character. But competition becomes toxic whenever a player experiences defeat as unbearable humiliation, usually because of toxic encounters with shame during early childhood that have shaped his or her personality.

In such cases the ruthless drive to win—that is, to defeat shame—overshadows the social values instilled by team sports: the pleasure of striving toward shared goals, the importance of discipline and hard work, and the need to accept that one is important but no more important than anyone else on the team. Players overly driven to win usually struggle with self-esteem issues and unconscious shame, often because their parents have similar problems. If your children play team sports, you're no doubt familiar with this type of parent—the one heckling a referee or yelling at his kid from the sidelines.

Sometimes boys and girls are poor sports because their parents continued to idealize them long after it was time to discourage their "all about me" grandiosity. Because the self-esteem movement has focused on unconditional love and largely overlooked the importance of conditional approval in building self-esteem, parenting infused with the movement's precepts has failed an entire generation of children. Influenced by the anti-shame zeitgeist that characterizes our age, the self-esteem movement has unwittingly encouraged these young adults to expect nonstop admiration and to respond defensively to any encounter with shame. And sometimes it turns them into ruthless competitors unable to cope with defeat.

Once again, self-esteem does not mean freedom from shame. The person with authentic self-esteem can endure the inevitable experience of shame in everyday life, learn from it when necessary, and continue pursuing goals.

In part 2, I describe the defensive ways that people typically attempt to avoid, deny, or control the experience of shame rather than weathering and potentially learning from it. These defensive maneuvers, what I refer to as the "masks of shame," make us less able to endure the shame inherent in everyday life; they prevent us from learning the lessons that shame sometimes has to teach us. As a result these masks of shame impede the development of lasting self-esteem for people of all ages.

SEE EXERCISE 3, PAGES 269–270

Part II

THE MASKS OF SHAME

As a central issue in psychotherapy, shame often shows up in disguise. Some people begin treatment consciously aware that they struggle with shame; many others are focused on their maladaptive strategies to avoid, deny, or control shame without being aware of what drives them. For these latter clients the shame they feel is almost entirely unconscious, masked by their defensive strategies to evade it.

Psychological defense mechanisms are lies we tell ourselves to evade pain. When the emotional truth seems unbearably painful, when we feel hopeless about the possibility of alleviating that pain, we often try to hide it from ourselves or to disguise it, relying on a variety of defense mechanisms that shunt awareness into the unconscious. This is especially true for clients who struggle with the agony of core shame, or a feeling that one is broken, defective, ugly, and unlovable—the legacy of early childhood experience that departs dramatically from the norm. Most of the clients I describe in the chapters that follow have struggled with core shame.

These nine case studies are grouped in three sections, each focused on a different strategy for coping with shame, by avoiding, denying, or controlling it. In each section three separate case studies provide background history and describe the course of treatment as my clients and I learned to understand their defenses against the awareness of shame. As they became more self-aware and able to bear their shame, these clients also learned ways to build authentic self-esteem in order to mitigate the shame.

Following the chapters that present the case studies in each section is a chapter that describes the ways all of us attempt to avoid, deny, and control the experience of shame in our every-day lives. In part 1, I discussed how the capacity to feel shame is an integral part of our genetic inheritance and an unavoidable aspect of the human condition. On a regular basis each of us encounters the shame of Unrequited Love, Exclusion, Unwanted Exposure, and Disappointed Expectation. Because those experiences are painful, we understandably try to avoid, deny, and control them whenever we can. There is nothing pathological per se about trying to minimize our exposure to shame.

Only when our efforts to evade shame become so pervasive that they stop us from forming intimate relationships and achieving our goals do they create problems in their own right. The nine clients I describe in part 2 defended so heavily against shame that they became isolated and unfulfilled, unable to feel a sense of belonging and connection to other people in their lives, and they were stunted in their efforts to fulfill their dreams.

Presenting detailed clinical material from my practice raises important ethical issues and potentially threatens the trust I developed with my clients over the years. At the same time, to be of value to readers, a psychological profile must be detailed and include authentic truths uncovered through psychotherapy. I've dealt with these competing challenges in several ways.

Whenever possible, I alter details that might enable readers to identify my clients. All therapists who write about their clients follow the same procedure. We change names and ages, of course, but also give them different occupations and subtly alter their family backgrounds. Because I've worked for many years as a distance therapist through videoconferencing, fulfilling this responsibility is a bit easier: in addition to the other changes I make, I can locate a client in a different city or country.

In writing this book I was always conscious that past or current clients might read it and feel betrayed to see themselves in these pages. For this reason I've also added events and exchanges from my work with other clients who struggled with similar issues, making the individual cases less specific to any one individual.

While each person is unique, the different types of early life experience that lead to core shame have much in common. People who struggle with shame try to avoid, deny, and control it in similar ways. The myriad insights and emotional exchanges I've experienced with many clients resonate with each other, enabling me to enrich these profiles with harmonious detail. In writing this book I've distilled the emotional truths from thirty-five years of clinical experience into the nine case studies you are about to read. They span my entire career, from my many years of working in person one on one while I lived and practiced in Los Angeles to more recent cases conducted by videoconference.

AVOIDING SHAME

seven

SOCIAL ANXIETY

IN HER FIRST EMAIL LIZZIE asked whether I'd be willing to consult with her by telephone rather than videoconferencing. She told me she'd been reading my blog for months and would like to begin therapy but didn't think she could bear direct visual contact. Would I talk to her on the phone instead?

Although years earlier I'd worked by telephone with clients who came to my office for a time and subsequently moved away, I had since begun to use a videoconferencing platform and found the medium far superior to voice only. Humans empathize by reading one another's facial expressions and bringing our own into alignment, calling forth an affective echo of what we feel within our own bodies. I need to see a client's face to do my job.

In my email response I told Lizzie I no longer felt I could function effectively as a distance therapist without the visual component. Would she like to set up a video consultation instead? She didn't reply.

Months later I heard from Lizzie again. She had just read an article I'd written for *The New York Times*, about the unexpected role played by household pets in distance therapy, when clients most often connect from their homes. For some reason the thought of including her cat, Cleo, in a session made the prospect of meeting face to face more bearable. We set up an appointment for later that week, which she canceled twenty-four hours in advance, claiming illness. We rescheduled several more times during the next two weeks.

Based on our exchanges up to that point, I felt a little anxious when she didn't cancel our next rescheduled session. Given the dread she apparently felt at being seen, I wasn't sure what to expect. The profile photo she'd uploaded to the video platform showed a calico cat arching its back—said Cleo, I presumed. Minutes before the session was to begin, I had no idea what Lizzie looked like. Although she'd completed the new client questionnaire I had sent, her answers were terse and unrevealing. She was twenty-eight years old and lived in New York City, with one previous experience in short-term cognitive-behavioral therapy. She had decided to seek treatment because of "social anxiety." In the space provided for family background she wrote: "One living sister, both parents dead."

I initiated our video call at the appointed time and Lizzie answered right away. Cleo the cat dominated the frame, with the middle section of a woman's body positioned in a chair behind her. The laptop screen was angled so that the camera took in her torso only, bisecting her at the neck; I could see slender arms and long hands as she stroked her cat. Behind them was a blank wall, with no art or shelves or furniture of any kind. The background that clients choose for their sessions and the visual information they include in the video frame often provide important information. This absence of visual detail seemed telling in a different way.

"I can't see your face," I said.

"Sorry."

Lizzie's hands reached for Cleo, relocating her offscreen, apparently to the floor. The cat meowed in complaint and jumped back onto the table. Lizzie then shifted Cleo to the side, out of view, and repositioned the laptop screen so that the frame included her face. Nothing exceptional or shocking. Short flat hair, blond in color; an extremely pale face; a body that appeared to be of average size. She wore a short-sleeved tee shirt in muted green. Her eyes, wide and brown, looked frightened. Although she lived thousands of miles from me and our connection was virtual, she couldn't bear to maintain eye contact and quickly glanced away.

"Nice to meet you," I said. Cleo's meows of complaint continued off-screen.

Lizzie nodded. I could read the fear in her expression and sensed my own face tightening up. I have a list of questions I usually ask during an intake session—about a client's reasons for seeking treatment and what they hope to get from it—but I decided it would be a mistake to begin in so direct a fashion that day.

Another meow from offscreen.

"She's chatty," I said.

A faint smile crossed Lizzie's face. She reached for Cleo and placed her in her lap. "She just wants attention. She doesn't like that I'm talking to you."

"How old?"

"Five years. I've had her since she was a kitten." Lizzie was stroking Cleo's fur and smiling down at her. "Such a pretty girl," she crooned. When I'd owned cats years earlier, I'd spoken to them in that same tone of voice. Loving. Parental. Through the speakers on my laptop I heard the jagged rumble of Cleo's purr, oddly disjointed instead of the usual rhythmic pulse, and I laughed.

"That may be the loudest purr I've ever heard."

Lizzie laughed, too, although she kept her gaze downcast. "Her funny little broken motor," she said. "She's always been that way."

And so we began.

LIZZIE'S BACKGROUND

I learned about Lizzie slowly, over time, because she found it difficult to collect her thoughts and speak during our sessions. We often sat together in anxious silence. Sometimes I asked simple questions and she gave me simple, unrevealing answers. Much of the time her cat meowed and purred and filled up the screen. Discussing Cleo often gave us a way to make contact without approaching painful subjects too directly. Between our appointments I occasionally received long, highly articulate emails in which Lizzie divulged information she'd remembered only after the session was over, about things too painful to describe to me by videoconference.

Lizzie suffered from social anxiety that seemed to be growing more intense with each passing year. As a technical writer she worked mostly from home, alone in her tiny apartment, and had organized her life to reduce interactions with other people as much as possible: her groceries were delivered and laundry picked up; she regularly ordered out. Weeks passed with only minimal human contact.

She'd always been shy and disliked social gatherings larger than two or three friends, but in recent years she'd grown to dread all contact with other people. Even a brief exchange with a convenience store clerk made her anxious. Once, when the guest list for a birthday dinner honoring a college friend unexpectedly grew from three to ten, she suffered a full-blown panic attack as she began to get dressed for it. Her heart raced, she broke out in a cold sweat, a nameless dread came over her. She finally texted the friend who'd organized the party, made an excuse, and begged off. Since then Lizzie continually worried that she might have another panic attack and arranged her life to avoid any situation that might set one off.

Influenced by the disease model of mental health that pervades our society, Lizzie believed she suffered from some type of anxiety disorder, a condition akin to physical disease, usually the result of a chemical imbalance or defective thought processes in need of correction. Her primary physician had prescribed different psychiatric medications, but she couldn't bear the side effects. Long-acting benzodiazepines gave her the most relief, and for a time she thought she'd found a cure. When she sensed herself becoming physically dependent upon them, she grew frightened about losing control, weaned herself off, and refused to try any more drugs.

She next found a local therapist who worked in a cognitive-behavioral mode. After a couple of months Lizzie discontinued treatment because she felt she'd made no progress. After reading my blog, she finally decided to try psychodynamic psychotherapy. My posts expressing an antimedication bias initially drew her to me. She hoped that psychotherapy might alleviate her anxiety without the need for psychiatric drugs.

During the first few weeks she never mentioned any members of her family, living or dead. When I finally inquired about her childhood, she seemed uncomfortable and again became terse. Both parents had died within the last few years. No uncles, aunts, or cousins. Distant relatives in Europe she didn't know. She did volunteer one unusual detail: she and her older sister, Jane, had been named after the elder Bennet girls in *Pride and Prejudice*, their mother's favorite novel. When Lizzie first read the book in her early teens, she decided that she should have been named after Mary Bennet instead. She saw herself as dull and unexceptional, entirely unlike Austen's spirited heroine. She added further details about her past quite reluctantly and only in response to my questions.

I eventually heard about Lizzie's childhood on New York's Upper West Side. From an early age she'd ride the subway home alone after school, quickly dispatch her homework at the kitchen table, then retreat to the bedroom she shared with Jane and disappear into a novel. Her mother, a librarian, was a voracious reader, too, and reared both girls on the classics of English and American literature. While Lizzie had read and enjoyed all of Austen's novels, she preferred George Eliot; her favorite author was Virginia Woolf.

During those afternoons of her childhood she was forbidden to enter the living room, which was dominated by two concert Steinways and curtained off from the rest of the house. Lizzie's father, formerly a teacher at Juilliard, now gave private lessons to gifted pianists aspiring to a professional career on the concert circuit. When she recalled her childhood, and especially those hours reading alone in her bedroom, her memories were accompanied by a soundtrack—demanding passages from Liszt, Beethoven, and Chopin, interrupted by her father's imperious voice and caustic corrections.

As a younger man Lizzie's father had concertized and seemed poised for an illustrious career as a solo artist when crippling stage fright cut it short. He was paralyzed by dread and nausea, and his hands trembled so violently before each performance that he finally gave up concertizing and became a teacher. From Lizzie's descriptions of her childhood, we eventually understood how a sense of his failure had pervaded family life, never mentioned yet an invisible part of the air they breathed, concealed behind feelings of artistic superiority and contempt for the unwashed masses.

Her mother, who was much younger than Lizzie's father, lived in awe of her husband—the "great man," as she thought of him, while she was merely a librarian. Neither parent took much interest in their daughters. Their father was preoccupied with his students and their mother devoted herself to his care. Jane and Lizzie showed little aptitude for music and abandoned lessons at an early age. Jane immersed herself in competitive sports; on those rare occasions when she made an appearance in his conversation, their father referred to Jane, with blatant disdain, as the "athletic one." Lizzie he described as bookish.

He had died of a sudden heart attack several years earlier. Their mother died not long thereafter of late-stage breast cancer; Lizzie believed her mother might have survived had she paid more attention to herself and caught it earlier, instead of slavishly devoting herself to the great man. Anger concerning her mother's self-abnegation opened the door to Lizzie's rage about her father, the way he'd always made her feel insignificant, entirely unworthy of attention compared with those adoring students who passed through the living room each day and often stayed for dinner.

Lizzie had excelled in high school, especially at those subjects requiring term papers. After a childhood spent reading novels, she'd developed a love of language and a gift for writing. English and history teachers regularly held up her essays as the standard of academic excellence; she hated being singled out. She also began writing short stories at an early age but never showed them to anyone. She aspired to emulate Henry James and unfolded psychological tales in baroque prose; her stories usually featured a shy heroine with keen and superior insights into other people. In later years Lizzie felt embarrassed by those stories—pseudomature and pretentious, as she thought of them.

Her mother, who knew nothing about her daughter's short stories, once came upon and read one of them while dusting the girls' bedroom.

"Why, this is really quite good!" she exclaimed to Lizzie. The look of surprise, almost shock, on her mother's face made Lizzie furious. Through our work she also recognized how much her anger had fueled her desire to become a successful writer. Even her father might hold her in higher esteem if she forged a literary career for herself. His daughter might not be a musician, but at least she could become an artist of some kind.

Lizzie told me that she'd always hated her sister, for vague reasons I didn't at first understand; the feeling seemed to be mutual. I was under the mistaken impression that Lizzie had broken off all contact with her sister since their mother's death, but one day she told me in passing that Jane was training to run the New York Marathon. The disdain in Lizzie's voice made clear that she'd absorbed her father's contempt for Jane's athleticism and her desire to compete. Lizzie despised all forms of competition . . . or so she insisted.

Behind those feelings of contempt we eventually uncovered rivalrous feelings toward her sister so intense we described them as murderous. In the atmosphere of emotional starvation that defined their childhood, it felt to Lizzie as if the attention or scant affection Jane received only deprived Lizzie of what she herself desperately wanted from their parents. Both sisters felt some obligation to maintain the family connection after their parents died, but a feeling of grudge bearing or grievance suffused their rare phone calls.

After a dozen or so sessions Lizzie still hadn't mentioned sex. With most clients I usually approach the subject directly, and much earlier during treatment, but with Lizzie I found myself hesitating. From her startled reaction when I finally asked, and the violent blush that spread from her collarbones up her neck, it was obvious the question made her uncomfortable. In a halting voice she finally told me that she hadn't dated at all in high school. As an English major at an Ivy League college, she'd had her first and only sexual experience during her junior year, with an awkward classmate from a seminar on the Victorian novel. She found their encounter distasteful. Disgusted by her own body and repelled by the dark moles on his shockingly white skin, she gave him the brush-off when he next approached her.

During her senior year an Irish novelist who'd recently won an important literary prize came to her college as writer-in-residence and offered a seminar on short story writing. To apply for admission to the class students had to provide a sample of their work for evaluation. Lizzie submitted what she considered her best short story and was rejected. She stopped writing fiction for nearly a year after that. In a tone of voice that mingled pain and contempt, she described the story to me as puerile. She said it was no wonder the professor had deemed her unworthy of participating.

Since then Lizzie had resumed writing fiction and had completed several short stories that she'd shown to no one and had never submitted for publication. About a year before our work together began, she'd started writing a novel and had completed nearly a hundred pages. She wanted to join a Meetup group of writers in the city, but the prospect of reading pages to strangers terrified her. At that point she lived in near-complete isolation.

THE EMERGENCE OF SHAME

"What are you scared of?" I asked. "When you imagine talking to the convenience store clerk, what are you afraid will happen?"

Over time I asked similar questions about many different situations, from rare social events at which she encountered strangers to those dreaded meetings with clients who preferred to discuss a new project in person. I did not regard her anxiety as an irrational response to be dealt with by using systematic desensitization or thought stopping; rather, I suggested to Lizzie that she might have a potent reason for feeling anxious in social situations.

"So what will the clerk think of you?"

"He'll think I'm weird," she said.

Or: "I'll do something to embarrass myself."

"I'll say something stupid or just clam up."

"They'll think I'm ugly."

"I won't fit in."

"They'll be bored."

"They'll notice that I'm blushing and assume I'm incompetent."

"She'll see there's something wrong with me."

The theme of damage, beginning with Cleo's "funny little broken motor," ran through her sessions, with dreams (usually related by email) featuring disease-ridden animals and children with handicaps. Early in our work Lizzie read Susan Cain's book *Quiet*, about the power of introverts in a world that values loud self-promotion; she wanted to see herself as a quietly creative person, different from, but not less than, all those attention-seeking extroverts. Instead, as she realized over time, she felt defective, like damaged goods. On an emotional level she felt herself to be ugly and misshapen, although she consciously knew better. She felt a deep disgust for her own body.

Lizzie eventually understood her "social anxiety" as the profound fear that she might experience one of the emotions in the shame family. Most of all she dreaded exposure as a freak—her word—someone damaged, defective, or hideous. I talked to her about the way core shame can take root in early childhood, when the sort of parent-child bonding we usually expect falls short, saddling you with feelings of inner ugliness. She thought that her mother might have suffered from postpartum depression. According to family lore, Lizzie had also been a difficult baby—colicky and inconsolable. Her mother had always described Jane as the easy one.

Although she'd known the truth on some unconscious level, Lizzie was eventually able to acknowledge that her mother felt virtually no interest in, or emotional attachment to, her children and had gotten pregnant only because that's what women of her generation were supposed to do after they married. Her father cared for nothing but his art. When I asked about experiences of joy, Lizzie told me she couldn't remember ever seeing a joyful expression on her mother's face. She did recall that her mother felt proud of Lizzie's writing but not in a way that made her feel loved and accepted for who she was.

Lizzie eventually understood how shame had always pervaded her family life, concealed behind a veneer of artistic superiority and contempt.

The unspoken shame of failure (Disappointed Expectation) haunted her father, although no one ever spoke of it. Lizzie began to feel some compassion for him when we made the connection between his stage fright and her own social anxiety. No doubt he had felt the same way she did—terrified that his image as a virtuosic pianist would be stripped away, exposing him as worthless and defective, an imposter without any real talent.

In short Lizzie came to understand her social anxiety as the dread of encountering shame (Unwanted Exposure). Over the years she'd organized her life to avoid that experience as fully as possible. While avoiding shame saved her a great deal of pain, it had also crippled her. With no relationships of any depth, and unable to make her writing public, either by submitting it for publication or sharing it with peers, she was an isolated, profoundly unhappy young woman. For years she had taken quiet refuge in superiority and contempt for the average person—attitudes she had absorbed from her family. Through our work she eventually recognized those attitudes as defenses against unbearable shame.

At that point Lizzie abandoned work on her novel for several months. The vision of herself as a writer seemed yet another kind of dodge, an idealized self-image meant to disprove all the shame she felt, just as her father had concealed his own shame behind a superior artistic persona. During this period she spoke with scorn about her early stories and even the opening of her novel. Becoming an artist represented a flight from shame in the family tradition; it also embodied her hope for redemption, proving herself worthy in the eyes of her parents.

At the same time her love and respect for good writing was sincere. Eventually she began to wonder whether she might try to write something more truthful.

COURAGE AND PRIDE

Like many clients Lizzie naturally hoped that psychotherapy would take away her anxiety and erase those feelings of shame. She finally accepted that I couldn't work such magic and that realistic progress meant gradually braving and learning to bear those situations that stirred up anxiety. It also meant setting realistic and attainable goals that might enable her to feel pride in achievement. All her strategies for avoiding the experience of shame had only deepened that shame and at the same time prevented her from building authentic self-esteem that might offset it.

Lizzie began with small steps. Rather than having all her groceries delivered, she decided to purchase some of her vegetables from the Korean grocer on the corner at least once each week. The first time she approached the store, she felt so full of dread that she gave up and hurried back to her apartment. When we discussed it during her next session, she derided herself as weak and cowardly. As is often the case with clients who struggle with shame, she despised herself as if from on high, viewing that other, defective self as contemptible. Such self-loathing is another kind of defense against shame: it puts distance between oneself as the superior observer and the shame-ridden self one is rejecting.

Lizzie tried again the next week and bought a single orange. At the register she fumbled for change from her coin purse until the stern-faced Korean woman finally counted it out for her. With sweaty hands and a racing heart Lizzie hurried back to her apartment. She couldn't bring herself to eat the orange until the following day. When she told me about it during our next session, she described the orange as surprisingly delicious, as if she'd expected it to taste bitter. She went back to the grocer several times during the ensuing weeks. One day the Korean woman must have recognized Lizzie and gave her a smile. It came as such a surprise that Lizzie couldn't smile back. For days afterward she tortured herself for being "so rude."

Eventually she worked up the nerve to ask the woman, "How are you doing today?"

"Busy," she answered. "Always too busy." The sense of burden made Lizzie think of her own mother.

"I'm sorry," she told the grocer, who brushed aside Lizzie's sympathy.

On the walk back to her apartment Lizzie felt an unfamiliar sense of pride about that exchange. She had accomplished something she'd set out to do, however small an achievement it might seem to others.

"Good for you!" I exclaimed when she told me about it. Although I was trained in the psychoanalytic method and encouraged to maintain a neutral demeanor with my clients, I've since learned that expressing my sincere joy when clients make progress plays a crucial role in their development. Shared joy—between parent and child or between therapist and client—contributes to feelings of self-esteem for both parties.

Sometimes clients who are desperate for dramatic change will eagerly view a success like Lizzie's as a turning point in their lives, as if everything thereafter will be different. Lizzie had no such illusions. She knew that each future challenge would be just as difficult; she also recognized the potential reward to be gained through perseverance. Although lasting self-esteem would have to be earned gradually over time, achieving that goal now seemed possible.

She eventually became more focused on joining a Meetup group for writers, although for a long time the prospect felt overwhelming, more an unrealistic fantasy than an attainable goal. Instead she decided to submit some of her work for publication—also frightening but less personal and immediate since it wouldn't occur face to face. The first form rejection letters devastated her; they also triggered self-loathing. During one of our sessions she parroted in self-mocking tones a letter she had received: "We regret to inform you that your story does not meet our current publishing needs. Best of luck in placing it elsewhere."

She obviously wasn't good enough, Lizzie sneered. What a pathetic waste of time, to believe herself a writer worthy of publication. She might as well give it up.

The shame of Disappointed Expectation. The shame of Exclusion from the world of published writers she longed to join.

By that point in our work Lizzie agreed right away when I pointed out her defensive response. As much as it pained her, she understood that renouncing her goals in order to avoid further shame would thwart any chance of success. After a string of further rejection letters, one editor from a small literary journal suggested changes to the story and encouraged Lizzie to resubmit. In fits and starts she revised the story and it was eventually accepted for publication.

When she read me the acceptance letter during our session, she wept.

THE ONGOING CHALLENGES

Lizzie eventually joined a Meetup group with about a dozen writers but couldn't work up the courage to read during the first few months. A somewhat competitive atmosphere and the presence of two difficult, dominant personalities made the prospect of exposure too threatening. When she finally did read, as she told me during our session, her halting voice and constant self-deprecating asides must have inspired the group to be gentle. "They went easy on me," she said. At first she dismissed all the positive comments they made about her story and focused exclusively on the negative.

Many weeks later she finally read a revision to the group and has since read them the opening chapter of her novel. Taking the stage continues to provoke deep anxiety, and she knows it will never be easy. For the most part she now values the members' suggestions and makes use of them. Lizzie feels that she's becoming a better writer as a result. She has resumed work on her novel and intends to complete it.

Another member of the group, a young man about her own age who writes well-plotted screenplays that Lizzie admires, asked her out for a drink after one of their meetings. She begged off with a fumbled excuse about having to feed her cat and felt socially inept. The prospect of dating still frightens her; she wonders whether she'll ever be able to have sex again. The very thought of exposing her body to another person's gaze feels humiliating.

Lately she has begun taking an evening yoga class twice a week. She unfurls her mat in the back row, as far from the mirror as possible. Because of the exercise she's lost a little weight and is growing fit.

"My form's not too bad," she says. "I'm getting better at it."

eight

INDIFFERENCE

IN HIS MESSAGE ON MY ANSWERING machine, Dean sounded flat and indifferent: "My mom says I should set up an appointment with you." My return call went directly to his answering machine. During the next few days Dean and I traded messages so many times that I wondered whether he was screening my calls to avoid direct contact. Did he really want therapy or was it only his mother's idea?

The respected colleague who'd referred Dean, his mother's therapist, described him as a twenty-year-old who lived at home with his parents after dropping out of college and who refused to get a job. He played video games, stayed out late most nights with his friends, and appeared to show no interest in his future.

Without ever speaking directly, Dean and I finally set up an appointment through another pair of messages.

At the scheduled hour I opened the door to my waiting room and found him seated in the corner chair; he was wearing flip-flops, baggy shorts, and a Pearl Jam tee shirt. A little overweight, with a bulge at his waist, he appeared to be older than his age. He hadn't shaved in a day or two, and his ash-blond hair looked dirty. In his lap he clutched a book with a pale green cover, unopened, its title obscured by his large hands.

Dean stood up and when we shook hands, his grip was slack. Then he walked ahead of me into the consulting room and dropped into the client chair opposite mine, placing the book on the floor between his feet. *The Selfish Gene* by Richard Dawkins. Dean had dark circles under his eyes and seemed tired more than depressed, maybe a little sullen. He crossed an ankle over his knee and began rhythmically snapping his flip-flop against the flat of his foot.

"Tell me about why you're here today," I said.

Dean shrugged without looking up. "Mom says I have to."

"Does that mean you don't really want to be here?" The snapping sound of his flip-flop quickly became irritating. He seemed unaware of it.

Another shrug. "I don't have a choice."

Therapy with clients compelled to attend, whether as part of a legal settlement or by family members as a condition of financial support, rarely succeeds without buy-in from those clients. I learned that lesson many years ago, during my first internship, when a young woman came to see me after her older sister insisted that she get help with her binge drinking. We met for three sessions marked by long periods of silence, terse replies, and her unspoken but clear denial that she had a problem. She failed to show up for her fourth session and never returned my calls.

"Why exactly does your mother think you need to come?"

Dean looked up briefly and squinted at me. Then he glanced off to the side and shrugged again. His attitude of detachment felt mildly hostile.

I decided to stop asking questions for a minute or two and watched him grow uncomfortable as the seconds passed. He finally seemed to notice the nervous energy in his foot and stopped snapping the flip-flop.

"Aren't you supposed to ask me stuff?" he said.

"Like what?"

"Like about my traumatic childhood and how my parents fucked me up. That Freudian shit."

"Why don't you just tell me what you think I need to know?"

The muscles along his jaw began to pulse, as if he was rhythmically clenching his teeth. He didn't speak.

A minute or two into the silence it crossed my mind that I was old enough to be his father. At the time I was in my early forties and had two small boys of my own. Until that point in my career I'd rarely worked with clients that much younger than I, so the age difference between us felt novel.

"I understand you dropped out of college and seem to have no interest in more education or getting a job. If you don't think that's a problem, and you're okay with where you're at, just say so and we can call it a day."

"I don't think it's a problem and I'm okay with where I'm at."

Fuck you.

"So would you like to stop then?"

"Stop?"

"This session. Therapy. We don't have to continue."

"I can't. Mom says—"

"Yes, I know. Your mother says you have to come. That's not a good enough reason. We'd just be wasting our time if you don't want my help."

Dean chewed on his lower lip, glaring at his feet. "I don't see what the big deal is. Why is it so important I get a job? Dad's fat."

It took me a moment. "You mean wealthy?"

He nodded. "He pays for everything anyway so why does she even care? Now she's threatening to take away all my cards if I don't do something. Like what I spend makes any fucking difference. She still gets her allowance. Maybe *she* should get a fucking job."

Anger was our opening. Dean vented at length about his mother and her expectations. Lots of his friends' parents supported their adult children and they didn't have to work. He mentioned the children of several Hollywood celebrities with whom he'd gone to high school in Beverly Hills. He told me about his best friend, Dylan, who lived off a trust fund from his grandparents and whose father was a big-shot litigation attorney. Dylan didn't work, would never have to work.

Most of his friends still lived at home or had their own apartments, paid for by their parents. If they did work, it was part time or at an unpaid internship in the film industry. Dean thought he might like to be a film director one day, but his parents didn't have the right connections to open those doors.

When you work as a therapist in a major metropolitan area, you sometimes get these glimpses into a world of wealth and privilege completely remote from your own life. Dean had grown up with kids whose parents appeared on the cover of *Entertainment Weekly*, owned second homes in Aspen, and always flew first class. He sounded dismissive when describing his own father's business, a chain of dermatology clinics across Southern California. His dad might be rich, but in Beverly Hills, where Dean had grown up, the children of celebrities had opportunities he would never enjoy. Or so he insisted.

In the gaps I asked background questions. He didn't seem as hostile now and answered in adequate detail, with snide commentary along the way, particularly about his mother.

His parents had divorced when Dean was nine years old, he had one younger sister by that marriage, and his father was now on his third wife. Dean's mother had never remarried. At one point she'd opened a clothing store in Beverly Hills and went out of business several months later. "She thinks she has such amazing taste," he said, rolling his eyes. According to Dean, his mother had since devoted herself to yoga and "minding everybody else's business." In the settlement agreement that she and her ex-husband had finally negotiated after a protracted legal battle, she was entitled to a monthly stipend and free housing for life. She often complained to Dean about his stingy father and periodically brought legal motions to increase her support payments.

"I'm not the one who needs a job," Dean said.

The way he presented himself and talked about his parents felt almost like a cliché. Rich-kid-surfer-dude with a chip on his shoulder, whose shallow mother was into glib self-actualization. A familiar type.

Except for that book under his chair. I knew Dawkins by reputation but hadn't read him.

"Your mother's in therapy with Dr. Kasich, right?" I said.

He shrugged. "All her girlfriends are in therapy. What else would they have to talk about at lunch?"

Because I knew my colleague to be serious, I didn't fully trust Dean's characterization of his mother. I studied Dean across from me in the client chair, once again snapping his flip-flop and scowling into his lap. He apparently sneered at therapy and insisted he didn't have a problem.

Sometimes you have an intake session with new clients and never see them again.

"I don't know, Dean. Maybe this isn't such a good idea, you coming here. I know your mother says you have to, but even so—"

"What're you going to tell her?"

"What do you want me to tell her?"

He stared down into his lap. "She'll just make me go to somebody else."

"That's the problem with being financially dependent—the strings. There're advantages to having your own money. Freedom to make your own choices, for starters."

"So *you* think I should get a job too." He sounded more resigned than bitter.

"I didn't say that. But in my experience you can't have it both ways."

My colleague Jim Grotstein has described certain clients who unconsciously long for a fantasized existence in which their needs are gratified without their having to ask, and at the same time they don't have to acknowledge their dependence upon anyone else. Such clients, he says, want "a womb with a view." Helping a client like Dean, who has been exposed to so much wealth and privilege, to face and accept reality can be difficult because he knows so many people who have apparently escaped that fate. Best friend Dylan lived off his trust fund and would never have to work a day in his life.

At that moment feeling optimistic about Dean's future in therapy was difficult. He seemed to despise what I had to offer. Then he surprised me.

"I could use some help with my weight," he said.

"You mean you want to lose some?"

He nodded. "I try going on diets but never stick to them. Late at night I just raid the fridge. The way I feel, it's, like, *fuck it*. I can eat a whole pot of pasta by myself."

EARLY SESSIONS

During the next few weeks Dean described this problem of controlling his appetite and how it had begun. He dated it to his parents' divorce when he was nine. His dad had moved out and closed all their bank accounts, withholding funds for weeks while the lawyers wrangled over temporary support payments. The nanny quit after a month without pay and so did the cook and the cleaning woman. From his description his mother seemed to have fallen into a depression so profound that she barely got out of bed. Dean wondered how he and his younger sister, Acacia, had survived when, so far as he could remember, their mother had never cooked. "Probably maxed out her credit cards on delivery pizza," he said. He couldn't recall how he and Acacia had gotten to and from school during those awful weeks.

One memory stood out. Dean was standing before the pantry, its doors wide open, searching for something to eat. He'd already finished off the peanut butter and all the crackers. There was a box of Frosted Flakes but no milk in the refrigerator. He finally found a tin of Hershey's cocoa powder, mixed it with sugar and water, and ate an entire bowl of paste in front of the TV while watching afternoon cartoons.

Finding comfort in food when you're miserable is a familiar story; Dean recognized how awful he must have felt during that period, although he couldn't remember feeling *anything*. He agreed that unhappiness might be driving his present-day struggles with overeating, but he couldn't feel it. Most of the time he felt numb, with a faint undercurrent of anger. Smoking pot with his friends usually enlivened him, although now and then it stranded him in a bleak, colorless world alleviated only by sleep. Sometimes he erupted in rage if his mother criticized him or asked for help. During our sessions he complained about her a lot.

I've noticed over the years that clients who begin therapy focused on their problems with one parent often have more profound, unrecognized issues with the other. Dean scorned his mother and often ridiculed her vacuous lifestyle, her shallow friendships, the way she clung to youthful styles of dress and behavior well into middle age. He complained about her hypocritical demands and the way she kept hounding him to get a job. Several sessions began with a heated account of their latest blowup.

Dean had virtually no relationship with his father, who now lived with his third wife and their two-year-old daughter. Dad paid all the bills and had always been fairly generous with Dean, even if the man otherwise ignored the children of his first marriage. But lately, when Dean had tried to circumvent his mother by going directly to his father for cash, his father had said, "Work it out with your mom. If I go against her, we'll wind up back in court. You know how she is." Although Dean was disappointed, he made excuses for his father. He knew his mother could be a "real bitch" and didn't blame his dad for wanting to steer clear.

Dean would have preferred to have a celebrity parent like many of his friends, but the more he talked about his father, it gradually became clear that Dean admired his wealth and professional success. With his primary practice in Beverly Hills, his dad's clientele included movie and TV stars. He often socialized with those clients, emulating their lifestyles as if he, too, were a celebrity. He went on lavish vacations and always flew first class, drove a top-of-the-line Range Rover, and owned a second home in Aspen.

Dean spoke with rare enthusiasm about his last Christmas holiday, spent with his father and stepmother in Colorado—private ski instructor, full-time cook, and a massage therapist who came to the house when the family returned each afternoon from the slopes. After he inherited money from his dad, Dean told me, he would be able to afford the same lifestyle. Or so he believed.

I also sensed that not far below the surface Dean felt angry with his father for neglecting him. They might have spent time together during the Christmas holiday, but he rarely heard from his father during the school year. At the occasional dinner in town at some trendy new restaurant, his father talked mostly about himself, the famous people he knew, and his intention to expand his chain of dermatology clinics. Dean's dad planned to sell the chain for many millions one day and then retire in style.

He also made sarcastic remarks about Dean's weight and complexion, the shabby clothes he wore, and the lazy way he expressed himself. His son's appearance seemed to bother him more than Dean's lack of ambition. Most of the time Dean would listen in silence while his father went on about his celebrity friends and the latest chic party he'd attended. If Dean tried to talk about his own life, his father soon changed the subject back to himself, almost as if Dean hadn't spoken. He felt hurt and angry but kept his mouth shut.

Dean didn't hear from his father on his twenty-first birthday. During our next session he made excuses for him—such a busy man, with all those clinics to manage—but obviously felt hurt. He couldn't remember the last time they'd spoken.

"He just forgets about you," I said. "You disappear from his thoughts for weeks at a time."

Dean flinched at my comment. On some level he'd always known the truth, but hearing it spoken aloud had shocked him. In the weeks that followed we pursued this topic of neglect and forgetfulness. What kind of a man, he began to wonder, withholds money in order to wound his wife without any concern for how it might affect his own children? Where was his father when Dean's mother was depressed and Dean had to look after himself? What kind of father talks constantly about his own life and takes no interest in his son? With only a little guidance from me, Dean began to understand that his father was entirely narcissistic and self-absorbed, incapable of caring about anyone but himself.

We returned several times to his memory of that bowl of cocoa paste eaten in front of the television. He got in touch with how desperate he'd felt—frightened and isolated, as if he didn't matter to a soul in the world. His mother eventually emerged from her depression, but without the full-time nanny and cook she could no longer afford was easily overwhelmed by the responsibilities of motherhood. After the divorce Dean's father had dropped out for months. He'd probably never cared much about his children.

Dean's friend Dylan had always been his greatest ally. They watched afternoon cartoons together in grade school, ran weekly experiments with their chemistry sets in middle school, and shared a passion for video games beginning in their teens. "A couple of math-science nerds," he said, laughing, "and really popular with the girls." More recently Dean and Dylan seemed to spend many days each week smoking pot and playing video games together or going out to all-night eateries when they had the munchies.

"Dylan's parents think he's a loser too," Dean told me. "They're always on his case to get a job. Lucky for him he doesn't have to."

Dean never mentioned girls or expressed any interest in sex. He didn't strike me as gay. He seemed almost asexual most of the time. Much later he confessed to me, with obvious shame, that he masturbated compulsively to video porn, multiple times per day. I could see that he expected me to feel contempt for him. He finally told me that he'd kept his masturbation a secret for so long during our work together because he dreaded my reaction. When I compared masturbation with his compulsive eating problem, linking them both to the pain of loneliness, he seemed relieved.

At one point Dean mentioned that he felt grateful for my interest in him, even if I charged money for that attention. He didn't fully trust it, though, and still doubted whether I really cared. Maybe nobody cared about him, not even his mother. She wanted him to get therapy not out of concern for his future but because he embarrassed her in front of her friends.

"I'm just some kind of slacker as far as she's concerned."

Only Dylan truly accepted him.

SHAME AND INDIFFERENCE

During the early months of our work together, Dean's numbness began to lift. From the outside he led the same indolent existence, but at least during our sessions he felt much more deeply than he used to. He was feeling hurt and anger about his father's neglect, sadness for his younger self, and mild compassion for his mother, whom he was coming to see as weak but well intentioned. He hadn't made any progress with his weight.

So far as I could tell, he still felt no interest in a job or further education, and I didn't see it as my place to apply pressure.

Then I received a phone message from his mother. "I need a progress report," she told my answering machine. "I'm not seeing any movement."

Working with clients whose treatment is paid for by a parent or other relative can be tricky. Parents worried about their child naturally want to know whether therapy is helping, and early on I learned to take that feeling seriously. I once declined to discuss a thirty-five-year-old client with his father, the source of his financial support, explaining that a client needed complete privacy for therapy to succeed. The father subsequently refused to pay my bill, and treatment eventually came to an end.

"I have to tell her *something*," I told Dean during his next session. "She doesn't see any change in your behavior and she wants to know why."

The news that his mother had called surprised Dean. It also made him angry. "Tell her it's none of her fucking business," he said.

"I don't think that would go over too well."

He was wearing jeans and black high-tops that day, their laces untied. He tugged listlessly at one of them. "Then tell her I'm going to night school."

"But you're not."

"I could sign up. Doesn't mean I have to go."

"I can't lie to her, Dean."

He scowled at his shoes. "I don't want her fucking nose in my therapy."

"She's just worried about you. You can understand that."

"That's what she wants you to think, like she's some kind of super-mom, so concerned about her children." His recently softening attitude suddenly hardened again. "*Bitch*."

"What if I tell her we've been focused on your feelings about the divorce and how that affected you? It's true, after all. I could say you've been thinking . . . well, what *are* you thinking these days about job or school? It's been a while since you mentioned it."

As soon as I'd spoken, I knew I'd said the wrong thing. A mild tone of frustration had crept into my voice. When I thought about it later, I realized I felt pressure from his mother to prove my effectiveness. I also wondered what Kasich, the colleague who treated Dean's mother and had referred him, would think of me.

I thought he looked hurt for a moment. I wondered whether his eyes were tearing up.

"Nothing." Then he shrugged with indifference, the way he'd so often done during our early sessions. "The fuck, tell her whatever you want. I don't really care."

He seemed quite young then. I thought of the way middle-schoolers will sometimes say "I could care less," asserting their indifference as a kind of superiority, when they don't want to admit feeling hurt or left out.

In *Understanding Shame* the psychologist Carl Goldberg writes that the experience of being in psychotherapy can be inherently shaming, because of the inequities in the relationship—therapists safely shielded by their professional demeanor, clients vulnerable with their secrets laid bare. Although clients enter willingly into this relationship, it may lead to the shame of Unwanted Exposure whenever therapists do their job and reveal some previously hidden psychological truth. When therapists make mistakes, or when they subtly express frustration or disapproval, clients may also feel shame. Not that day but eventually I realized that my tone of voice had caused Dean to feel shame. I felt shame, too, when I recognized the unintentional hurt I had caused him.

Dean's reaction also gave me a clue about what lay behind his apparent indifference concerning his future. During the next few months we revisited his childhood and uncovered how unbearably painful he had found it to love and long for contact, only to be left in near-complete isolation. The shame of Unrequited Love, the shame of Disappointed Expectation. Even when parents don't deliberately shame a child, their lack of involvement and emotional absence leads to feelings of shame. For Dean the divorce, his mother's depression, and his father's disappearance meant he must be defective and inferior, unworthy of love. He shielded himself from such shame by ceasing to care about *everything*, including his own future.

Aesop's fable of the fox and the grapes describes how painful it can be to long for what you can't have and the comfort to be found in renouncing it from a place of superior indifference. Over the years I've seen again and again how clients (my friends and acquaintances, too) will sometimes try to avoid the shame of Disappointed Expectation by taking refuge in defensive indifference. If you don't care what happens, you'll never be disappointed. Dean had no hopes or expectations for what he might achieve and therefore (he believed) could never feel let down by reality. For some people this defensive maneuver also leads to a kind of joylessness in their relationships. Allowing another person to be the source of joy feels threatening when your life history has forged too strong a connection between joy and inevitable disappointment (shame).

Recall the baby's distress in the Still Face Experiment.

As a result of our work during those months, Dean made some half-hearted resolutions to explore enrollment at a local community college but never carried them out. I've also found that the dread of shame sometimes lies behind problems with procrastination and follow-through. If you never really try, then you can never experience the shame of Disappointed Expectation. Grandiose fantasies of what might have been often coexist with such apparent lack of ambition. Dean believed he would have been a film director of great renown if only his father had worked in the industry.

From time to time Dean showed up for his session looking sad and depressed. On those days he sometimes spoke of himself with contempt, the fat boy stuffing his face and jerking off to video porn.

"What a fucking loser."

A TURN OF EVENTS

Dean showed up for one of our sessions looking more exhausted than usual, his face ashen, his clothes unkempt. He looked so despondent that after a minute or two of silence, I asked, "Did something happen?"

He shrugged. He couldn't look me in the eye. "Dylan got a job," he finally said.

Out of the blue—or so it seemed to Dean—his best friend had gone to work as a clerk with his father's law firm. "Menial shit," he sneered. "Sorts mail and works in the copy center. Like, why would you take some bullshit job like that when you've got your own money? I don't get it."

As much as he tried to disguise it with contempt, everything about Dean's demeanor told me he felt hurt, betrayed, and filled with shame. Together he and Dylan had turned their disengaged lifestyle into a superior kind of existence. Working was for losers who had no other choice and who for sure envied Dean and Dylan their freedom. As he kept talking, Dean finally revealed that Dylan planned to enroll in college. He thought he might like to become a lawyer one day like his father.

Dean shrugged. "Fuck him."

"He abandoned you," I said.

"We'll see how long it lasts." He laughed without real amusement. "Dylan getting to work every day by nine? What a joke!"

It took a few more sessions, but I helped Dean acknowledge the shame he felt. When he and Dylan had been partners in crime, Dean could more easily sustain the fiction that getting high and partying was superior to pursuing a career. Nowadays he spent more time than ever alone—more time overeating and compulsively masturbating, which only deepened his shame and self-loathing. He occasionally described himself as a "total dweeb" without a single friend, resorting to contempt (like Lizzie in chapter 7) to put distance between his superior critic self and the other Dean, that defective unlovable loser.

I eventually reminded him that he, like Dylan, had lately been talking about a college course or two. Might that make him feel better about himself, less alone and isolated, not an outcast, and more a part of the human race?

As with Lizzie, Dean's progress in building pride was slow and erratic. The first semester he enrolled in college, he dropped out after a few weeks, taking refuge once again in superiority and indifference. "What a fucking waste of time. And boring! I could barely stay awake." I helped him to recognize his defensiveness and acknowledge the shame (Disappointed Expectation) he felt for giving up.

"But maybe it was the wrong class," I added. "I don't think I've ever heard you say you were interested in American history. Didn't you decide on that class just because all the other ones you wanted were already closed?"

Dean, it eventually emerged, was fascinated by biology and especially the Human Genome Project, which was then just getting under way. On the day we first met, the Dawkins book he was carrying had been a clue. Dean had only a vague idea of the career options for someone in that field and what sort of degree you needed to pursue. He supposed he might start with an introductory course in biology. He brought in the catalogue for his local community college and read me the course description.

"That one doesn't sound too boring."

Although at that point in my career I didn't yet understand the role of shared joy in building self-esteem, I can see in retrospect how my paternal feelings for Dean and the happiness I felt whenever he did well must have supported him. Even a psychoanalyst trained to function as a blank screen can't help but smile when his young client hands him a successful report card. Even if I'd only said "Congratulations," my face would have told him the rest.

Years after his lengthy treatment had come to an end, I received a graduation announcement from Dean in the mail. He'd finished his degree at a four-year university. On the back was a handwritten note: "I thought you'd be happy to see this."

nine

PROMISCUITY AND ADDICTION

DURING THE EARLY YEARS OF my practice, when I saw all my clients in person, the ratio of women to men held consistently at about 80:20. Once I began practicing distance therapy, that ratio quickly reversed. It's impossible to know exactly why that should have been so, but I believe it's because of the absolute privacy afforded by videoconferencing: many men (especially non-American men) still don't want anyone, including strangers on the street, to know they're in treatment, and distance therapy allows them to avoid that particular type of shame (Unwanted Exposure).

For some other clients, like Noah, the depth of their personal shame is so profound that walking into a therapist's office and meeting the therapist in person would be unendurable. Therapy by videoconference obviously involves a kind of distance, and that distance made Noah feel just barely safe enough to sustain our work together. We lived thousands of miles apart with no overlap in our worlds; he knew he could always drop out and no one would ever know. I've had several distance clients disappear that way over the years when the work stirred up too much shame. For many months I worried that Noah would do the same.

The vibration of Noah's cell phone interrupted our initial consultation several times during the first fifteen minutes. He'd placed it on the wooden table beside him and I repeatedly heard it vibrate. Each time Noah would pick it up, briefly scan the screen, then swipe left. Although I'd never used such an app, I'd heard enough from the media to know what the gesture meant. As a thirty-two-year-old gay man, Noah was no doubt using Grindr or something similar. He didn't appear to feel self-conscious about it.

As cell phones have come to permeate modern life, I've tried to remain flexible about their presence during sessions, but after a few weeks I usually suggest to most clients that they turn off their devices while we're talking unless they need to be available for business reasons or in case of emergency. With Noah I asked him to switch off his phone during that first session because the ongoing interruptions kept breaking our contact, distracting him from what he'd been saying. This breaking of contact felt significant somehow; I wondered how it manifested in his outside life.

Clients will occasionally object when I ask them to turn off their phones, especially if they work in fields where they need to be continuously available; Noah powered off his phone and placed it on the table again without comment, but a look of discomfort or embarrassment flickered across his face. Although he was well dressed and apparently fit, he looked extremely tired. At the beginning of the session he maintained good eye contact for the most part, although he frequently broke it with little interruptions—a quick glance down at the table and back up again or off to the side—with a brief loss of focus.

"What was I saying?"

"Your head of production, the problem you're having."

Noah produced TV commercials for a large advertising agency in London. His last boss had recently left and a new head of production was hired in her place. Under those circumstances, Noah told me, it wasn't unusual for a new head to fire the existing production staff and bring on people from the last agency where the boss had worked. Noah believed it was only a matter of time before he lost his current job, especially since he and his new boss were butting heads. Noah's ongoing problems with lateness and absenteeism made matters worse.

"To be honest, I'm not sure why I haven't already gotten the sack." He laughed in a self-deprecating way. Although Noah had a youthful appearance, his eyes had an old-before-his-time look. He had a few gray hairs at his temples and in his closely trimmed beard, reddish brown in color.

Noah told me that this problem of showing up on time or even getting to work some days was one of the main reasons why he'd decided to enter therapy. Despite repeated resolutions to do better, Noah kept sleeping through his alarm or hitting the snooze button so many times that he regularly arrived at work an hour or two late. As a producer who spent much of his time outside the office, he had more freedom than most other agency workers, but he'd recently slept through an important meeting on a Monday morning.

"It was a busy weekend," he said, laughing again in that self-deprecating way. He glanced at his phone, as if he wanted to pick it up.

"Busy?" I repeated. He seemed to have underscored the word, giving it a special weight.

With the guarded air of someone taking care not to disclose too much information, Noah told me that he'd hooked up with "a few" different men during the weekend. "And then I went to a chill-out in Vauxhall on Sunday and barely slept that night. Should've known better."

All I knew of Vauxhall was that an American friend had been mugged there while visiting London.

"What's a chill-out?" I asked.

Looking uncomfortable, his gaze downcast, Noah reached for his phone and began spinning it between his fingers.

He didn't tell me everything that first day—he didn't yet trust me, of course. He also felt such deep shame about the role of drugs and group sex in his life that he found it hard to be open. During the weeks that followed, he gradually filled me in, testing the waters to see whether I would disapprove or feel disgusted by new details.

"Does that gross you out?" he often asked me.

Between our sessions I educated myself about this small and largely hidden sector of gay life. I read some news articles on the subject as well as a professional study from the London School of Hygiene. I watched a documentary film entitled *Chemsex*, about a growing mental health–care crisis in London. I spoke with other gay men I knew.

Chemsex refers to the use of drugs to enhance sexual pleasure, usually in group settings. Through websites or Grindr and other hookup apps, private house parties ("chill-outs") are arranged and drugs sold. I knew about crystal meth, of course, but GHB (gamma hydroxybutyric acid, a psychoactive drug) and mephedrone, a powerful synthetic stimulant, were new to me.

These drugs are imbibed or smoked and sometimes injected, often in combination; in the short term they reduce inhibitions and heighten sexual pleasure, prolonging orgasm for hours. Overdosing and slipping into unconsciousness is common and death from overdose not unusual. The psychological side effects include drug-induced psychosis, paranoia, heightened aggression, and reduced empathy. In the chemsex world sexual violence, exploitation, prostitution, and rape are endemic.

Over the years a few clients like Noah have made me feel naive, as if I lead a sheltered existence and understand little about certain dark corners of life. From my earlier practice and personal life, I knew about group sex and the use of recreational drugs within segments of the gay community, but I was unprepared for the details of Noah's sex life. Frightened too. He told me he was HIV negative, but I worried that he wouldn't remain so for long. Later in our work together, when he hadn't logged on to his account by session time and hadn't emailed beforehand with an explanation, the thought would cross my mind that he might be in the hospital. Or dead.

Recreational drugs and alcohol have been fueling casual sex for decades, of course, but the chemsex world makes one-night stands and impersonal hookups seem tame. Noah sometimes spent the time from Friday evening after work to early Monday morning using a cocktail of different drugs and moving from sex party to sex party. During our first session he was evasive and minimized the number of his sexual partners.

As he grew to trust me, he eventually explained that a typical weekend involved sex with ten to twenty different men, sometimes more.

Noah told me that he'd repeatedly tried to give up chemsex parties and to stop using drugs but had always gone back. Although he couldn't bring himself to tell me so during our initial session, this was the real reason he'd reached out for treatment. Over time he eventually disclosed his full background, including his sexual and relationship history; it seemed clear that he'd never felt truly intimate with anyone.

Part of him longed for a traditional and monogamous relationship—home, commitment, and a shared life. Another part of him felt contempt for "breeders" (straight people); he mocked the gay marriage movement. Sex without drugs felt boring, he said, and he could never imagine restricting himself to one person. At the same time he was finding it increasingly difficult to maintain an erection during these sex parties. He'd added Viagra to the mix. Sometimes he seemed resigned to an early death.

At times I felt the sudden urge to ask Noah if he was out of his mind, putting his life at such serious risk. Now and then I wanted to take him by the shoulders and shake him. I insisted we meet twice weekly, to which he readily agreed, and even then I wondered if it would be enough. Money didn't seem to be an issue and I was never entirely clear about his sources of income. His job apparently paid well, but sometimes I wondered whether he was also selling drugs.

"Are you sure you don't want to see a therapist in person?" I asked, more than once. "I'm sure I could find someone for you in London."

Noah always refused, offering the same excuse: because he traveled so much in his line of work, he'd miss too many sessions if he had to show up in person. He needed a therapist who practiced online and could therefore meet with him whenever he had to go on location. I gradually understood that telling the full truth to a local therapist felt too threatening and literally too close to home.

Thanks to guidance from early clinical supervisors and my own analyst, I've always been clear that worrying about my clients between appointments won't help them; only when we're working together in person can I offer meaningful help. But in the first months after Noah began treatment I often worried about him between sessions. He told me he'd recently begun taking PrEP, an antiretroviral drug that prevents HIV infection when taken daily, but he could still overdose. He might meet with sexual violence. Through my research I'd read about predators who deliberately drugged their victims and raped them after they became unconscious, sometimes killing them by overdose in the process.

I also asked if he would consider entering a residential rehab setting to help him get off the drugs. He shook his head and looked a little angry.

"Trying to get rid of me?" Noah was always on guard for any sign that I had tired of our work together or felt repulsed by the details of his sex life.

I dropped the issue for the time being but never felt entirely comfortable with my decision to accept Noah as a client. Given his near-complete isolation, I thought he needed more solid and immediate contact. I'd located a clinic in London affiliated with the National Health Service that offered free guidance to men with chemsex issues and mentioned it one day during our session. Noah told me that he already knew about it but refused to go there, for vague reasons he couldn't make clear to me.

NOAH'S PAST

Noah had grown up in a middle-class family in southwestern England, the youngest of three children. On the surface his childhood and family history were unremarkable. His father had been an affable, hard-working man who loved his children but left parenting almost entirely to his wife. Noah described his mother as chronically bitter and consumed by grievance, as if life had somehow cheated her. She'd never been affectionate and he couldn't recall ever being touched by her. Both his much-older sisters had struggled with substance abuse during their teens but were now married with children—happily so, Noah believed. Given the large gap between his and their ages, Noah suspected that he'd been an accident—that his mother hadn't wanted a third child.

When he was fifteen years old, Noah began having sex with his school math teacher, a man in his late twenties who'd offered private tutoring when it looked as if Noah might fail his class. Noah didn't think of it as sexual abuse because he looked up to Tim and had been fantasizing about him for months before they actually began having sex. Their relationship continued off and on for two years. From his adult perspective Noah could see that Tim had been a selfish predator who didn't care about him, exploiting Noah's hero worship to make use of him sexually.

Sometimes, when Noah's parents went away for the weekend and left him home alone, Tim would sleep over. When his mother finally realized what Noah and his teacher were doing on those weekends, she stopped speaking to Noah. She wouldn't even look at him. Giving her husband and children the silent treatment had always been her preferred method of expressing disapproval, but it usually lasted only a day or two. This period of silence went on for weeks and Noah had no doubt about the cause.

Whenever she couldn't avoid speaking to him, she became terse, her voice stripped of emotion. Neither of his parents ever talked to him about his sexual involvement with this teacher or intervened with authorities to stop it. As an adult Noah still wondered what his father, now deceased, had felt about it. Perhaps he hadn't even known. He hoped he hadn't known. Noah felt certain that his sexuality disgusted his mother.

After several months he finally told her, "I'm not seeing him anymore." They never spoke of it again. His mother stopped giving him the silent treatment but still found it hard to maintain eye contact. Ever since she'd had a way of addressing Noah that made him feel as if he were not quite there.

At university he tried to lead a heterosexual lifestyle. He dated women and slept with some of them, although without much enjoyment. From time to time he'd go to a gay club, get drunk, and hook up with a stranger for one night. The morning after, he'd be full of self-loathing and would recommit himself to the straight life. He felt convinced he was unattractive to both men and women, despite evidence to the contrary. He eventually began working out regularly, to make himself appear more manly (his word). Growing up, he'd learned to suppress any mannerisms that might identify him as gay, and at university he successfully passed as straight.

In recent years the term *internalized homophobia* has gained currency in the realm of psychology and sociology, and it has been defined as "the personal acceptance and endorsement of sexual stigma as part of the individual's value system and self-concept."[1] Shame lies at the heart of internalized homophobia. Because of his mother's lack of engagement early on, her later rejection of Noah through silence (Unrequited Love), and his growing up in a social milieu that condemned homosexuality (Exclusion), Noah felt damaged, defective, and unlovable. I've rarely met a client so burdened with core shame.

Because he rejected his own sexuality, Noah had never allowed himself to integrate into the gay community and find support there. He didn't have a single gay friend and viewed the gay life he'd experienced up to that point as emotionally shallow, preoccupied with promiscuous sex, and focused almost entirely on appearances. Noah loathed the idea of leading such an empty lifestyle. At the same time he could no longer feign an interest in dating women and having sex with them. After graduating from university, he took a job in advertising and led an extremely isolated life, interrupted now and then by those one-night hookups that filled him with shame.

Noah encountered the world of chemsex during his late twenties when he hooked up on Grindr with Ed, a somewhat older man, and fell hard for him. Unlike those obviously gay men Noah despised, Ed came across as stereotypically masculine, with no identifying mannerisms—the sort of regular "bloke" Noah aspired to be. When Ed asked him to drink a glass of wine laced with "G" (GHB), Noah agreed only because he was afraid Ed would dump him if he said no.

Before then Noah had smoked pot and occasionally drank to excess, but the idea of using hard drugs had always frightened him.

On G he felt beautiful and free of inhibition for the first time in his life. Being penetrated by another man had always been mildly painful; completely relaxed now, he couldn't get enough of it. They had sex for hours that night and for much of the following day. Ed took him to a group sex party the next week, and Noah again took G and smoked crystal meth for the first time. He'd never felt such ecstasy and intense sexual pleasure. Ed dumped him not long thereafter but Noah was hooked. Sex parties became a regular part of his weekends and gradually consumed more and more of his life away from work.

At the point at which he reached out to me for treatment, Noah had no real friends and virtually no social life apart from sex hookups on Grindr, always involving drugs. Whenever he tried to stop taking drugs and avoid sex parties, he slipped into a depression thick with self-loathing. He sometimes thought of killing himself but didn't have a plan. He'd probably die soon from a drug overdose anyway, he told me. During the last year several men he'd met through chemsex parties had died that way. He believed it was only a matter of time.

In our work together I often spoke to Noah about shame. I helped him understand how drugs and sex with strangers helped him to escape from deep feelings of shame, often experienced as inner ugliness or a conviction that he was disgusting to other people. He feared that if anyone got close enough to know him, they'd inevitably reject him. Tracing the origins of his shame, I linked it to his mother's early disengagement, his conviction that her third pregnancy had been accidental and that he'd been an unwanted burden to her. The emotional absence of his father during his early life contributed to Noah's feeling of defect and unworthiness.

As a kind of leitmotif in the treatment, we repeatedly came back to his mother's use of the silent treatment to punish him, linking it to present-day events such as being ghosted by a new sex partner he liked. What could be more shaming, I often remarked, than to make a child feel so repulsive, so completely outside the realm of the acceptable, that he must be utterly shunned?

"You sound like you don't much like my mum," he once said, after I'd spoken again of her cruelty and the ways it had damaged him.

Choosing my words carefully, I said, "I'm angry on your behalf. What an awful way to treat your own child."

But Noah was right about my feelings. The image of the objective and dispassionate therapist is a myth. As you come to care for your clients, you sometimes can't help but have feelings about the way other people have treated them. His mother's deliberate use of silence to shame her own child, with no show of concern for his welfare, made me dislike her.

A CRY FOR HELP

Several months into our work together Noah appeared on-screen for one Monday session looking depressed and exhausted, with black circles under his eyes and days-old stubble. He wore a sleeveless tee shirt, and I could see what appeared to be large bruises on his arms, bluish black against his pale skin. He made no mention of those bruises, but I wondered whether he had worn that shirt so that I'd notice. When I asked about the bruises, he shrugged and did not answer. In a flat, exhausted voice he went on to describe another weekend entirely consumed by sex and drugs. He'd lost track of the number of his sex partners but believed he'd been penetrated by more than thirty men.

He thought they'd all used condoms but couldn't be sure because he'd "gone under" for a couple of hours and didn't know what had happened to him during that time. "Going under" meant using too much G and then passing out. From my research I'd learned that people who go under will sometimes slip into a coma and need to be hospitalized. Sometimes they die. As Noah described his weekend, he seemed numb at first. Then he began to cry in a strangled sort of way. He desperately wanted to give up the chemsex life but couldn't stop.

He went on to tell me that he'd lost his job on Thursday, just as he'd been expecting all along. He called himself a "totally fucked-up wanker" and told me the idea that he could ever have a healthy relationship was a joke. His voice mingled agony with sarcastic self-loathing. "Might as well call it a day," he said. Overdosing was so common within his world it wouldn't look like suicide . . . nobody would even notice. He sounded full of self-pity but also like he despised himself.

Clients like Noah can easily make a therapist feel scared, helpless, and incompetent. Their despair can infect you, causing you to doubt your skills and your ability to help. After checking to make sure he had no plan and didn't actually intend to kill himself, I reminded Noah of some earlier ideas we'd discussed—how he took refuge in contempt and self-loathing to distance himself from that "totally fucked-up wanker," how self-pity could sometimes be a substitute for self-esteem when shame ran deep. Nothing I said that day felt particularly helpful or effective.

When he logged on at the beginning of our next session, the second for that week, he looked even worse. His face dark with despondency, he gazed into his lap, seemingly immobilized.

"Are you all right?" I asked. He made no reply.

After a few minutes of silence he glanced up for a moment, made intense eye contact, despairing and angry, then abruptly disconnected the call.

When I tried to reinitiate, he didn't answer. I sent several emails that received no response. From my office I called his mobile number and tried again later from my cell phone. Both calls went straight to voice mail. For hours after that aborted session I felt anxious and worried. I also suspected that Noah intended for me to feel that way, even if he wasn't consciously aware of what he was doing.

The concept of projection long ago entered the mainstream, and most people understand the meaning of the expression "the pot calling the kettle black": we sometimes criticize others for faults we don't want to recognize in ourselves. Projection also has other complex motivations and uses. Sometimes clients will project unbearable emotion onto their therapist so they don't have to feel it themselves, and sometimes they'll do so in order to provoke a desired response. Noah's dramatic rupture felt like a call for help.

I'm at the end of my rope. Do something!

I debated contacting the local police department in London. During the weekend I researched local UK suicide prevention hotlines. I sent Noah another email and made more calls. After a day and a half he finally sent me a text message:

I'm not going to kill myself. Speak to you tomorrow at the usual time.

When he answered my video call at the beginning of our next session, Noah didn't look as bad as I'd feared. He appeared less exhausted, as if he'd finally gotten a decent night's sleep. I felt immensely relieved . . . angry, too, for complicated reasons. Noah had put me through an ordeal the last few days, but I was mostly feeling angry with myself, questioning my judgment in taking him on. As I'd struggled with my anxiety during the weekend, I'd concluded that we couldn't continue as we'd been doing.

"I'm not ending your treatment," I told him, "but you need some local support. We can keep working together if that's what you want but only on the condition you contact that clinic we've discussed. You need more help than I can offer." I spoke more insistently than I usually do with clients. It must have been obvious that the last few days had unsettled me.

I reminded him that the London health center held a walk-in clinic, no appointment necessary, the following night from 5:00 to 7:00 p.m.; with little resistance he agreed to go. I think he felt relieved that I was upset and so certain about what he needed. Much later he told me that my reaction had made him believe for the first time that I cared about him.

A SENSE OF COMMUNITY

Our work together had laid the groundwork, but his involvement with counselors and other patients at the clinic supported his efforts to grow in ways that distance therapy could not. As part of the clinic's program he made an abstinence contract: without committing to anything further, he agreed to spend a single week without using drugs and to refrain from sex during that period. He lasted only three days, but the nonjudgmental encouragement he received from his counselor at their next appointment enabled him to try again rather than succumbing to shame (Disappointed Expectation). Eventually he managed to make it through a full week, and the pride he felt in his success helped him refrain for longer periods. He suffered setbacks, of course; it was a lengthy process.

Noah also attended group support sessions each week. For a long time he held himself aloof from other members, telling me about those "losers" in sarcastic detail during our sessions. I helped him to understand his retreat into superiority and contempt as a defense against shame. When he finally told his own story during one of those group meetings, he surprised himself by crying. The empathy and support he received from other members felt like an entirely new experience to Noah. A few of them invited him to join them for coffee after the meeting.

"I guess I'm part of the loser group," he told me with a smile. He didn't sound aloof or contemptuous. We both understood he felt happy to belong.

ten

AVOIDING SHAME IN EVERYDAY LIFE

MANY INSTANCES OF WHAT WE call social anxiety would be better described as shame anxiety, the fear or dread of encountering shame through Unwanted Exposure. As psychoanalyst Léon Wurmser writes, "Shame is a specific form of anxiety evoked by the imminent danger of unexpected exposure, humiliation, and rejection." Shame anxiety signals an impending threat, which anxious people subdue by avoiding those situations in which they feel overly exposed.[1]

The case studies presented in this section portray clients who so extensively tried to avoid shame that their efforts stopped them from forming relationships and achieving their goals, but most people regularly try to minimize exposure to the shame family of emotions. Of course they do: at the very least embarrassment feels uncomfortable, and humiliation can be excruciating. Attempting to avoid shame is thus normal and understandable. Lizzie (chapter 7), Dean (chapter 8), and Noah (chapter 9) relied on defensive maneuvers that, for the most part, differed only in degree and intensity from ways that all of us behave from time to time.

Consider the following examples from everyday life that might seem familiar:

You choose clothes to wear to a social function based on how
   dressed up or down you expect other guests to be.
Although you've been planning for a couple of days to extend an
   invitation to a new friend, you try to make it sound casual and
   spontaneous.
You decide not to attend a big party because you don't know
   anyone else who is going.
At the staff meeting you don't speak up because you're new and
   haven't yet gotten a feel for team dynamics.
You refrain from telling that risqué joke because the crowd
   strikes you as a little reserved.

Modulating our behavior to avoid an experience of Unrequited Love,
Exclusion, or Unwanted Exposure often makes sense. The shame of
Disappointed Expectation feels painful, and we regularly devise ways to
circumvent it. There's nothing pathological about trying to avoid shame,
provided our efforts don't stop us from forming relationships and pursuing important goals. But as these case studies show, pervasive efforts to
avoid shame usually isolate people and impede their development of
self-esteem.

The desire to avoid shame may encourage conformity, of course. This
makes sense when you recall that shame evolved as a means to enforce
group values and promote survival of the tribe. Widespread efforts to avoid
shame through conformity may encourage a sense of community through
shared values but can also stifle individuality when those values are too
narrowly defined.

Even in less restrictive societies opportunities to feel shame abound.
Whenever we seek contact with other individuals, put ourselves forward
in group settings, set goals, or express desire, we risk an experience of
shame. The preceding case studies described the strategies used by clients
who struggled to avoid core shame, but all of us confront similar issues
in our daily lives as we strive to limit exposure to everyday, ordinary
shame.

PERFORMANCE ANXIETY

Although some extremely self-confident (and occasionally narcissistic) individuals truly enjoy the spotlight, many people experience occasional discomfort, from mild to intense, whenever they become the object of group attention. Lizzie's father was crippled by stage fright, but the prospect of appearing onstage as an actor, musician, or other type of entertainer stirs up some degree of anxiety for most of us. Even successful public speakers may feel anxious before they address an audience. We usually refer to this as performance anxiety, but again, and as Broucek says, *"shame anxiety* would be a more accurate term."[2]

> *What if the audience dislikes my performance?*
> *What if I forget my lines or make mistakes?*
> *What if I appear foolish or incompetent?*

To avoid potential exposure to shame, many (and perhaps most) people will not place themselves in such a situation to begin with. This isn't pathological. Unless you feel a strong desire to appear onstage, it makes sense to spend your energies on endeavors that don't risk so much exposure to shame. Some people may easily shrug off a disappointing performance, but appearing inadequate or unqualified in front of an audience would make most of us feel embarrassed and perhaps humiliated.

Over the years I've appeared on dozens of radio shows and a few TV programs. I've grown accustomed to answering questions on-camera and fielding calls from radio audiences. I always feel some degree of anxiety before each appearance, even when the questions have been provided in advance and I'm speaking on a familiar subject. Whenever I make a public appearance, I run the risk of embarrassing myself or appearing unprepared (Unwanted Exposure). So far my anxiety hasn't stopped me from making these appearances, but I know that low-level dread will always be a part of my experience.

Giving a presentation in class or at a meeting of coworkers will usually stir up some degree of anxiety for most people. We naturally want to make a good impression; we hope to win the esteem of our teachers, colleagues, bosses, or classmates. Fearing that we might fall short (Disappointed Expectation) or embarrass ourselves (Unwanted Exposure), we sometimes avoid situations in which shame might arise. At work we might keep a low profile and refrain from voicing our opinions. We may decline high-profile assignments or sit in the background while others on our team take the microphone.

Once again, none of this is pathological per se. Only when performance anxiety or fear of shame prevents us from achieving cherished goals does it become a problem. If we avoid taking risks to such a degree that we thwart those goals, we may eventually feel even worse about ourselves, a vicious cycle in which intense performance anxiety leads to shame avoidance, resulting in more shame.

In his classic sociological study *The Presentation of Self in Everyday Life*, Erving Goffman analogizes face-to-face interactions between two people and a stage performance in which both individuals are adjusting their appearance and behavior to guide the impression formed by the other.[3] According to Goffman, whenever we come into contact with other people, we attempt to control or guide the impressions they form of us by modifying our appearance and manner, often without conscious awareness that we are doing so. Those others will simultaneously behave in a similar way while trying to obtain information about us from our performance.

Goffman holds that a desire to avoid embarrassment, for oneself as well as the other person, motivates such a performance. From this perspective all social interaction potentially involves a degree of performance anxiety, motivated by the desire to avoid shame.

SHYNESS

As Susan Cain has described in her book *Quiet*, some people are introverted by disposition and not because they struggle with self-esteem issues. They're quite content to listen while others speak or to spend time in solitary, creative activities. For these people, as social historian Joe Moran notes, shyness can be something that you are, rather than a trait or inhibition that prevents you from becoming the person you'd like to be.[4]

For many other people, however, as Moran observes, shyness is "often reactive and damage-limiting: fearing that others will share our own disapproving thoughts about ourselves, our goal is often to not make a mistake, to avoid censure rather than go after praise."[5] To be shy, bashful, or overly self-conscious means to be on constant guard "against the risk of being humiliated, a risk viewed as continually present."[6] In other words shyness as a defining and pervasive personal trait reflects an ongoing effort to avoid the shame of Unwanted Exposure, as in the case of my client Lizzie.

Many otherwise confident people may become shy in specific situations. Confronted with a group of strangers, for example, they tend to become more reserved and less expressive than they'd be with people they know well. Imagine you are attending a party where most of the other guests are unfamiliar, for example. You will probably be more self-conscious than usual and less effusive than you'd be among close friends. Such reserve seems natural. Knowing your crowd well and feeling certain of their friendship allows you to express your personality without restrictive self-reflection, but until you can assess your safety level within a new group, you naturally modulate your behavior to avoid the shame of Unwanted Exposure or Exclusion.

For the same reason many of us will become shy when asking someone for a date. At that point it's too early to speak of Unrequited Love, but when we feel and express interest in another person, we run the risk that it won't be reciprocated. Although we are lively and engaged with our friends, we may become reserved with a potential romantic partner. We may hedge our bets and show less interest than we actually feel as we search for clear welcome signs before we proceed. The dating world is rife with opportunities to experience shame.

Among the other uses of dating and hookup apps like Tinder or Grindr is the help they offer users in avoiding the full-on experience of shame by diluting it. Even if you express an interest in someone's profile and that person doesn't respond, you can swiftly move on to another prospect. Many people make connections and form long-term relationships by using such apps. Others, like my client Noah, become lost in a world of shallow contact, avoiding the prospect of shame through superficial and short-lived hookups. At the same time such defensive behavior often leads to its own type of shame when we violate our values and behave in ways we don't respect.

PROCRASTINATION AND ARTISTIC BLOCK

For a variety of reasons many people procrastinate more than they'd like or can't bring their creative projects to completion. A ruthless perfectionism inhibits some of them. Others have low frustration tolerance for the long hard work involved in creating and revising. Still others, like Lizzie, become mired in artist's block because they dread the *prospect* of shame, always a possibility when you complete a work and make it public (Disappointed Expectation, Unwanted Exposure). If they never complete and expose it, such individuals unconsciously believe, they won't ever have to experience shame.

As in Dean's case, such blocks often coexist with, and are compounded by, grandiose fantasies. One of my clients with only rudimentary musical skills, who rarely practiced despite repeated resolutions to do so, fancied herself a musical genius whose compositions would one day earn her worldwide renown. (She often made me think of Lady Catherine de Bourgh, from Jane Austen's *Pride and Prejudice*, who felt certain she would have been "a great proficient" at piano if only she had learned to play.) Such grandiose expectations, impossible to fulfill, intensify the dread of shame; one reaction is to remain in a perpetual limbo state between conceiving and executing a project (like Edward Casaubon in George Eliot's *Middlemarch*); another is to make endless small changes without completing it.

Have you ever resolved to make an important change in your life and failed to execute it? Perhaps you came up with an exciting idea for a new side business or creative venture, one that seemed like a surefire winner you could manage in your spare time, but you let it languish and fade. Such lack of follow-through can occur for many reasons, but avoiding shame often plays a part. The so-called fear of failure reflects a dread of the shame that might arise from Disappointed Expectation and Unwanted Exposure.

Difficulties with procrastination and follow-through don't afflict only writers and other artists. Many people struggle to complete and hand in school or work assignments, for example. Once again, various psychological factors may play a role in such difficulties, and shame is only one of them. If a dread of prospective shame drives people to procrastinate, they often commence work at the eleventh hour once sufficient pressure has mounted and then dash off a paper or cram for an exam. After they receive a middling grade, they mitigate their shame by telling themselves they would have done much better if only they had tried.

Sound familiar?

One of my clients, unemployed at the time, found the prospect of applying and interviewing for an open position so threatening that he took many days and sometimes weeks to complete his application—so long, in fact, that the position had often been filled by the time he applied for it. In addition to procrastinating and avoiding the application itself, he spent hours revising his cover letter and résumé in the hope that making it perfect would guarantee success. This client struggled with profound lifelong shame, had suffered a couple of serious career setbacks, and dreaded the prospect of encountering even more shame through the job application process.

The risk of shame becomes greatest, of course, when we commit to a project and work as hard as we can to complete it. But when we do, we also stand the greatest chance of earning our own self-respect, as I show in part 3 of this book.

INDIFFERENCE AND CONTEMPT

My client Dean avoided the prospect of shame by renouncing all ambition. If you never aspire to achieve anything, then you can never feel shame if you fall short. People who lack motivation, who are unable to plan for the future, or who appear to be lazy all may be driven by a dread of shame that might arise from Disappointed Expectation: if you expect nothing, if you have no goals, you can't ever be disappointed.

An apparent lack of interest in dating or forming friendships may also be fueled by a fear of shame. Many people become socially isolated because they find it impossible to express interest in other people; rather than expose themselves to the possibility of rejection (Unrequited Love), they become loners or workaholics. They take refuge in indifference when longing for human contact feels too threatening.

From time to time most of us avoid shame through indifference in less pervasive ways. Did you ever disguise your interest in another person because you believed it wasn't reciprocal (Unrequited Love)? Did you ever try to appear nonchalant when you found out you hadn't been invited to a friend's party (Exclusion)? Did you ever say "I didn't want the job anyway," when you found out another colleague was promoted instead of you (Disappointed Expectation)? Most of us have expressed indifference at one time or another as a means of mitigating shame.

A hidden sense of superiority often lurks behind such apparent indifference, sometimes mingled with contempt. Dean viewed his carefree lifestyle as superior to a nine-to-five job and expressed contempt for his friend Dylan when he took one. Although Noah longed for a shared home as part of a committed relationship, he belittled heterosexuals and insisted that sex without drugs was boring. When high on chemsex drugs, he felt ecstatic, on a plane far superior to that inhabited by ordinary mortals.

While indifference expresses a lack of desire, contempt goes a step further and insists that the desired object actually has no value and isn't worth desiring. Joe Moran, a shy man himself, believes "that what sustains the shyness of many people is that conceited part of us that finds much social conversation to be an empty ritual, a mere filling in of awkward silence." He also speaks of "that weird overconfidence that can afflict shy people, the sense that they are escaping the cant and evasions of social life."[7] Shy people, like everyone else, long for human connection and to be part of a community; when the pain of not belonging becomes unbearable, they may take refuge in arrogance and contempt for the world that excludes them.

Unconventional teens rejected by their peers sometimes take refuge in superiority and contempt, viewing the popular kids as bimbos or lugheads. Like my client Noah, gay men who feel themselves to be outsiders will sometimes express contempt for the heterosexual world (breeders) that excludes them. Many people find ways to belittle others who make them feel inferior, with scornful epithets like "pointy-headed intellectuals" and "yuppie scum."

Aesop's scornful fox who dismisses those unattainable grapes as sour could stand in for most of us at one time or another. Indifference and contempt help us to avoid shame when we feel excluded, inferior, unwanted, or less successful than we'd like to be.

PROMISCUITY, DRUGS, AND ALCOHOL

Like my client Noah, some men and women often prefer one-night stands or casual sex because they minimize the risks of shame. Such impersonal connections deprive the other person of emotional standing to arouse shame. Because anonymous sex partners never get to know you, they can't pass judgment about your shortcomings. Without emotional engagement they will never form expectations that you might disappoint. When casual sex becomes compulsive and promiscuous, core shame usually drives it.

At the end of a painful breakup, struggling with feelings of rejection (shame), many people seek to avoid a repeat by deciding not to date or to date widely and not look for another committed relationship. You probably have friends who have told you for months after their last relationship ended badly that they are "not looking," or you might have gone through such a phase yourself. Such self-protective measures are normal and understandable, provided they don't become a permanent way of life. Avoiding shame as a temporary strategy often makes sense but can lead to loneliness, isolation, and a deeper sense of shame when it becomes entrenched.

Alcohol and recreational drugs often reduce social inhibition, which is another way of saying that they make the prospect of shame more bearable. Party hosts will provide alcohol in order to loosen up their guests, to free them from the shyness they naturally feel in the presence of strangers. As Donald Nathanson has noted, "One of the primary actions of alcohol is to release us from the bonds of shame."[8] A glass of wine or a cocktail at the end of the day may also help us to weather a blow to our self-esteem, and recreational drugs may serve the same purpose.

When avoiding shame becomes a person's central goal, as in the case of Noah, he may abuse alcohol or drugs as an ongoing method for coping with shame. When afflicted by shame at our core, we easily come to rely upon those drugs for ongoing, continuous relief. A pernicious cycle sets in: We turn to our drug of choice to escape from shame, often using more of it than we intended; once it wears off, we feel even more shame for having disappointed our own expectations. Because the compounded shame feels unbearably painful, we once again turn to our drug for release.

Alcoholics refer to this dynamic as the "squirrel cage," because the search for release in alcohol leads to shame and a further need for alcohol to relieve it, producing more shame, and so on. John Bradshaw, author of *Healing the Shame That Binds You*, has written extensively about the relationship between shame and various forms of addiction; he believes that shame afflicts anyone who engages in compulsive or addictive behaviors. Within that group he includes gamblers, workaholics, sex addicts, and those who struggle with an eating disorder. Most of us have comfort foods we enjoy as an occasional form of solace, a normal and nearly universal response to pain and disappointment. When relying on food for relief becomes chronic, the drive to avoid and obscure shame usually plays a part.

Many people will occasionally rely on food, drugs, or alcohol to escape from shame if they've suffered a setback like losing a job (Disappointed Expectation) or experienced rejection (Unrequited Love, Exclusion). We sometimes refer to this as drowning our sorrows or eating our feelings.

Nothing is inherently pathological about such behavior, provided it's a temporary measure to avoid shame and we eventually go on to face it. Only when avoiding shame through substance abuse becomes chronic, as it was for Dean and Noah, is it a source of grave concern.

SECRETS AND WHITE LIES

As many shame researchers have noted, the "notion of *hiding* is intrinsic to and inseparable from the concept of shame."[9] Perhaps the most obvious and common strategy for avoiding shame is to keep secrets, to conceal the truth from other people who might judge or reject us. Because shame arises from Unwanted Exposure, we can avoid it by making sure the truth never comes to light.

Perhaps you've had a conversation like this one.

"Did you remember to change that doctor's appointment?"
"It was superbusy at work today. I'll call first thing tomorrow morning."

In truth you may simply have forgotten that you'd promised to call the doctor's office, but because you're embarrassed to admit it, you concoct a white lie about your hectic day at the office. Your answer implies that work commitments prevented you from fulfilling your promise.

Sometimes we avoid acknowledging shame even to ourselves by focusing instead on the disappointment or contempt we imagine that someone else might feel if they knew our secret. We might conceive of that person as especially harsh or judgmental (which may actually be true). A psychological sleight of hand, shifting the focus from *our* Disappointed Expectation to *her* judgmental nature, helps us to avoid directly confronting our shame.

Imagine the conversation about the medical appointment continues, and your partner sighs with exasperation.

"The appointment's in two days. Do you want me to take care of it?"

"I told you—it was crunch day at work. Get off my back!"

As we focus on the other person, especially when we begin to blame them for some defect of character instead of owning up to our mistakes, we move from merely avoiding our shame to denying that it exists. I address strategies for denying shame in the next section.

SEE EXERCISE 4, PAGES 271–272

DENYING SHAME

eleven

THE IDEALIZED FALSE SELF

Endearing.

I often use this word to describe those clients who, for sometimes ineffable reasons, inspire feelings of deep affection. Looking back over my career, I believe I have been most successful in helping those clients whom I find endearing, especially when it seems clear their parents didn't feel that way about them. When parents fail to find joy in a child, even when they are not abusive or grossly negligent, it instills feelings of shame that may last a lifetime. Psychotherapy helps the most when insight unfolds within a relationship in which the client senses a therapist's affection, even if it isn't always voiced.

I found Anna endearing from the beginning of our work together. She was in her midthirties and lived in Houston; she reached out to me for help with "depression and self-esteem issues." During our first session she seemed preoccupied with my impressions of her, often asking whether I thought something she had said sounded stupid. She wondered whether she might be feeling sorry for herself and simply needed to get her act together. She believed she came across as unlikable and had always felt that way. Sometimes a client's obvious suffering makes her endearing and inspires in me the wish to help alleviate it.

Anna was seated before her laptop in her private office and appeared to be tall, with high cheekbones, a narrow face, and auburn hair pulled back in a way that gave her a somewhat old-fashioned appearance. She sat with the kind of erect posture and straight back that does not come naturally to most people. Although she was born and raised in Texas, she spoke with no trace of a drawl. She later told me she'd worked hard at Bryn Mawr to alter her speech patterns and shed her native accent. Without sounding pretentious she came across as refined and well educated. At the same time she seemed ill at ease during our sessions and found it difficult to maintain eye contact.

Anna suffered from the sort of punitive superego that finds constant fault and insinuates contempt into self-reflection. Feelings of fraudulence plagued her, which is often the case with people who struggle with shame. She was a probate lawyer and worried that her colleagues and partners disliked her, for reasons she struggled to articulate. "Maybe because I have no sense of humor?" she offered. "Or because I'm so uptight? I don't know why."

Despite her statement that she lacked a sense of humor, Anna came across as witty and made frequent mordant observations, most often directed at herself. The video interface I use displays the other person full screen, with a small box in the lower corner that shows you yourself. Now and then she'd abruptly focus on her own image and make a sarcastic aside: "God, this blouse. I look like somebody's grandmother." Sometimes she described her colleagues with keen and unsparing insight, referring to them with her own special epithets: "the snake," "Uriah Heep," "Brad Pitt manqué." I gathered that only close friends and family knew this acerbic side of her.

For months before beginning therapy she had felt profoundly depressed, although she had not allowed herself to indulge that feeling, as she put it. She worried that she was a burden to her husband and savagely berated herself for being a terrible mother to their young son—too impatient, too self-absorbed, with little tolerance for his needs or emotional ups and downs. Her primary care physician had prescribed antidepressants, but Anna could not endure the side effects, especially the weight gain, which made her feel disgusted with her body.

In our early sessions Anna felt some relief when I drew attention to the brutal way she treated herself. Clients like Anna, who have spent their entire lives subjected to harsh self-criticism, do not always recognize how badly they treat themselves. As I described it to Anna, "It's like the air you breathe, so pervasive you don't even notice it." Our early sessions focused on helping her to become more conscious of this contempt and self-criticism and to begin standing up for herself.

Most psychodynamic psychotherapists are familiar with this phase of treatment. Earlier in my career I focused on this kind of savage perfectionism without fully understanding the unconscious shame behind it. Over the years I've learned that unbearable feelings of defect and unworthiness, rooted in early life, drive expectations that one conform to an ideal self-image. When core shame takes hold during childhood, people sometimes take flight into an idealized self that is meant to disguise and disprove the sense of damage.

This dynamic lies at the heart of narcissism. Men and women who more successfully embody their idealized false self typically defend it with arrogance, contempt, and feelings of superiority; they often blame other people for their own mistakes, shoring up their winner status at the expense of the losers they despise. These narcissistic individuals rarely seek psychotherapy, although I discuss one such client in chapter 12.

In contrast Anna suffered from depression and self-esteem issues because, in her view, she consistently fell short of expectation. She believed that the other members of her family of origin—her parents and her older brother, Aidan—had achieved a level of success and accomplishment she could not attain. Although she recently had made partner at a law firm where she specialized in estate planning, she felt herself to be a failure, a disappointment to her parents, a lackluster child with nothing special about her. She covertly competed with Aidan, her parents' pride and joy, but she felt she could never win this competition.

As a child she'd taken ballet lessons, studied violin, and learned French from a succession of au pairs. I had the distinct impression that Anna's parents had groomed their children to embody an ideal of sophistication that only Aidan (apparently) had fulfilled. Anna gave up ballet in her early teens and not long thereafter resigned from the statewide youth orchestra of which she had been concert mistress. Her parents made empty supportive remarks about its being "her own choice" if she wanted to quit, but Anna knew they disapproved. She had since forgotten most of the French she'd learned.

Clearly Anna led a fairly joyless life. She took occasional pleasure in her son and usually cried when she did because she felt so relieved to have normal maternal feelings. She loved music but rarely found time to listen. The one place she felt at peace, unburdened by expectation and a sense of failure, was the yoga studio. Anna struck me as about as far from a New Age type as I could imagine, but she was passionate about yoga. She often felt selfish and guilty about it, but she made time for class twice a week, usually in the morning before she went to the office.

ANNA'S FABULOUS FAMILY

Early in his career Anna's father had worked as a corporate lawyer on Wall Street, then went in-house with one of his firm's clients and relocated to Houston, where the corporate headquarters was located. He eventually advanced to senior vice president and earned, according to Anna, close to a million dollars a year. Her mother had inherited family money and didn't work. She sat as a director on boards for the symphony and ballet, devoted herself to several high-profile charities, and managed their extensive social life. They kept a pied-à-terre in New York City, traveled extensively in luxurious style, and knew many prominent figures both locally and in Manhattan.

"You sound like you're in awe of your parents," I said.

"They're just so glamorous. As opposed to dowdy humdrum me with my boring job. Estate planning! Now don't get too excited."

Brother Aidan was an investment banker who lived in Paris with his French wife, Liliane, who was "drop-dead gorgeous," had a master's degree in comparative literature from the Sorbonne, and spoke four languages fluently. Aidan and Liliane lived an opulent lifestyle, with a large apartment in the Sixteenth Arrondissement and a summer home near Nice. Mom and Dad took frequent trips to France and had traveled throughout Europe with Aidan and Liliane, who had no children. Anna and her husband, Dan, lived in the same city as her parents, but they rarely saw one another.

"They're nice to Dan but they think he's boring," Anna told me. "They wish I'd married Seth."

Anna had met Seth during college and dated him off and on for several years while attending law school on the East Coast. She rarely introduced her boyfriends to her parents, fearing their disapproval; when she finally flew with Seth to Houston for a visit, she worried about the impression he would make and coached him on how to behave, which subjects to avoid, and those opinions that would win him favor. He succeeded beyond her expectations.

"They liked him better than me," Anna said. "When they found out he'd sold his novel, they went into raptures. You would have thought he was being published by Knopf instead of some small literary press! Let me tell you, I definitely earned some status points that day. I might be a disappointment, but at least I had good taste in boyfriends. His glamour made me look less dowdy."

The theme of glamour and dowdiness ran throughout our work together. Anna as the drab, unexceptional, and therefore unlovable child. Aidan, Liliane, and even Seth as the glamorous ones who deserved all the attention and acclaim.

During the several years they dated, Anna increasingly felt in competition with Seth because (she believed) her parents found him more exciting. When his book was released, they hosted an event in Houston for their wide social circle. During visits to her parents' house Anna would meet old friends of the family who invariably told her they'd "heard so much" about Seth's book and sometimes had even read it. If he accompanied her on those visits home, she frequently slipped and called him Aidan, the rival for her parents' affection. She usually returned to New York feeling angry and depressed.

Seth might have been an up-and-coming young writer, but he made a lousy boyfriend. Charming but self-absorbed, occasionally unfaithful, financially unreliable. The sex, she told me, was the best she'd ever had. Passionate, inventive, uninhibited. But Seth was moody, too, and prone to black depressions that went on for weeks during which their sex life came to a halt. One of Anna's healthier choices in her life was to cut Seth loose, leave New York, and eventually find a more stable partner to marry.

Dan taught high school English. According to Anna, the only glamorous thing he'd ever done was work in Morocco for two years while in the Peace Corps. A passionate liberal, he cared deeply about many issues, especially poverty and early childhood education. It seemed apparent to me that Dan loved his wife and son. He shared in household responsibilities and undertook more of the cooking and child care than Anna, who worked longer hours. He didn't mind doing laundry, which Anna refused to do because it made her feel like a failure. She wanted to send their laundry out to be done as her parents always had, but Dan insisted it was a waste of money.

While the healthier part of Anna valued Dan's steadiness, another part of her, which was aligned with her parents, looked down on him. Although she never gave voice to her views, she frequently mocked him in her thoughts—his utter lack of style, the excess pounds he carried, his low-status job. She felt ashamed of their sex life too. Since the birth of their son, both stretched thin, sex had become an infrequent event. Even in the beginning, their sex life had lacked the passion of sex with Seth.

Spending time with her parents only made her feel worse about her marriage. Still handsome in their sixties, obviously attracted to one another after so many years together, her mother and father embodied everything she and Dan were not.

After listening to her go on at length about her fabulous parents and their amazing marriage, I once remarked, "I hear they have great sex up there on Olympus. Down here on Earth, we're just so boring."

She laughed but it brought her no relief. She suffered deeply from this image of the ideal parents leading the ideal life, while she plodded through in abject mediocrity. From that point on we regularly referred to the Olympians versus the humdrum mortals as a kind of shorthand.

"They don't even like my kid!" Anna cried. "Aren't grandparents supposed to dote on their grandkids? Whenever I ask Mom to babysit Nick, she's having lunch with some columnist or they're going to a gala event they can't miss. They almost always have a good excuse for missing his birthday parties too."

"Children are so unsophisticated!" I said. Sometimes these descriptions of her parents activated my own sarcastic side. "He's only two years old. Just wait till he's grown up, then your parents will take an interest. As long as he's not too boring."

Unlike everyone else, Anna's parents consistently referred to their grandson as Nicholas.

Her parents never forgot a birthday and gave thoughtful gifts at Christmas. They paid for Nick's preschool when Dan and Anna couldn't afford it. Despite their emotional shortcomings in regard to Anna, they came across as fascinating people: thoughtful, well read, brilliant conversationalists so long as you didn't demand too much from them. I've known other people like Anna's parents, delightful to know on a social level but who make terrible parents. In large part Anna owed her wit and insight to the cultivated atmosphere in which she'd grown up.

A FAMILY VACATION

During the first year we made some steady progress toward helping her to understand how "Ideal Anna," the person she was supposed to be, corroded her self-esteem and undermined her relationships. With time she was learning to value the real instead of the ideal, suffering periodic setbacks whenever she spent time with her mother and father. I had little success in challenging this view of her parents as perfect.

Anna appeared for one of our sessions looking both excited and on edge. "We're going to France!" she told me. It would be their first real vacation in years. Because Dan didn't earn much as a schoolteacher, and they had a young child, international travel had seemed impossible. Now her parents had offered to fly her whole family to Nice, where they would spend a week at Aidan and Liliane's villa, the whole family together for the first time in years.

"Doesn't that sound incredible!?" Anna asked. She seemed more agitated than I'd seen in some time, her back more erect than usual, her shoulders lifted and tense. Her enthusiastic smile seemed forced.

"Sounds like a nightmare to me," I said. "Spending an entire week with the Olympians, Aidan the Magnificent, and Liliane the Polyglot. And weren't we talking about you and Dan finding some time alone together? Didn't you tell me just the other day you needed to get some rest?"

Anna visibly relaxed but her smile vanished. She found it hard to relinquish this image of their glamorous vacation in the South of France.

"I was going to ask Liliane if she could spot Dan and me a night on our own. She sent me an itinerary of all these activities we can do with Nick while we're there. I think she gets how important it is to keep him busy. And it would be for just one night. I bet she wouldn't mind."

Most people would have a hard time turning down an all-expenses-paid trip to the South of France. My suggestions that she might be exposing herself to a toxic environment had little effect. During our last session before she left on vacation, she seemed intensely excited and out of reach, as if running from everything she'd learned about herself and her family dynamics. We met on a Thursday afternoon and their flight left that night. We weren't scheduled to meet again for almost two weeks.

On Tuesday, only five days after our last session, I received an email from Anna, asking if we could schedule a session as soon as possible, she hoped that very day. She told me she'd make it work whenever I could be available, despite the time difference. She obviously felt desperate. I found a time that afternoon, which meant she'd be connecting from France at midnight.

When she appeared on-screen at the appointed time, she looked more distraught than I'd seen her. Exhausted, with a gaunt, haunted look. She'd obviously been crying and her eyes were red.

"You look like you've been through hell," I said. She burst into tears.

From the moment they arrived in Nice, everything had gone wrong.

Her parents had promised to meet their flight, but when she eagerly scanned the waiting crowd as they emerged from the jetway, Anna couldn't find them. After the long flight Nick was exhausted and fussy. Despite Dan's efforts to arrange international cell phone coverage before they left Houston, neither of them could make an outgoing call. Anna snapped at Nick and told him to hush in a hissing whisper charged with fury. She accused her husband of not taking care of their international coverage as he should have. She felt hot with exhaustion, shame, and rage.

Dan finally received a text from Anna's father on his phone, which for some reason had successfully connected to the local carrier for data service but not voice calls.

Long lunch! Just take a cab and we'll pay you back.

Anna felt hurt, forgotten, and left out, feelings that only deepened during the next few days. Her parents had arrived in France a week earlier, spent a few days in Paris, and had since been staying with Aidan and Liliane, having a "fabulous time"—dinners out at their favorite restaurant in Nice, a visit to Cannes for the music festival, a day trip to Vaucluse, including lunch at a restaurant recently awarded its first star from the Michelin guide. It felt to Anna as if her parents, her brother, and her sister-in-law had strong bonds, sharing interests that excluded her and the rest of her family.

"I feel like such a loser," she told me, sounding bitter and resentful. "Trying to schedule things around Nick's nap—excuse me, that's *la sieste de Nicholas*—is such an obvious inconvenience to everyone. They're always speaking French, by the way, or slipping back and forth. When I suggest an outing for all of us, one of those things from the list that Liliane sent, nobody wants to go. Mom, so very thoughtful, says, 'Don't let us hold you back.' Nobody asks about us, nobody wants to play with Nick. I wish I'd never come."

I hurt for Anna. Nobody likes to hear "I told you so," and of course I didn't say it.

"And get this," she went on. "While they were in Paris, they had dinner with Seth! His new book is coming out in French, and I guess he had some promotional appearances there. They didn't say it, but I knew what they were thinking: 'You should have married Seth. That could have been your life—in Paris for the debut of your husband's new *roman. Quel dommage!*'"

Anna had never been one to drop French expressions into her remarks; her use of them felt sarcastic in part but also an effort to assimilate into the bilingual clique that excluded her.

The event that precipitated her email to me had occurred earlier that morning when she came silently downstairs and overheard a conversation the others were having in the kitchen. Anna didn't tell me so, but it seemed clear that she'd approached the kitchen in stealth with the intention to eavesdrop. Her worst fears had been confirmed. In lowered voices Aidan and Liliane, her mother and father were discussing the defects in Anna's parenting.

"You'd think no one had ever had a child before."
"Why does she cater to his every whim?"
"Poor Dan seems to do most of the work anyway, so why does
  she seem so stressed?"
"Motherhood clearly doesn't suit her."

To hear yourself discussed in such unflattering terms would humiliate anyone. The shock to Anna felt like a physical wound. It also infuriated her. She stepped into the kitchen and glared accusingly from face to face.

"You're talking about me," she said.

As might be expected, none of them showed the least remorse. Anna couldn't recall exactly how they had done it, but they soon turned the situation around to make it her fault. She had misunderstood. She shouldn't be so sensitive. Why had she been listening outside the door like some pathetic sneak? Rendered speechless with pain and rage, Anna fled the kitchen and retreated to her bedroom for the rest of the day. She'd eventually reached out to me by email.

She and I spent the rest of our time devising self-protective measures. I stressed the importance of shielding herself, her husband, and her child from contempt. Within twenty-four hours, although they could ill afford it, Anna and Dan had found a hotel in Nice and spent the rest of their vacation alone.

ORDINARY ANNA

Nice was a pivotal event that confirmed insights we had developed in therapy, and it provided Anna with the impetus for greater change. Anna's glorification of her parents and brother had persisted despite many interpretations concerning its toxic effect on her self-esteem, but this disastrous vacation finally began to loosen idealization's hold upon her psyche. Back in Houston she distanced herself from her parents and drew closer to Dan. She began to value his down-to-earth qualities more than she had before. She started to focus on what felt truly meaningful in her life, rather than struggling and always failing to become Ideal Anna.

As Nick grew older, Anna found parenting easier. I've often seen how parents overwhelmed by infants and toddlers feel more competent as their children age, finding new pleasure as well as some relief at having more normal feelings for their kids. This was especially true for Anna. As her parents' critical and sophisticated views lost their hold, she became more accepting and tolerant of Nick's childish ways.

She also became increasingly aware that she hated her job. Years earlier Anna had decided to follow in her father's footsteps by becoming a lawyer, hoping for his approval, but had then chosen to specialize in an area of law he scorned. She didn't despise probate law but found it dull and overly procedural, focused on compliance with an arcane and tedious legal code. Over time she realized she valued the interpersonal aspects of her job—the meetings with clients, helping to assess their goals, bearing witness to the family resentments and feuds that often motivated their choices. It wasn't enough.

After several years in therapy Anna decided to give up the law, take a yoga teacher training course, and eventually open her own studio. Dan supported her choice, but the rest of the family believed she had taken leave of her senses. She loved her new work. With managerial skills that surprised her, Dan took over the business end of her studio when Anna was struggling with it. Together they opened another and then a third yoga studio in the Houston area. Dan eventually gave up teaching to manage their growing "yoga empire" full time.

During a stop in Houston as part of a book tour, Seth contacted Anna and they met for coffee. She hadn't seen him in a few years, and he'd "gone to hell," as she put it. Divorced for the second time, struggling with alcohol and depression, he confided his troubles to Anna over coffee and shed a few self-pitying tears. Although she felt sorry for him, she admitted to a certain relieved pleasure. If she'd married Seth as her parents had wished, her own life might be part of the wreckage he left in his wake.

It would be misleading to say that Anna never again suffered from shame and self-loathing. Whenever she heard about her parents' glamorous exploits, or Aidan's most recent accomplishment, she could easily lose touch with what mattered most to her. She might succumb to the feeling that she'd failed in life, viewing herself once again as boring and unaccomplished compared with the Olympians. That savage, self-critical voice never entirely disappeared.

She would eventually rescue herself from despair, sometimes with Dan's help. She'd recover a sense of joy in her work and once again feel pride in what she and her husband had accomplished together. Although Ideal Anna continued to cast a faint shadow over her life, she'd learned to appreciate how much better it felt to be ordinary, humdrum Anna, down here on Earth with all the other flawed mortals.

twelve

SUPERIORITY AND CONTEMPT

WHEN THERAPISTS PRESENT THEIR cases in professional papers to their colleagues, or in books like this one intended for a larger audience, they usually describe their success stories, putting their work forward in its best light. Therapy often falls short, of course, and more often than we like to admit. Sometimes we fail to form an emotional connection with our clients, or the limits in our understanding prevent us from helping them. Sometimes we make significant mistakes. And sometimes a client's defenses actively thwart the insights and emotional support we offer them.

I think the case I describe in this chapter reflects all those failures. At the same time it illustrates the challenges involved in working with clients who massively deny shame. I never found Caleb endearing in the way I did Anna (chapter 11). His arrogance and contempt were off-putting at times, and he rejected his own vulnerability so decisively that I struggled to connect with him on a deeper level. As a result I sometimes intervened too early or made interpretations that were too assertive, probably colored by my own wish to counteract his devaluation of me. At that point in my career I didn't understand how core shame drives the narcissistic defenses.

I was trained in the object relations school of psychoanalytic thought, which locates the root of most mental health problems in the early maternal-infant relationship. It focuses primarily on how it feels to be utterly helpless and dependent upon another person for everything you need. "Good enough" caregivers inspire confidence that, when you need other people, you can depend upon them to give you what you need, at least most of the time. When that early experience of need and dependency goes badly awry, however, according to object relations theory you will develop defenses against the awareness of such need.

Denial: *I don't need anyone.*

Projection: *You're the needy one, not me.*

You may take flight into a grandiose fantasy of having everything you need within yourself or try to possess and assert control over those you depend upon so you don't have to feel helpless.

In my work today I focus less on defenses against need and more on the defenses against shame that lie at the heart of narcissism. The narcissistic defense reflects a complete denial that the person has any reason to feel shame. It does not arise from a self-aware choice but from the unconscious and lifelong rejection of a self that is felt to be defective, ugly, inferior, and unworthy of love. The haughty, I'm-better-than-you personality that the narcissist presents to the world masks profound shame, concealing it from himself and from everyone else. Unlike the shame experienced by clients whom I discussed in earlier chapters, Caleb's shame was almost entirely invisible.

Caleb, who was in his late twenties, was a therapist in training, working at a community mental health clinic whose interns I occasionally supervised. While personal therapy was not a requirement of his degree program or his internship, the clinic strongly recommended that its students enter therapy. For fledgling therapists, their first encounters with clients usually stir up so many strong feelings, tapping into their own emotional struggles, that therapy ought to be a requirement for anyone entering the field. Before he worked with me, Caleb had never seen a therapist. When the director of the clinic suggested he enter therapy, he resisted for many months and agreed only when she insisted.

In a personal communication before Caleb called, the director told me he was universally disliked by other interns at the clinic. During staff meetings and group supervision he condescended to his peers, criticized their work, and continually tried to demonstrate superior insight. In group and individual supervision interns trained in psychodynamic psychotherapy present line-by-line accounts of their sessions, which they have usually transcribed from memory rather than audio recordings. When other interns in his group read their notes, Caleb often highlighted what he thought they had missed and showed them what he thought they should have said—and not in a way that felt particularly helpful. He competed with the group supervisor for prominence. After numerous complaints from other interns as well as his group supervisor, the director gave him a list of several therapists he might contact.

No therapist wants to believe he was chosen for his lack of experience, of course; it has taken me decades (and some lessons in humility) to see that Caleb probably chose me because I was the youngest therapist on that list, without the professional stature of the others. I was only seven or eight years his senior. A highly competitive young man, he probably would have chosen a therapist whose level of experience he could more easily challenge and whom he had a good chance of defeating. From the beginning of our work together, Caleb's desire to render me useless, with nothing of value to offer, felt clear.

Most of us form quick impressions based on our first encounters with a stranger; therapists are no different, even if we're more conscious of the observations we make and what we deduce from them. The clinic director's description of Caleb had already colored my expectations. When I opened the door to my waiting room that first day, he was reading a magazine, a copy of *The New Republic* I kept there with some other reading material for my clients. He didn't immediately glance up as I opened the door, as other clients typically do. With his gaze fixed on the page, he hesitated a few seconds, as if finishing that particular paragraph were of paramount importance. When he finally looked up, he smiled faintly.

"Dr. Burgo," he said, rising from the chair. In some ineffable way, the way he said my name felt condescending or ironic.

Tall and well built, with broad shoulders, Caleb wore khaki pants, a starched white shirt, and a tie with deep blue lines against a vivid red background. His closely cropped blond hair gave him a vaguely military look, accentuated by his erect posture. (He had served in the army, I learned later in that session.) He cut an imposing, and subtly intimidating, figure.

When he shook the hand I offered him, he barely took hold, gripping and soon letting go. He walked past me into my office, glanced around him in a leisurely way, as if assessing my furniture and wall art, then settled into the client chair opposite mine. He placed his right ankle over his left knee and gave me a look of mild expectation.

"So tell me about why you're here," I said.

With a sober expression Caleb nodded. "Of course. Dr. Lewis suggested some personal therapy would help in my work."

"What about you? Do you think it will be helpful?"

"I'm willing to give it a try." Again the faint smile.

Like Dean, Caleb hadn't come for therapy of his own volition, at least not entirely. I had similar doubts regarding the success of our work together.

I asked about his family background. He willingly answered my questions but with minimal detail, in terse summary fashion, and almost as if he were doing me a favor. This impression became clear only much later. At the moment, inexperienced in dealing with the subtle devaluation of clients like Caleb, I felt mildly ill at ease, not quite able to connect with him.

Caleb had grown up in the rural South, part of a large dysfunctional clan he described with clear disdain. Drug addicts and losers living on disability benefits—aunts and uncles, cousins, siblings—most of them unemployed and unemployable. Teen pregnancies, spousal abuse, and serial divorce were the norm. He was one of five children from his mother's several marriages and had always felt like an outsider. Unlike everyone else in his family, he did well in school and took part in the ROTC program as a teenager. He spent four years in the military and later went to college on scholarship.

The armed services provide stability and routine for many enlistees who come from chaotic family backgrounds. Sometimes it saves their lives. It also helps them to build pride through achievement, recognition, and a sense of belonging to a group whose values they respect and adopt. I believe the army had rescued Caleb from the horrible dysfunction of his family, but based on the few details he gave me, I gathered that he'd never made it a home the way many recruits do. He'd felt like an outsider in the army, too, never quite able to feel that he belonged. He made no close friends and formed no lasting bonds.

"What about romantic relationships?" I asked.

The military, college, and now graduate school had left him little time for such involvements, he told me, at least until recently. His current girlfriend, Katia, had been born in El Salvador and came to the United States with her parents when she was a small child. "She works as a property manager but goes to school at nights," he said. "She won't be satisfied to stay where she is. She's ambitious. We wouldn't be together if she weren't."

Caleb's words inspired a number of impressions I could sort out only later, after the session had ended. He seemed embarrassed that Katia was of Hispanic descent and worked at a job he clearly viewed as beneath her. He was quick to justify it as temporary, to align himself with a partner who shared his ambitions. As I grew accustomed to Caleb's contempt and superiority, I began to feel sorry for Katia. He clearly viewed her as inferior; I suspected that those ambitions for her future were his and not hers.

"How did you decide to become a therapist?" I asked. It seemed an unlikely choice of profession.

"I've always wanted to help people," he said. "Nobody ever helped me find a way. I had to do it all on my own, as crazy as it was. If I can make the struggle easier for other people, that's got to be good." He intended to work with inner-city kids eventually, he told me; he'd already begun to outline the type of program he wanted to establish. He couldn't see himself fitting into the existing social services network operated by federal, state, and local government, which he dismissed with vague contempt. Funded by "forward-thinking philanthropies," he wanted to found a private network of community centers integrating individual and group therapy in their offerings.

I'm sure Caleb consciously believed what he said; on another level a kind of grandiosity fueled this vision of his future. Just as he fought against being "just one" of the interns at the clinic, he could never envision himself as a mere "cog in the wheel," as he once put it. He couldn't accept being part of an existing system and therefore planned to found his own network.

"You see yourself as a leader and not a follower," I said.

"Exactly."

"Has it always been that way?"

"What do you mean?"

"How did that go in the army? I've never served, but I gather there's an emphasis on hierarchy and following orders. What was that like for you as a new recruit?"

"I understood my duty. I did what I was told."

"Any problems with authority?

Caleb visibly stiffened. He didn't like the question. "No."

At that point, based on what I'd heard from the clinic director and reinforced by what Caleb had told me himself, I made my first intervention. In retrospect it was probably premature. I no doubt wanted to demonstrate that I had something to offer and assert the authority I unconsciously felt him subverting.

"It sounds to me like you have a hard time being young and inexperienced. Given your childhood, being small and dependent can't have been easy. I wonder if you wanted to grow up all at once so you wouldn't have to feel small."

Even if accurate, this wasn't a particularly good interpretation. In the school of thought in which I trained, therapists are encouraged to provide insight before clients grasp it themselves, to shed light on the unconscious aspects of their communications that we hear and they don't. Given that Caleb was a therapist in training, I also assumed that need and dependency issues would be familiar to him, a part of his own theoretical toolbox.

"Interesting," he said, with an interest that felt feigned. "How would I know if that's true?"

The question took me aback. "What do you mean?"

"You say I don't like feeling small and needy. That doesn't fit with my experience of myself. But you may have greater insight than me. So how do I know if you're right and I'm just missing something?"

"If it doesn't feel true, then it's not helpful. It's *your* experience and it's ultimately up to you to decide. I can only tell you what I think might be true."

"But you have more experience than I do and you might see things that I don't. Maybe I'm just being defensive."

"Possibly."

"So how can I tell if I am?"

This particular interaction encapsulates my work with Caleb throughout the several months we worked together. When I made an observation, he often would wonder aloud how he was to know whether it was accurate. Sometimes he would offer an alternative hypothesis: "Couldn't that just as easily be true?" he'd say. On one level he seemed cooperative and engaged, conceding that my experience as a therapist might enable me to observe things he couldn't see; at the same time he usually insisted that my interventions didn't "feel true," sometimes offering an alternative hypothesis as if we were cotherapists.

Eventually I began remarking on the nature of those interactions. In psychodynamic psychotherapy the relationship between therapist and client sometimes becomes a focus: clients bring their emotional issues and styles of relating into the consulting room, interacting with their therapists in ways that shed useful light on their other relationships. Caleb's view of himself as visionary leader, his condescension toward the other interns, his competition with his supervisor, and the way he reacted to my interventions felt all of a piece.

"I think it's hard for you to let yourself be a client," I said more than once. "You'd rather be my peer than turn to me for help."

"I suppose that's possible." Caleb never contradicted me directly but instead raised doubts in a reasonable tone. "How would I know for sure that I'm doing that?" He appeared cooperative, willing to consider anything

I might have to say, even if he never accepted any of it. His attitude toward me felt vaguely patronizing, as if I were his inferior and not terribly bright. The person who relies on narcissistic defenses against unconscious shame often offloads or projects his shame into other people around him, forcing them to feel it.

"That sounds familiar," he once said in response to my comment. "We were reading [Melanie] Klein's paper on that subject in class last week. I think it's 'Envy and Gratitude.' She says something very similar to one of her own clients."

Caleb frequently shifted the focus from personal to intellectual. If I pointed out the subtle ways he dismissed and devalued me, he'd relate it to some theoretical paper he'd read. If I suggested that he found it humiliating to admit he needed help, he'd say how interesting he found the idea, then relate it to one of his own clients from the clinic. Over the years many of my clients have been therapists, and now and then they bring to our session their feelings of anguish or concern about their own clients. Caleb regularly discussed his clients in our sessions but never with any implicit bid for help. He recounted his fascinating insights and told me how much his clients felt helped by him.

"Seems like you want to show me what a good therapist you are, rather than turning to me as your own therapist."

"Don't other therapists you see talk about their cases? Dr. Lewis told me personal therapy would be a good place to talk about these things."

Such interactions made me feel useless and ineffective. Nothing I said seemed helpful. I had no doubt that Caleb was devaluing and competing with me, but I couldn't find a way to help him see it. Because I was aware that he made me feel competitive in return, I was more cautious than I might have been in confronting him.

He talked about one particular case more than the others. Celine, a young and apparently beautiful actress, formerly featured on a soap opera that filmed in New York, had recently moved to Los Angeles after being written out of the plotline. She was currently working part time as a cocktail waitress and chose the clinic for therapy because it charged clients on a sliding scale according to what they could afford. As the on-call therapist that week, Caleb had spoken to her on the phone and accepted her as a client.

When he discussed Celine during our sessions, he seemed enchanted by her. Smart, well educated, lively, open, and willing to do the hard work of psychotherapy. She readily accepted his insights and made good use of them during the time between their sessions. She often told Caleb how much she appreciated his help and considered herself fortunate to have wound up with such an excellent therapist, even if he was still in training. According to Caleb, she considered him brilliant.

On the one hand this description of his sessions with Celine continued the pattern of one-upmanship in our work together: he was brilliant and insightful, I was ineffective. On the other I worried that this client was unconsciously playing to his narcissism because of her own needs and issues. For complex reasons some clients idealize their therapist during the early phases of treatment; they may feel a kind of elation at having found a savior. Especially for beginners in the profession eager to feel proficient, the experience of being worshipped by a client can be quite seductive. For Caleb it seemed like a kind of drug, confirming his idealized view of himself.

I couldn't speak with authority about Celine's issues, of course, but in addition to his competitive feelings I did try to address Caleb's wish to be idealized. I mentioned the anxiety and inevitable confusion that comes with being a fledgling therapist and how good it can feel to work with a client who reveres you. I talked about idealization as the flip side of hatred, a description I'd heard from my own supervisors. Caleb found this idea deeply interesting.

"Klein writes about that," he told me. "Splitting and idealization as a means of coping with ambivalence. Of course, that assumes she's actually idealizing me."

What I didn't yet understand in my career was the role of unconscious shame in fueling this wish to be idealized. Hidden feelings of defect, ugliness, and inferiority may drive you into the arms of someone willing to agree that you are perfect.

It should come as no surprise that Caleb abruptly terminated his therapy without notice. He left a phone message on my machine, telling me how much he appreciated my efforts but that he'd decided to seek help from someone "more senior." He wished me the best of luck in my career.

Because we worked in the same profession and he was an intern at a clinic where I occasionally supervised, I heard about Caleb from time to time. According to the clinic director, he waited months to mention that he had stopped treatment, and when it finally came out, he refused to pursue further therapy. He continued to be an irritant to staff and the other interns. Everyone looked forward to his departure from the clinic at the conclusion of his internship.

Toward the end of his tenure one of his clients (I had no doubt it was Celine) filed an ethics charge against him for unprofessional behavior. According to the affidavit she filed with the board, Caleb had suggested they discontinue treatment and pursue a romantic relationship. He left the clinic not long after that, and I never heard from or about him again.

Although some predatory therapists deliberately exploit their position of influence to take sexual advantage of their clients, others unwittingly succumb to the kind of idealization Caleb found so intoxicating. Based on their own emotional issues and needs, some clients unconsciously attempt to seduce their therapists; others idealize the person who helps them because of a deep longing to be rescued. When an idealizing client encounters a therapist in flight from shame, the results can be traumatic for the client and professionally ruinous for the therapist.

thirteen

BLAME AND INDIGNATION

I WORKED WITH NICOLE OFF and on for many years, first in person in Los Angeles, then over the telephone after she was married and her husband received a transfer, and finally by videoconferencing once technology made it possible. Most therapists have worked with long-term clients like Nicole who have played a central role in their professional development. She entered treatment when my views still adhered closely to my early training, which was grounded in object relations theory and focused on difficulties in enduring need and dependency; she stayed with me as my views on shame evolved. Sometimes clients must wait for their therapists to grow enough to be able to help them.

Nicole also helped me to understand the importance of shared joy in developing self-esteem. In the early days of our work together, I functioned sort of as a blank screen; over time I began to convey my own affection more openly and to express my sincere joy when she made progress or achieved an important goal. Through my work with Nicole and a few other clients, I eventually learned that the love you feel for your long-term clients (and they for you) is the single most important factor in their development of self-esteem. Helping such clients to grow makes therapists feel good about themselves too.

THE EARLY YEARS

Nicole was referred to me by a psychiatrist who felt she needed intensive psychotherapy rather than medication. Eighteen years old, angry, and depressed, she abused drugs and cut herself with razor blades. She suffered from debilitating insomnia, sleeping no more than a few hours each night. She struggled with gender identity issues, wondered whether she might be a lesbian, and often expressed the wish that she had been born a man. Something about the way she carried herself—a kind of swagger to her walk and a stiffness in her posture—made her seem a bit mannish.

During our first session Nicole barely looked at me. When she answered my questions, she spoke to the floor, the walls, at her animated hands with their noticeably long fingers. I now know that the inability to maintain eye contact usually reflects profound shame at being seen, and even then I intuited what she felt even if I didn't yet have a way to conceptualize it. For some clients like Nicole, to sit in a consulting room while a stranger gazes intently at them and asks deeply personal questions feels almost unbearably humiliating (Unwanted Exposure). Throughout that first session and for months thereafter, she fidgeted and shifted positions, bouncing her knees up and down. Now and then she yanked on her helmet-like hair in a way that looked painful.

Nicole displayed most of the traits and behaviors associated with borderline personality disorder, a difficult clinical issue that most therapists prefer to avoid because clients who struggle with BPD can be so challenging. They typically call between sessions, sometimes in the middle of the night, and engage in self-destructive and impulsive behaviors that can easily make you worry about them between sessions. They shift between idealizing you as a therapist and hating your guts. At times they can be extremely abusive, screaming and calling you names while you try to stay calm and not react defensively.

No one in my life—client, friend, or family member—has ever treated me with such blatant hostility and scorn. She sometimes stormed off midsession, screaming "Fuck you!" as she slammed the door behind her. She left insulting messages on my answering machine. She frequently criticized my "superior attitude"—the supposed belief that I was special and better than her because I was her therapist. From time to time she told me with heartfelt emotion that she hated me.

Even so, Nicole was the most endearing client I've ever worked with. You may find it hard to understand how I could feel that way about her. Although I didn't yet grasp the role of shame in her attacks, I always understood her abusive behavior as defensive. Despite our volatile and painful relationship, I recognized that an agonized, needy person kept showing up for her appointments and turning to me for help. For ineffable reasons, we connected during our first session, in part because she reminded me of myself at a younger age. During the early years of my own analysis, as I struggled with unexamined shame, I gave my therapist a hard time, even if I didn't abuse him quite so vocally.

Much later Nicole told me that during our first session she had felt like crying. She'd had several consultations with other therapists before coming to me; each one, she sensed, had kept her at arm's length, as if they found her distasteful or dangerous, especially when she showed them the scars on her arms where she had cut herself. In part because of my own overconfidence, Nicole didn't frighten me; I felt certain I could help her.

She came from an intact middle-class family with a history of mental illness on both sides. Schizophrenic grandfather, a cousin who had committed suicide, more than one case of major depression. From Nicole's description I gathered that her mother was uncomfortable with affection and prone to brutal sarcasm. Her father came across as jovial, a kind of jokester who appeared warm but was actually quite remote and self-absorbed. She had a jealous older brother who had tortured her throughout childhood—deliberately waking her with loud noises, pinning her to the ground and farting in her face, poking her with sharp objects, and the like.

Although she hadn't been sexually molested as a child, Nicole had always felt confused and frightened by ambiguous sexual boundaries in the family—frequent parental nakedness, deliberately on display, and a sense of being ogled by her father; the feeling that she had to be a "sex slave" to her mother, not in the literal sense but more in terms of servicing her need for companionship, emotional support, and pity. Some of her sexual anxiety arose from her own sexual fantasies; early in life Nicole turned to masturbation for comfort in the face of terror and confusion. Several months into treatment she confessed her belief that she and I would eventually have sex and that our intercourse would "cure" her, to use her word.

Even more than the average teen, Nicole felt passionate about rock music. She possessed an encyclopedic knowledge of eminent and obscure musicians. With two of her friends she went on long road trips to attend concerts in distant cities, following their favorite bands on tour. She revered a few famous lead singers and indulged fantasies of meeting them or having sex with them. Most of all she wanted to be a star herself. Although she had never taken guitar lessons and knew only a few rudimentary chords, she saw herself as a major talent. It was only a matter of time, she believed, before a scout for the record companies would sign her up and make her a star.

Nicole composed many songs and sometimes played them for me during our sessions—simple pop tunes demonstrating an ear for catchy phrases but too undeveloped to achieve true melody. She had no background in composition, nor had she ever played with other musicians in a band. She frequently told me, with obvious pride, that she had perfect pitch. Whenever she brought her tape recorder to a session and played songs for me, she obviously expected me to be overcome with admiration.

Although Nicole viewed herself as a "secret genius" destined for greatness, she had no idea how to develop as a musician. She often talked of forming a band but never did so. On occasion it occurred to her that she should take lessons, and she eventually did find a teacher. She studied with him for only a few months and then dropped out because the difficulty of practicing and the slow pace of her progress enraged her. She believed she shouldn't have to work at it: a musical genius would simply know how to play.

In the beginning Nicole's parents paid for her sessions, but a year or so into treatment they refused to continue because of her abusive attitude toward them and her involvement with drugs. By that point I had already reduced my fee substantially so she could come several times a week. Given the severity of her difficulties and especially my concerns about her self-injury, I knew we needed to meet that often. When Nicole informed me that her parents would no longer pay, she asked, "What am I going to do now?" She sounded both angry and afraid. She knew she needed her sessions even if she rarely acknowledged it.

"I guess you'll have to get a job and pay for them yourself."

My answer infuriated Nicole. She expected me to see her for free; the very idea that she would now have to take financial responsibility for herself struck her as an outrage. "You're a fucking leech!" she screamed at me. "You're a parasite who feeds off people like me!"

We had several difficult sessions about the issue, some cut short when Nicole stormed out of my office, hurling abuse at me and slamming the door behind her. She always came back. Despite the enraged sense of entitlement, she understood on some level that I cared about her and was trying to help. Eventually she began looking for work. At first she earned money by posing nude for art classes and imagined that she might become a highly successful runway model. She enjoyed having the artists in class look at her. Maybe one of them would tell an agent-friend about this great beauty he had found in art class.

Nicole later found a job in retail and managed to keep it, despite the anger she felt about having to work at a job she considered beneath her. During this time our sessions focused on her rage and sense of entitlement. She continued to insist that I should work for free and that someone else should cover the rest of her bills. She should have become a rock star by now, living an opulent, privileged life. I made many interpretations about her hatred of reality—the long, hard work involved in achieving anything of value in the real world. I often said, "You feel you should just have what you want when you want it." I talked about running from the experience of being small and helpless, becoming big all at once—a rock star, a top model, a musical genius.

During this period Nicole brought in a revealing dream image. She doesn't appear in the dream. Rather, a scientist with large black glasses stands onstage behind a podium, delivering a lecture. He sports a white lab coat, with a mortarboard on his head. Beneath his lab coat, invisible to the audience, he is wearing diapers that need to be changed. The image reminded Nicole of Mr. Peabody, a character from a favorite childhood cartoon, *Peabody's Improbable History*. In this cartoon Mr. Peabody is a beagle who happens to be the smartest being in existence and has accomplished incredible things in life as a business magnate, inventor, Nobel laureate, and two-time Olympic medalist, among many other achievements.

Nicole's dream conveyed the sense of a grandiose but fraudulent self, a baby masquerading as a scientist of note. In those days I hadn't yet evolved the views about core shame that I currently hold. We talked instead about her hatred of being small and needy. In terms of our relationship we talked about the rage she felt at being dependent upon me. She often threatened to quit treatment, insisting I was useless and that she no longer needed me. She remained committed to our work and never missed a session.

Today I would make a different sort of interpretation to a client like Nicole: "You're afraid you're so damaged that there's no hope of getting better. The only way out seems to be by magic, to suddenly change into somebody completely different—a 'winner' who has it all." I would have spoken with feeling about the agony of shame, too, and hoped that it would convey my empathy with the depth of her suffering.

The original interpretations I did make to Nicole were not incorrect. They reflect a different but compatible perspective on the emotional issues involved. Yes, Nicole struggled with feeling small, needy, and helpless, but that experience also fueled her profound sense of shame and a fear that she was damaged beyond repair. She equated neediness with being a "fucked-up loser" and then took flight from shame into a fantasy of having it all—being a winner. This dynamic lies at the heart of pathological narcissism.

THE MIDDLE PHASE

Nicole's therapy lasted many years. Over time she learned to tolerate feeling small and inexperienced, to endure the frustration involved in persistent work rather than taking grandiose flight. Within the context of a psychotherapy relationship in which she felt seen, understood, and accepted, she eventually faced the underlying shame about her psychological damage, even if we didn't use that particular language in those days. Self-injury, partly an expression of rage and partly emotional release, receded as she learned to think better and tolerate her emotions when they flooded her.

Nicole had several short-term sexual relationships with women during her late teens and early twenties, but her strongest attraction was to men, although for a long time she found that difficult to acknowledge. She equated her own femininity with defect and inferiority, viewing her vagina as a disgusting smelly hole full of unbearable need (full of shame, too, I would add today). At the same time she idealized men and their "no-need" penises. Why would any man want to have sex with her, or with any woman, for that matter? She believed that all men were secretly gay, enjoying their superiority in group "penis parties," disdainful of all those gross and needy women who wanted them.

This description might sound like classic Freudian views on penis envy; it actually reflects a confused and false equation of shame with femininity, where having a penis represents the idealized magical antidote to shame rather than a desire for male anatomy. Helping Nicole to sort out that confusion and eventually value her own femininity was a long journey and one of the most moving experiences of my professional career. In her midtwenties she began to date men and eventually married a young professional. They had children together.

After many years of therapy Nicole had built a successful life and a good marriage. I felt proud of her achievements and proud of our hard work together. Many therapists would have considered her treatment a success and brought it to a close. But while Nicole had made great progress, her earlier issues still played an outsized role in her life, in ways that could occasionally be quite destructive to her marriage, her children, and her ability to function as a professional. We agreed that, before we could terminate, she needed to have a better handle on these issues.

During this phase I was coming to terms with my own shame and the superior postanalytic self I had built in order to deny it. I recognized myself in the way Nicole so badly wanted to look as if she'd grown up in a healthy family with caring parents. Denying her ongoing struggles, she took refuge in a postanalytic self that she viewed as superior and more enlightened than other people, even those, like her husband, who had grown up in normal families.

IDEAL NICOLE

Following a heated argument with her husband, Eric, Nicole would spend sleepless hours reviewing the exchange in a highly accusatory way, going over all his faults and progressing to total character assassination in her mind. She'd spend the opening minutes of her next session recounting the fight in black-and-white terms: Although she didn't always spell it out, she believed that, by virtue of her many years in therapy, she possessed greater insight and self-awareness than Eric, who supposedly knew nothing about himself or the destructive ways he behaved. She was superior and enlightened while he remained in the dark. She was right and he was wrong.

As a younger woman, she had often felt inferior to other people because of her troubled family background and early struggles, but she now saw herself as superior (a psychoanalytic winner) as a result of all the insight she had gained through our work together. Unenlightened Eric often found himself cast in the role of loser, an object of scorn. Nicole's descriptions reminded me of fights I'd had with my then wife and the way I tried to use my analysis against her, a realization that filled me with shame.

Because I was coming to terms with that shame, I was finally able to help Nicole face her own.

In her relentless goal to become Winner Nicole, she refused to recognize her limits and the ongoing role of Borderline Nicole in her life; she often took on more than she could manage and suffered as a result. She wanted to view herself as hypercompetent, superior to those other mere mortals in her life, able to juggle the challenges of career, marriage, and children with ease. As a result she took on too much and tended to deteriorate under pressure, becoming more forgetful, irritable, prone to angry outbursts, intolerant of the emotional needs of her family, and so on. Bouts of insomnia would plague her, during which she'd hallucinate spiders or feel persecuted by endless song loops in her head. Instead of feeling regret about poor choices she had made, she would find fault with Eric, nitpicking endlessly until she provoked a fight.

In Nicole's view only two scenarios were possible: either she was entirely right and Eric was to blame for everything; or she was such a messed-up nutcase that we might as well give up and flush her down the toilet. Because acknowledging her own contribution to these fights reconnected her to shame, she usually defended her self-image as Winner Nicole with great zeal. Under assault Eric often responded in kind, calling her crazy and treating her with reciprocal contempt. If I tried to promote a more nuanced view, she would turn on me as well, accusing me of insensitivity or of "teaming up" with Eric against her.

Together Nicole and I eventually recognized and accepted that no one ever completely heals from core shame, despite years of successful therapy. We can build pride to offset it and share the joy of achievement with those who matter most to us. But someone who comes from a chaotic family background like Nicole's or mine will always bear the scars. For us, preserving our mental health means keeping Borderline Nicole (or Borderline Joe) in mind, accepting that in moments of deep pain or profound emotional stress, we tend to fall back on our old defenses, especially when we feel shamed or humiliated.

When they were on the verge of divorce, Eric entered therapy with one of my closest colleagues, a woman who understands shame on a deep level. Nicole and Eric's marriage survived because they both learned to defuse the winner-loser dynamic that characterized their fights and become more authentic with each other. Over time Nicole learned to endure her shame, acknowledge her limitations, and take better care of herself. She became a better mother to her children too.

In the final stages of our work together, she recovered her love of music and pursued it in a nongrandiose way. She found a new guitar teacher and after several years became quite proficient. She studied composition and put her gifts to good use, writing more complex and musically satisfying songs. Although she did not pursue a career in music, she formed a band with friends and occasionally played small clubs in the city where they lived. Mostly the members played together for their own enjoyment, sharing the joy of music they made together.

fourteen

DENYING SHAME IN EVERYDAY LIFE

PEOPLE WHO EXTENSIVELY DENY SHAME usually escape from it into an idealized false self. Whereas Anna (see chapter 11) consciously and quite painfully fell short of the ideal exemplified by her parents, Caleb (chapter 12) believed he had achieved his own ideal. He had left his chaotic family (and his own shame) behind in the rural South and saw himself as an enlightened therapist revered by his clients, more insightful than his teachers, his supervisors, and his therapist. Nicole (chapter 13) likewise viewed her postanalytic self as superior and refused to acknowledge the lasting impact of a traumatic childhood on her psyche.

As Francis Broucek writes, "Shame is the instigating force in the creation of the idealized self," a dynamic that lies at the heart of pathological narcissism.[1] In less dramatic form most of the narcissistic behavior and defenses against shame discussed in this book are quite common, a part of everyday life, and not necessarily pathological. To some degree all of us try to deny shame whenever we can, at least temporarily.

NARCISSISTIC DEFENSES

As Ervin Goffman notes in *The Presentation of Self in Everyday Life*, interpersonal interactions resemble a stage play between two characters, each trying to influence how the other perceives them. A few people, as I show in the section on controlling shame, intentionally shoot themselves down or deliberately try to elicit negative reactions, but most of us want to put our best foot forward and present ourselves in a favorable light. We prefer that other people think well rather than ill of us.

At the same time most of us recognize that, in addition to our best foot, we also have a worst one—that is, we accept that we have faults and limitations, some of which might arouse feelings of shame if they were exposed. In contrast a group of difficult individuals—those to whom I refer as extreme narcissists—will insist that they have no such faults or imperfections and therefore nothing to feel ashamed about. To carry the analogy further, extreme narcissists want you to believe they have two best feet, both of which are far superior to either of yours. Caleb and Anna's parents were such people. Nicole often tried to see herself that way.

In our all-about-me age many people tend to think a little too well of themselves and exploit social media to make themselves look good—everyday narcissists, if you will. Extreme narcissists go even further, striving nonstop to present themselves as winners, building themselves up at the expense of the losers they despise. In flight from unconscious feelings of defect and inferiority, extreme narcissists inhabit an idealized false self that is (unconsciously) designed to deny any feelings of shame. They vigorously defend their superior self when threatened, making use of a characteristic trio of defenses to defeat anyone who challenges them: blame, contempt, and righteous indignation.

During arguments with her husband Nicole made consistent use of these defenses. She held him in contempt and blamed him for her own shortcomings; she attacked him with righteous indignation because he couldn't face the truth about himself. With subtle contempt Caleb neutralized anyone in a position to challenge his superiority. Anna's parents blamed her for being a "pathetic sneak" when she overheard the contemptuous way they were discussing her.

From time to time most of us use similar strategies to deflect or deny shame, although we do so less pervasively than extreme narcissists. Occasional reliance on blame, contempt, and righteous indignation when we feel criticized differs only in degree and intensity from pathological forms of narcissism; these defenses can be considered normal if they don't define our character or dominate our relationships.

A blow to one's self-esteem (a narcissistic injury, as we call it in my profession) is difficult to bear and always arouses some member of the shame family of emotions. The following vignette portrays the typical ways that all of us defend against a narcissistic injury, usually brief and transient reactions that are not necessarily pathological. It describes one particularly awful day in the life of Natalie, a young woman in her midtwenties who works as a legal assistant at a midsize law firm in Atlanta.

A DAY IN THE LIFE

Natalie awakened in a bad mood because she had once again slept through her alarm clock and was going to be late for work. She had a vague recollection of hitting the snooze button more than once . . . she probably should've gotten to bed earlier, instead of watching those two episodes of *Homeland* on Netflix. Natalie took a quick shower, wolfed down a protein bar, and was about to leave the apartment when she spotted a note from her roommate, Selena, on the kitchen counter. Selena was an assistant producer for one of the morning programs on CNN and usually started work before dawn.

"Hey Natalie," the note read. "Just a quick reminder that it was your turn to clean the bathroom this week." Natalie felt irritated by the row of smiley faces that Selena had placed above her signature. "Neat freak," she said aloud, on her way out the door.

As she climbed into her car, Natalie recalled with a smile that she and Brian had a date scheduled for that night. They had been going out for only a couple of months but she felt it was starting to get serious. Brian was an attractive guy with an offbeat sense of humor and a great job at Ernst & Young. She and Brian had a lot of interests in common. Lately she had begun to wonder whether he might turn out to be marriage material.

Because she did not leave home early enough, Natalie ran into the worst of the commuter traffic on the interstate and arrived at work even later than usual. She always made up the missed time at the end of the day (plus, her bosses, Dan and Matthew, usually rolled in much later than she), but she still felt bad that she could not get to work on time, despite repeated resolutions to do better. Nina the receptionist smiled and said, "Forty-five minutes—now that must be a record!" Feeling hot and irritable, Natalie shot back, "There was an accident on I-75—it's not my fault!" Even though she knew this was a lie, she felt justified in her self-defense.

As she settled down at the computer, she pulled up her calendar and noted that her annual performance review with Barbara, the office manager, was scheduled for eleven. She'd forgotten all about it. With a lot of work in her in-box, the morning passed quickly. Natalie was a little nervous about the performance review, but mostly she was looking forward to a raise. She had been with the firm for two years and hadn't had one since she started. Of course there had been some glitches in her work product—nobody's perfect—but all in all she thought she'd done a pretty good job. She *deserved* a raise.

Barbara, the office manager, called Natalie into her office at 11:00 on the dot. Barbara was extremely punctual, almost to a fault, and a stickler for details. She gave Natalie one of those big phony smiles that were her trademark and launched into the review, handing a single sheet of paper across the desk so that Natalie had a copy of the evaluation.

As she ran her eyes down the column, Natalie saw a fairly straight line of threes—*satisfactory*. She also saw notations of "needs improvement" in a couple of areas: "punctuality" and "attention to detail." Overall her performance received a three, but there was a short minus sign after the number. Natalie felt the heat in her face and scalp; tears filled her eyes but she fought to maintain a placid exterior. For a moment she had the panicky urge to run. She kept her eyes downcast because she found it hard, almost painful, to meet Barbara's gaze.

"The lateness isn't a major concern," Barbara said, "not in and of itself. As you know, we're fairly casual around here and we all appreciate that you're so careful to make up any time you miss." When Natalie looked up, Barbara was smiling at her with sympathy. She could sense that Barbara was trying to be gentle, but it only made Natalie feel worse.

"We're more concerned about the number of unnecessary mistakes in your work product. Both Dan and Matthew feel you tend to rush through things. Maybe it's because you're so often late and playing catch-up, but we'd all like you to slow down and double-check your work from now on." A memory sprang suddenly to mind—last week the messenger service down at court had called because she'd forgotten to include a check for the filing fee along with the Davis complaint. She'd come in late that day, too, and had felt frazzled all morning.

Back at her own desk, Natalie had a hard time focusing. Barbara's words from the performance review kept intruding in her thoughts, disrupting her concentration. She tried to remember whether she had told Selena or Brian about the upcoming performance review. Maybe she wouldn't have to say a word about it to either one. As the afternoon wore on, Natalie wondered whether she should start looking for a new job, a better job with a higher salary. Law firms are so stuffy, lawyers so boring. This had not turned out to be the exciting place she imagined when she started. Maybe Selena could help her get a job in television. She'd probably do better surrounded by more creative types.

Near quitting time, Natalie decided to cancel her date with Brian. Given her dark mood, she'd probably make poor company. She might start crying. If Brian asked her why, she wouldn't be able to avoid telling him about the performance review, and she was afraid he might think she was a loser. Right then all she wanted was to go home, curl up in bed with a pint of Häagen-Dazs, and watch the final few episodes of *Homeland*. She reached for her cell phone and saw that Brian had called earlier in the day, during her meeting with Barbara, and had left a message. Her heartbeat speeded up a little at the sound of his voice.

"Hey, Natalie, it's me, Brian. Calling about tonight. Listen, I'm not going to be able to make it. Actually . . . God, I really don't want to do this over voice mail. Call me back when you can—we need to talk."

Hearing those four dreadful words, "we need to talk," Natalie felt as if the bottom had dropped out of her world. The pain of the day overwhelmed her. She stifled a small scream as her eyes welled up with tears. When Nina, the receptionist, walked by, Natalie startled her by snarling, "Men are such assholes! It's just not fair!"

SHAME AND NARCISSISTIC INJURY

Like all of us, Natalie must cope with the shame family of emotions as an inevitable part of life. This particular day may have proved especially painful, piling up the challenges to her self-esteem one after the other, but there was nothing unusual about the narcissistic injuries she experienced or the ways she reacted to her transient encounters with shame.

She began her day feeling bad about herself because she had not yet found a way to wake up and get to work on time (Disappointed Expectation). On some level she knew that her lateness was the result of poor choices she had made (deciding to watch *Homeland* instead of turning off the lights and going to sleep). Her roommate's reminder that she had forgotten to clean the bathroom only made Natalie feel worse, but she deflected that feeling with a critical thought about Selena: "Neat freak." *It's not that I dropped the ball; the problem is that Selena is a perfectionist.* At work when the receptionist made a crack about Natalie's lateness, she took similar evasive action: "It's not my fault!"

Shifting blame is one of the most common strategies for evading the pain of narcissistic injury and the shame it arouses.

She had been looking forward to a positive evaluation and a pay raise but instead was devastated by her performance review (Disappointed Expectation once again). Tears came to her eyes; she felt hot and humiliated in the face of Barbara's sympathy (Unwanted Exposure). While Natalie had successfully warded off the earlier challenges to her self-esteem, she couldn't escape this time and felt trapped (at least for the moment). She knew that what Barbara had told her was true. As the day wore on, however, she began to recover: she belittled the stuffy, boring nature of law firms and persuaded herself that she was a more creative type who'd do better in a different environment.

Taking refuge in superiority or contempt for the source of a narcissistic injury is another common strategy for evading the pain of shame.

Despite these efforts to shore up her self-esteem, Natalie's day had shaken her badly. She felt as if she were a loser, although she attributed that thought to Brian (that is, how he might view her if he knew about her poor performance review). Overwhelmed by her painful day, she wanted to cancel their date and retreat to her bed-nest for comfort. When she heard the voice message and realized that Brian intended to dump her, she felt shattered (Unrequited Love). She almost immediately warded off the pain, however, by taking refuge in feelings of rage and indignation at the way women are treated in the dating world: "Men are such assholes!"

Righteous indignation is a third common response to narcissistic injury, an attempt to evade the pain of shame by going on the attack.

Unlike Natalie, who relied on these three defensive maneuvers for temporary relief from shame, extreme narcissists make extensive and continuous use of them. In constant need of support for their inflated self-image, they can't tolerate even the smallest criticism and may launch an aggressive attack against the person who threatens to stir up feelings of shame:

Like Anna's parents, they will turn the tables on you if you fault them.

Like Caleb, they will treat their rivals with superiority and contempt.

Like Nicole, they may become enraged and respond indignantly to even the smallest challenge to their self-esteem.

Extreme narcissists make constant use of these defenses, but, like Natalie, each of us will occasionally rely on them to manage our shame if it feels unbearable. The defenses against shame used by clients in the preceding chapters eventually dominated their lives, but all of us resort to such defenses from time to time. In other words temporarily defending against shame is normal.

DEFENSES AGAINST SHAME IN DAILY LIFE

Reacting defensively to criticism is an extremely common response, one might even say a universal human reaction. Dale Carnegie made this point long ago in his 1936 classic, *How to Win Friends and Influence People*, one of the most misunderstood and underrated books of the last century: "Criticism is futile because it puts a person on the defensive and usually makes him strive to justify himself. Criticism is dangerous, because it wounds a person's precious pride, hurts his sense of importance, and arouses resentment."[2]

Criticism can be dangerous primarily because the person you have criticized often feels attacked, no matter how sensitively you try to phrase your comments, and may retaliate in kind. Because you've wounded his pride, he may feel as if you deliberately intended to humiliate him and then he'll try to hurt you in retaliation. When Natalie read Selena's gentle reminder note, it made her feel bad about herself. On some level she felt attacked, as if Selena intended to shame her (despite those smiley faces!) and mentally retaliated: *Neat freak*.

Natalie's reaction should be familiar to you. Especially in relationship squabbles, many people respond to criticism with denial, insisting that it is unfounded; they often turn the tables and blame the other person or deflect attention onto their partner's faults. Over the years I've heard many clients begin a session by berating their partner in response to a well-founded criticism. During those years when I was in flight from my own shame, I used the same unfortunate tactic on my friends and loved ones. To deny shame and blame someone else is commonplace and not pathological, provided it's a temporary measure and we eventually own up to our shame.

Sometimes we respond with indignation when a partner faults us, especially if we have been harboring grievances of our own. "How dare you criticize me because I forgot the dry cleaning when you *always* leave your dishes on the counter instead of putting them in the dishwasher?" To hear that we've disappointed the expectations of a loved one, no matter how gently the message is delivered, might feel like a kind of Unrequited Love and will usually arouse some member of the shame family of emotions. Most people will try to ward off such a painful experience, at least temporarily, by denying that they have any reason to feel shame. Blame and indignation come to the rescue. "I'm not the one who should feel ashamed—*you* are!"

Relationship squabbles often intensify when both partners trade shame back and forth like a hot potato.[3] When words like *never* or *always* dominate such an exchange, it may escalate to complete character assassination. I invite you to think back on one of your own arguments. Did anger mount as each of you insisted the other person was to blame for the conflict you were having? Even in healthy relationships, such disputes easily become heated when both partners are defending against shame. As tempers cool down over time and we recover feelings of love and affection, we may eventually own our part, apologize, and make efforts to repair the damage.

When shame trading dominates a relationship and neither party can back down, both may rely on contempt, a more powerful weapon, to annihilate their shame and inflict it on their partner. While blame and indignation often fall within the normal range of defensive reactions to shame, contempt represents a more serious form of denial, one with the potential to inflict greater damage on a relationship. Like Noah's mother (chapter 9), people who extensively deny their own shame often express contempt for their partners or family members by giving them the silent treatment.

You're so despicable that you're unworthy of human contact.

As I described in the first section of this book, some mild and strategic forms of shame may have a positive influence on undesirable behavior; contempt, on the other hand, inflicts a global kind of shame upon the other person, pronouncing that person's entire self to be unworthy, unlovable, and even disgusting. When contempt dominates marital relations, it rarely bodes well.

Bitter divorce and a vicious legal battle often ensue. Because divorce means love has failed, it always involves shame of a deeply painful kind, especially when infidelity (Unrequited Love) is involved. When that shame feels unbearable, a blaming, self-righteous, and contemptuous assault on the ex-partner with every means available is too often the cure. You probably know someone who went through such a divorce. It's not uncommon. Vengeful use of the legal system often reflects an attempt to prove that the ex-partner has no value, that they are beneath contempt and therefore the rightful repository for all that unbearable shame.

THE DENIAL OF SHAME IN FANTASY LIFE

A group of your friends has planned an evening out and they didn't invite you. You tell yourself they've known each other far longer, and of course there's no reason why everyone has to be included in every single social event; all the same you're home alone that night and hurting (Exclusion). You have the TV tuned to your favorite program, but you can't concentrate because you keep drifting off into fantasy scenarios.

By coincidence you show up at the same club as your friends with an amazingly attractive date at your side. They're surprised and envious at your good fortune.

At the last moment you're unexpectedly invited to a fabulous party full of hip, attractive people, and now you're glad you didn't go out with your friends.

The band playing the club that night is terrible; your friends end up having an awful time and go home early.

At one time or another most of us have retreated from the shame of Exclusion into such fantasy consolation. It's a harmless way to deny that we feel hurt or to imagine making other people feel envious and excluded instead or to spoil their experience so we won't care so much that we weren't a part of it. Through such fantasies we deny shame and take refuge in feelings of superiority, a mild version of the way Caleb inhabited an idealized false self to deny his more profound experience of core shame.

In short we deny our feelings of shame on a regular basis without quite realizing it. We tell ourselves we have no reason to feel shame or we blame other people for our own shortcomings. We become indignant when criticized and take refuge in superiority or contempt for those who challenge our self-esteem. The drive to deny shame may influence our overt behavior and the way we treat other people, but more often the denial of shame unfolds within the private theater of our fantasy life. None of this is pathological per se, provided it is a temporary means to find relief rather than a pervasive way of relating to other people that damages our relationships in the long run.

Some people profoundly burdened by shame can neither avoid nor deny it; instead they have developed methods to control and predict their encounters with shame. In the next section I introduce you to those methods.

SEE EXERCISE 5, PAGES 273–274

CONTROLLING SHAME

fifteen

SELF-MOCKERY

WHEN I WAS STARTING MY private practice early in my career, I worked with many people at a greatly reduced fee because they couldn't afford what an established therapist would charge. I believe this is what most fledgling therapists do. On the one hand this can feel like a deprivation, especially when we're still in treatment ourselves and paying several times as much for our own sessions as our clients pay us. On the other it's an opportunity to take on fascinating and unusual cases, to work with people whose difficulties have seriously handicapped their ability to thrive, both personally and in their careers, unlike the successful lawyers, doctors, and other professionals who can afford to pay our full fee once we're more established.

People who lead marginal lives financially often struggle with the kind of personal issues that make them difficult to treat. In those early years I worked with several clients who would probably be diagnosed as suffering from borderline personality disorder. Volatile, sometimes angry and abusive, or prone to drug abuse and self-injury, such clients sometimes disrupt your private life after hours with emergency phone calls, personally attack you during a session, and lead such chaotic lives that they often lose or quit their jobs and can't afford to pay even a reduced fee. Nicole (chapter 13) was such a client during the early years of our work together.

Nora presented an entirely different set of challenges. Her difficulties did not truly conform to the diagnostic criteria for borderline personality disorder, although the referring therapist described her as borderline and almost apologized for sending her my way. In retrospect I think Nora frightened my colleague; he probably wouldn't have accepted her into his practice even if she had been able to afford his fee. When I describe my first session with Nora, you may feel some sympathy for him.

At the appointed hour I went out to my waiting room to greet her. Nora wore blue jeans, canvas high-tops, and a baggy tee shirt; her brown hair was cut in a military buzz cut. She appeared to be in her late twenties. As if startled, she jumped up as I opened the door. Her body appeared lean and wiry, full of nervous energy. She couldn't look me in the eye and hurried past me into my consulting room.

In those days most of my long-term clients would lie on the couch, my chair and ottoman behind them, with another client chair placed at right angles for those who preferred to sit up. Nora scanned the room, looked at the client chair, then plunged the crown of her head into one of the couch cushions and did a headstand on it. I stood in the center of the room, at a loss for what to do.

Her elbows propped against the seat cushion, body supported by the back of the couch, she brought her hands to her face, shifting her head from side to side with a dramatic expression of surprise upon her face.

"Such a change of perspective!" she said. She sounded like a middle-aged Jewish woman from New York. "I never looked at it this way before, Doctor. No, really—I mean it. You've opened my eyes! You're a genius, let me tell you!"

Despite feeling a bit alarmed, I also found Nora funny. I struggled not to laugh.

This was my first encounter with Jewish Lady, one of several oddball characters generated by her active imagination. Even then I knew this was not a classic case of multiple personality disorder. I sensed that, for Nora, meeting a stranger at the outset of therapy made her deeply anxious and playing such a character helped her to cope. In those days I didn't think of her behavior as driven by shame anxiety—the shame of Unwanted

Exposure—but it was obvious that my observing eyes made her extremely uncomfortable. I sat down in the client chair and waited.

After a minute or two Nora deftly flipped onto her feet and sat back down in the center of the couch.

"So, Doctor," she said, fluffing an imaginary hairdo and primping as if before a mirror. She continued with her Jewish New York accent. "Whaddya think of my new hairdo? Too poufy? I can't make up my mind. The girl said I'd love it, but I don't know. I just don't know. Tell me the truth. Does it make my face look fat?"

Still fighting the urge to laugh (it would have felt unprofessional), I said, "I guess you're uncomfortable being here in the room with me."

"Brilliant insight!" she cried. "You're a gem, Doctor, one in a million, let me tell you. Oy, and what a *shayna punim*. I don't want to embarrass you, Doctor, but you are a cutie pie."

She hadn't once looked at me. I'd been assigned a role in the comic scene she was enacting, her way of coping with this unfamiliar and probably frightening situation—frightening, I can add in retrospect, because it risked exposure to intense shame. Jewish Lady kept talking nonstop, constantly shifting her gaze around the room without making eye contact. She gathered her legs beneath her and sat cross-legged on the couch.

"Love your office! Such tasteful décor! Did you bring in a decorator or did your wife take care of it for you? No offense, dear Doctor, but it has the woman's touch, if you know what I mean. My Marvin, God rest his soul, he had no taste whatsoever. *Oy vey ist mir!* Dressed like a schlub every day of his life. But he let me have my way when it came to the home. 'Inferior decorating' he liked to call it—that was his sense of humor. Not so funny to most people. But such a good man!" She dabbed with an invisible tissue at the corner of her eyes, then glanced up to the heavens. "Wait for me, Marvin—I'm coming! It won't be long!"

What is a therapist to do with such a client? How do you even begin to make contact? Her obvious discomfort made me uncomfortable, too, but she also made me want to laugh. Nora had a comic gift for impersonation and a range of vocal tones that made almost everything she said sound funny.

"Maybe you could tell me why you decided to come for therapy," I said. To my own ears it sounded weak.

Nora abruptly unfolded her legs, planting her feet widely before her on the floor. She propped her hands upon her thighs and thrust her chest forward in a way that felt assertive, masculine somehow. She lowered her brow and nodded toward me, gaze askew, as if sizing me up. When she spoke, her voice sounded gruff and deep.

"You got the gift of the gab, Doc. I can see that right away. Don't take a genius to spot real talent. I could use a guy like you down at the lot—no, seriously. Just say the word and the job is yours. Bet you'd move the cars off the lot like it was Christmas!"

Here was Used Car Salesman, another of her funny characters I would come to know well. Nora puffed on an imaginary cigar and pretended to blow smoke from the side of her mouth. "Don't say it! I'm beggin' ya. Wife gives me enough grief. Look, I know I ought to give it up, but I do love myself a good stogie. And what's the harm? Seriously. You tell me, Doc, who am I hurting but myself?"

The idea of self-injury crossed my mind. I tried to put together my various impressions thus far but fell short of coherence. I also felt the presence of mental observers in the room, my own analyst and some of the other senior therapists I respected. They were wondering what I would do with such a client, feeling doubtful about my ability to handle this case. I'd never read about a client like Nora and had no idea how to respond to her.

"Is this something you can control?" I asked. I wasn't sure if this was the right thing to say, but all those mental observers expected me to say something. "Could you stop acting this way if you wanted to?"

Nora abruptly slumped, as if caving in upon herself. With the hardened flat of her hand, she began striking her head—above the temple, not quite at the crown. Tears abruptly sprouted at the corners of her eyes and slid down her cheeks. She looked both miserable and angry. Then she shifted again, lifting one elbow high and pointing an index finger toward her nose while contorting her face in a grotesque way.

"She's got a big honking zit right there at the center of her face! Can you see it?"

Contact.

At that point in my career I had no idea about core shame and how it makes you feel ugly, but I understood that Nora was suffering in ways that made her feel hideous. Anyone sitting in that room would have felt her pain. When I finally put my thoughts and feelings into words, I framed them from my accustomed perspective on need and dependency issues, the one that had dominated my training and my own analysis.

"I think needing to get help in therapy makes you feel hideous and so ugly that nobody who sees you would truly want to help."

Inexact interpretations are often good enough. Many months later Nora told me that during our first session she had been relieved and grateful that I didn't want to turn her away. My willingness to stay in the room with her and try to understand what she was feeling seemed like a gift. Throughout my career I've met other difficult clients with whom I failed to connect, clients who stayed for only a few sessions. Although Nora was profoundly troubled, I also found her—once again for ineffable reasons—endearing.

Over time I understood that Jewish Lady and Used Car Salesman were not merely comic impersonations; they embodied a kind of self-mockery, a way to ridicule personal and physical traits that filled her with shame and made her feel ugly—her Jewish background and the size of her nose, the stiff way she held her body, and the lack of a waistline that often made her feel like a freak, sort of half man. Nora misidentified the core shame she felt with her nose and somewhat masculine body posture and then made fun of herself, a protective kind of self-mockery intended to preempt ridicule (shame) from the outside.

THE CLASS CLOWN

Despite the troubled, somewhat chaotic personality she showed me during that session, Nora had attained a fairly high level of responsibility while working for a medical equipment supplier. She lived an isolated life with few friends and no close ones. She was unmarried, and her experience with sex had been limited and not satisfying. At work she made people laugh and otherwise kept her head down, focused on her work.

Alone at home she wrote and illustrated what she referred to as comic books but today would be considered graphic novels. Although she couldn't focus on television long enough to watch even a sitcom, she would immerse herself for hours in drawing and concocting elaborate storylines for her comics. She wrote poetry, too, and sometimes devised entertainments for her two cats, stand-up comedy routines performed in her living room. Nora was a woman of many talents, an artist who hadn't yet found a way to share her gifts with the world at large.

She had always been funny. For as long as she could remember, she'd known how to make people laugh, usually with one of her many impersonations. Making her widowed mother laugh helped alleviate her depression. Making other kids laugh made Nora feel like less of an outsider. From an early age she'd felt like a freak, utterly different from other children in part because she had no father, in part because her mother was a drug addict, but mostly because she felt fundamentally bizarre, like an alien from a different planet. Because she felt so different from everyone else, she constantly struggled with feelings of shame (Exclusion).

When she walked into a room, you felt her presence in ways that could be uncomfortable—she was, after all, so eccentric, and so deeply uncomfortable in her own skin, that she could easily make other people around her feel anxious too. When ill at ease, she would simulate facial tics that captured how odd she felt, drawing attention to herself in a self-mocking way. At those moments I found her extremely funny, although I never lost sight of her pain. I didn't yet conceive of that pain as an almost unbearable type of shame.

Trying to capture Nora's humor is almost impossible. We've all known people who are indescribably funny, for reasons we can't express. During a therapy session she could contort her face in ways that made me laugh. She could say something utterly mundane in a tone of voice that made it seem hilarious. Or she could slip into one of her many characters, the cast of oddballs that filled her head, including Valley Girl.

"Oh, my God, Dr. Burgo! Like, wow, that is so amazing! No, wait! Oh, darn, I forgot. What did you say again?"

"Unfortunately for you," I repeated, "you're very good at making me laugh."

I often said this to her because she used humor to keep me at such a distance that I was unable to make contact and help her.

When we speak of psychological defenses, the connotation usually is negative, as if facing the pain of emotional truth is much healthier than being so defensive. While on some level this is true, many people from disastrous backgrounds such as Nora's have no other way to cope with their pain than the defensive strategies they cobbled together as they grew up: by and large Nora had no "healthier side" to which she could turn. Under optimal conditions babies and children learn to manage their emotions with the help of their parents; when those parents utterly fail to provide the support necessary for psychological growth, as in Nora's case, children must find other ways to cope. Those methods may be maladaptive and usually give rise to a different kind of pain, but in some way they do work. They often represent quite creative solutions to intractable problems.

Nora's father had died of a drug overdose when she was an infant, leaving her in the care of a woman utterly unequipped for motherhood. A depressed drug abuser, Nora's mother led an itinerant life of serial relationships, intermittent employment, drug abuse, and emotional chaos. While not exactly a prostitute, she lived off and on with men who supplied her with drugs in exchange for sex. Nora didn't have a single memory of her mother preparing a meal for her, although she knew she must have eaten or she would have died. Hunger pervaded her recollections of childhood. It wouldn't be much of an exaggeration to say that Nora brought herself up.

Human infants are born into the world with an innate need to love and be loved. Think back on the Still Face Experiment. It may not yet be love in the fully adult sense, but this drive for joyful interaction with caretakers represents a precursor of love. As I discussed in chapter 5 infants also depend upon such joyful interaction for their brains to develop normally. In Nora's case such interaction was almost entirely absent. As a result, rather than feeling beautiful and worthy, at the center of her mother's emotional world, she felt ugly, deformed, and adrift in an impersonal universe.

Core shame.

She sometimes described herself as jerry-rigged: tenuously held together by wires and string and tape, constantly at risk of falling apart. On some level she felt unbearably hideous and unlovable. Like my client Lizzie, the aspiring writer afflicted by profound social anxiety (chapter 7), Nora usually isolated herself in order to avoid an encounter with shame—head down at work or alone in her apartment. On occasion, when she couldn't avoid being seen (during our sessions, for example), she took control of that experience by deliberately making herself appear to be bizarre, ugly, or misshapen in a manner that could be extremely funny. She would force people to laugh at her, thereby preventing them from mocking or shaming her in a way she could neither anticipate nor control.

Nobody wants to be laughed at or made fun of. Most of us do whatever we can to avoid such an experience; a few people, like Nora, intentionally seek it out, deliberately making themselves ridiculous to others and inspiring their laughter. The agonizing shame of Unwanted Exposure becomes bearable when it is intentionally produced and controlled. To entertain an audience and hear their laughter may also evoke a kind of pride that is not merely defensive in nature. When artful and well crafted, what starts out as a defensive strategy to control shame might eventually become a source of self-respect, as was the case with Nora.

THE ONE-WOMAN SHOW

My work with Nora lasted nearly two decades, and the primary healing took place within the context of our relationship. Beyond offering insight and understanding, I provided an emotional environment that compensated, to a limited extent, for what she had missed as a child. Psychotherapy can't work miracles, and even a successful, strong bond such as ours could not transform Nora into the adult she might have been had she grown up within a more reliable environment. All the same, I made her feel safe, seen, and eventually loved for herself.

She grew enormously through our work, even if she remained a somewhat eccentric person who struggled to be vulnerable in her friendships and later romantic relationships. It's hard to capture in summary the love and respect we came to feel for one another over many years. Nora eventually developed strong feelings of pride for her growth in therapy and what she had accomplished in her life. As I grew more confident and relaxed as a therapist, I was able to share the joy in achievement that she felt and to tell her so.

Early in our work together Nora often took flight into grandiose fantasies of wealth and fame through which she would triumph over her sense of defect and ugliness. Although she loved to draw and illustrate her stories, she also wrote traditional fiction, starting and quickly abandoning several novels. Sometimes she imagined herself as a writer of great renown whose books were translated into fifty languages and adapted by Hollywood. In those days I would interpret these flights of fantasy as a kind of omnipotent denial of her own neediness: when she couldn't bear feeling small and dependent, she'd magically and instantly transform herself into a literary star. Today I would describe those fantasies as a flight from shame rather than from neediness.

In the later stages of our work I also learned that her grandiose fantasies were not merely defensive; they also embodied a profound admiration for creative people and her desire to join their ranks, even if she found it hard to sustain the hard work necessary to do so. She admired writers whose works had stood the test of time. She revered painters who had changed the way people looked at their world.

She also felt a deep respect for a few stand-up comics she viewed as artists in their own right—in particular, the brilliant Andy Kaufman from *Saturday Night Live* (and, later, *Taxi*), whose extreme eccentricity made him seem, as she put it, like some kind of relative. One of our final therapeutic tasks was to sever the link between grandiosity and art so that she could undertake the long, hard work of achieving her own brand of excellence.

For people like my other client Lizzie, who consistently avoid encounters with shame, publishing their work in whatever form presents a huge emotional challenge because it might lead to the shame of Exclusion or Disappointed Expectation if their efforts meet with rejection. Going forward despite their fears depends upon having a great deal of courage. Nora might have staged comic routines for her cats within the privacy of her apartment; going public was something altogether different and frightening. She also had no idea how to enter the world she longed to join. She had no mentors, no teachers, and no one to guide her toward her goal.

As with Lizzie's, Nora's path was long and complicated. A pivotal event occurred when she found a throwaway circular for adult education courses offered throughout Los Angeles. She eventually enrolled in a course on improvisational theater, although she'd never felt an interest in that type of performance. She dropped out and later reenrolled for the next semester. Eventually she joined a new company that gave regular performances in a converted storefront in a marginal part of town.

Nora asked me many times to come watch her company, and I eventually agreed to attend a performance. By that point I'd invested many years and a lot of emotion in Nora's progress; I naturally felt curious to see how she performed outside my office. Onstage she was hilarious, so compellingly bizarre that her colleagues found it hard to stay in character and often broke into laughter. I could see that Nora also irritated them for that reason.

Seeing this performance eventually led me to focus on some ways in which she continued to be controlling in our work together, keeping me at a distance with humor in less obvious ways than before. In most respects she appeared to be entirely different from the young woman who had long ago entered my practice. Now she dressed well, wore her hair longer in a stylish cut, and was no longer afraid to make eye contact. Witty and intelligent, she was a pleasure to work with. She still knew how to make me laugh. No doubt because I enjoyed our sessions so much, I had failed to notice the way she continued to use humor to modulate the degree of our intimacy.

When I made an interpretation that surprised her, she'd often remark, "Now that was a good one," and laugh. On the one hand she meant this as sincere appreciation; on the other this comment on my craft distanced her from the feeling my interpretation had addressed. Her laughter moved us away from pain and the lingering shame at her core. I also began to focus on how she carefully organized our sessions, moving from topic to related topic in way that sometimes marginalized me, as if I'd been relegated to the role of audience.

Much of the work during that period focused on our relationship—how difficult she still found it to take in what I'd said in an unguarded way and to respond authentically, without making our exchanges into a source of humor. I finally recognized this control as a defense against the shame of Unwanted Exposure: despite all those years we'd spent building trust, she still feared that I might unexpectedly laugh at her. We eventually linked this controlling form of interaction to her work onstage and how it isolated her from her colleagues.

As much as Nora longed to succeed at her craft, she also needed to belong, to feel herself a true member of a community. In the final stages of our work she learned to restrain her humor and make room for the other players onstage to express themselves. She learned to do something that seemed entirely novel and frightening: to focus on the other actors and react to what they had actually said, rather than taking control of the stage with her domineering brand of humor. For obvious reasons Nora found it hard to trust that other people, including members of her company, would come through for her. She'd always had to do everything for herself.

Nora eventually went on to write plays for local theater groups and gradually built her reputation as a playwright. She dated, married, and divorced after several years. The last I heard, one of her plays was being developed as a series for television.

sixteen

SELF-HATRED

AT ONE POINT LATE IN MY career, I found myself working simulta-neously with three men who had been bullied during middle school. As a psychoanalyst steeped in object relations theory, which locates the roots of mental illness in the earliest years of life, I had not fully realized how profoundly a later trauma such as bullying can affect a person's psyche. This was especially true in the case of Ryan, a young man in his late twen-ties who sought treatment because of self-hatred so profound it sometimes left him almost catatonic. During middle school Ryan had been bullied, mocked, and ostracized in a way that had scarred him for life.

Bullies often target individuals who already struggle with shame and self-esteem issues. While this was true in Ryan's case, I doubt that self-hatred would have taken hold were it not for the abrupt and unforeseen way his peer group turned against him in middle school. For all three of my clients the sudden and unexpected aspect of the bullying they expe-rienced had a decisive impact. Up until that point in their lives, they had assumed they were safe. They believed that they had a place in their so-cial world, even if they weren't especially popular. Then one day they were abruptly afflicted by the shame of Exclusion. Ridiculed by their peers, they felt the unforeseen shame of Unwanted Exposure. This trauma shaped their personalities for the rest of their lives; its impact cannot be overemphasized.

During the year and a half that I worked with Ryan, I never once saw him smile. I never heard him laugh. One of the most joyless human beings I've ever met, he seemed remote and unreachable. During our sessions, held by videoconference, he usually appeared in the same cramped location: at a small desk with a bookcase at his back, so close that he seemed trapped by it. Ryan kept the lights in the room low. He spoke in a restrained, soft voice, as if afraid that someone would overhear him, even though his roommate worked the night shift and was away from their apartment when we held our sessions.

Ryan was good looking in an exotic sort of way, with the almond-shaped eyes and complexion of his Taiwanese mother. Although he apparently believed himself to be ugly, he was aware from time to time that one girl or another found him attractive. Usually too shy to respond when they flirted with him, he'd withdraw in a way that must have made him appear conceited. He desperately longed to date, to have a girlfriend, in part because he was so profoundly alone, in part because his isolation made him feel even more like a loser. Most of his contemporaries had coupled up and begun to marry.

Ryan had a small circle of friends he'd known since high school and throughout college, socially marginal men his own age with whom he'd played video games, taken drugs, and enjoyed rock music. For a time during college he'd played keyboard in a band, but appearing in local clubs had brought on such acute attacks of self-hatred that he finally gave it up. He loved playing music (he told me in a joyless tone of voice), loved belonging to the band (he flatly stated), but the agonizing anticipation before every performance eventually became unbearable.

At the time his therapy began, Ryan worked at a marketing firm, part of a team whose dominant male players were outgoing, boisterous, and self-confident—"overgrown frat boys," he called them. They joked and ribbed one another throughout the workday. Their banter made him feel on the outside, an object of derision, rather than a participant in the needling sort of humor adolescent boys and young men sometimes use to cope with their insecurities. Ryan despised himself for being meek and felt he ought to be more like his colleagues. Whenever one of them teased him for being so quiet, it revived the trauma of middle school, filling him with shame and self-loathing.

Although he faithfully appeared online for all his sessions, he seemed entirely indifferent to me and our work together. He often described himself as a kind of alien, different on the inside from real human beings, even though he resembled them on the outside. It felt to me as if Ryan existed in a lonely, dark cave of his own devising.

One particular session brought his isolation home to me in a visceral way. When he appeared on-screen at the usual time, he was seated behind the steering wheel of his car rather than at his desk. In the dark of night a nearby streetlamp shed an eerie, otherworldly light through the car windows. It was a lonely, haunting scene. I've since met by videoconference with other clients who spoke from their cars—in the parking lot at work because they could find no other private space or parked at the curb like Ryan when family members were at home—but this was my first such experience. It startled me.

"What happened?" I asked.

"Dennis changed to the day shift," he said. When we began working together, Ryan's roommate had never been at home when we talked.

From time to time during that session, the headlights of a passing car would illuminate Ryan's face. With a suddenly alert expression, as if prepared for a threat, he would stop talking. Several times he imagined hearing footsteps along the pavement outside his car and would again break off, cocking his head to the side and listening carefully.

"It's okay," he'd eventually say. "There's no one there."

MIDDLE SCHOOL TRAUMA

As a young man Ryan's father had worked in the oil and gas industry and spent many years living in Asia. When he returned to the United States to take a job in his native Colorado, he brought with him a Taiwanese wife and their infant son, Ryan. The father's new employer was located in a small city whose population was largely Caucasian, with some Hispanics and few people of Asian descent, its economy dominated by military installations and the national headquarters of a conservative religious foundation. Within a few years another son was born—Ryan's brother, Hunter.

Ryan believed his early childhood had been unremarkable, with no major family traumas, relatively normal. I saw it otherwise. His father was a timid, disengaged figure eclipsed and dominated by Ryan's mother, a formidable woman who clearly viewed her husband as a failure and treated him with blatant contempt. She was prodigiously ambitious, had founded a property management firm not long after her arrival in the United States, and grew it into a highly successful enterprise. Along with two sisters still living in Taiwan, she also ran an import-export business. Preoccupied with her business ventures, she took little emotional interest in her sons, although she directed and controlled virtually every aspect of their lives.

Even during elementary school Ryan felt somehow different from his peers, and not merely because of his half-Asian appearance. Shy and soft-spoken, with few friends, he saw himself as lacking some essential quality, the confidence and vitality he could identify in many of the other boys. His mother signed him up for the soccer league and insisted he continue playing, year after year, even though he didn't enjoy the sport. When it was his mother's turn to provide refreshments for a match, Ryan felt embarrassed by the Taiwanese treats she sent along—pineapple cake and *gua bao* (pork belly buns)—rather than the prepackaged snacks brought by the other mothers.

Yet he felt he had a place within his community, albeit a marginal one. His peers regularly invited him to their birthday parties even if no one considered him their best friend. When his classmates chose sides for team sports, he always found himself in the respectable middle. Teachers called on him during class and he answered without much discomfort. He sometimes wished he was more popular but the idea didn't torment him.

Ryan was twelve years old and had entered middle school when his brother, Hunter, was formally diagnosed with Asperger's syndrome. Hunter had always seemed unusual, with his strangely formal speech and refusal to use contractions, the odd bouncing way he walked, on the balls of his feet and leaning forward. Some boys would taunt Ryan about his brother and called Hunter a freak. Or they would mimic Hunter's speech in Ryan's presence, emphatically pronouncing the words *will not* instead of *won't*, or *cannot* instead of *can't*. Later the teasing focused on the shape of Ryan's eyes. Even the other boys on his soccer team, teammates for several years, began to mock him. The newly elected captain of the team, a boy named Danny, became head bully and relentlessly persecuted Ryan.

Before he reached adolescence, Danny had been a small and physically uncoordinated boy. Although his parents had divorced many years earlier, when Danny was only two, they continued feuding, publicly and through the court system. Ryan recalled one soccer match when both of Danny's parents showed up (they usually took turns) and humiliated Danny by screaming at one another on the sidelines. Early on Ryan had felt a kind of distant kinship with Danny because they both seemed like outsiders, different from the other kids. Middle school changed everything.

During the summer before seventh grade Danny shot up several inches and put on muscle. His looks improved. In the major reshuffling of social status that is middle school, he became one of the cool kids, highly popular with both boys and girls. When Danny mocked Ryan in the hallway, calling him a gook, other kids followed his example. When Danny told friends he thought Ryan must be gay, the rumor quickly spread. Boys began shoving Ryan into his locker as they passed. Groups of girls would point and snicker from adjoining tables in the cafeteria. At soccer practice his teammates would deliberately trip him and laugh when he fell.

Despite his mother's objections Ryan quit soccer. When he finally told her about the bullying, she shrugged and told him he needed to get tough. He felt that she viewed him with contempt—as a weakling, like his father. Ryan knew better than to ask for help from his dad, who seemed increasingly remote from the rest of the family. As the bullying continued during the next two years, Ryan's shame and sense of humiliation became so acute that he considered killing himself. He wished he were invisible; most of the time he shunned involvement with other kids.

With yet another change in the social landscape in high school, Ryan suddenly found he was no longer a target, although the legacy of shame and humiliation haunted him throughout his teens and into adulthood. Late in his twenties, Ryan finally sought professional help; by then he was afflicted with self-hatred so profound he felt crippled by it. He'd already tried cognitive-behavioral therapy. After reading some of my blog posts on the topic of shame, he reached out to me.

A NEW PERSPECTIVE

"When you say that you hate yourself," I once said, early in our work, "what exactly do you mean? What are you thinking when these bouts of self-hatred come on?"

Although we were thousands of miles apart in different cities, connecting by videoconference, I felt him tense up on-screen. He fell silent.

"Just telling me about it must feel humiliating," I finally said.

He gave me a tight nod. As usual he kept his gaze downcast. At last he told me what he was thinking: "*You're a fucking loser. You're pathetic. You're ugly. Nobody likes you. You might as well die. You're stupid. Why bother doing anything? You know you'll fail.* It goes on and on like that for hours, repeating the same things. Relentless, like I'm always being watched and judged. *You're pathetic. You're ugly.* Over and over."

He winced, as if an attack were coming on at that moment. Telling me had taken some courage, and now he felt like he was paying the price for daring to speak.

Although it was fairly late in my career, I'd never encountered such a profound case of self-hatred. From the beginning of my work with Ryan, I recognized that my primary theoretical model for understanding it—the punitive superego and its perfectionism, which usually serves as a defense against need and dependency—wouldn't help me. Something more profound and mysterious seemed to be at work in Ryan's self-hatred; over time he helped me to understand it.

Although Ryan felt shame about many issues, he focused in particular on his body: he believed that disgusting thick hair grew along his back and shoulders, across his upper chest. Before we started working together, he'd spent thousands of dollars on electrolysis to remove some of it, although much more work (he told me) remained to be done. This intense shame concerning his body had prevented him from having more than occasional sex, and only when he'd had quite a lot to drink. When sober, the prospect of appearing naked before another human being felt unbearable.

Given the degree of shame he apparently felt about his body hair, it surprised me that from time to time he'd appear on-screen for our sessions wearing a tank top or sleeveless tee shirt. As far as I could see, his arms, shoulders, and upper chest appeared entirely smooth. When I pointed this out, he insisted that his condition was much worse than it appeared and that I should have seen him before electrolysis. Although I never found a way to articulate this view during our sessions, I believe Ryan wanted to be found beautiful, in an innocent and not sexual way. Because of his dread of the shame it might arouse (Disappointed Expectation, Unrequited Love), he couldn't acknowledge this longing, to himself or to me. And so he bared his skin, proclaiming himself to be ugly before I or anyone else could do it.

You might have known people who regularly put themselves down in social situations. Sometimes they make self-mocking jokes, and sometimes they make derogatory remarks about themselves that inspire feelings of discomfort in those around them. We typically describe such people as having low self-esteem and being too hard on themselves. Ryan helped me to understand that self-deprecation is also a means to control shame. Rather than making yourself vulnerable (thereby risking an experience of shame) in the hope of being found beautiful or funny or clever, you shame yourself beforehand so that no one else can do it. As painful as such shame might feel, at least it isn't unexpected.

This insight came relatively early in our work together. It took me longer to understand its connection to those vicious attacks of self-hatred that occasionally paralyzed him. Although I tried to help him confront this ruthless internal critic, we made little headway. Every month or so he would savage himself so brutally that he could barely struggle out of bed and make it to work. Whenever Ryan appeared for a session while in the throes of self-loathing, he seemed encapsulated and remote. I wanted badly to help him find relief.

I began to discern a pattern: the attacks of self-hatred regularly came on whenever he entertained the prospect of emerging from isolation and putting himself forward. At work he was planning to apply for a promotion, but when he imagined the interviews involved, he berated himself so savagely that he shut down with migraine headaches and stayed in bed for two full days. When he met a young woman at work and wanted to ask her out, he repeatedly imagined scenarios in which she rebuffed him with contempt, so he never worked up the nerve. Something as little as wanting to tell his colleagues a joke he'd heard could bring on a paralyzing attack of self-hatred that silenced him.

It occurred to me one day that these attacks might represent a type of psychological defense mechanism, as counterintuitive as the idea at first seemed.

According to psychodynamic theory, all human beings resort to defense mechanisms to protect themselves from unbearable pain. Everyone relies upon such defenses to one degree or another; much of the time they help us to cope when we feel overwhelmed, usually on a temporary basis. Only when they become deeply entrenched and pervasive do our defense mechanisms stand in the way of personal growth.

While self-hatred shut Ryan down and paralyzed him, it also prevented exposure to ridicule or rejection. In other words he shamed and humiliated himself as a self-protective measure, a defense mechanism to shield himself from an experience of shame he could not control.

During our next session Ryan was talking once again about his team at work and, in particular, a boisterous colleague who was applying for a job opening, one that Ryan also wanted. He told me about his sleepless nights that week, long hours spent in darkness brutalizing himself for his shortcomings. He despised himself as a weakling who lacked the courage to apply for the new job. At that point I made a tentative suggestion: I wondered whether these attacks of self-hatred, as painful as they might be, also protected him from potential shame by shutting him down. So long as he didn't put himself forward, he would never encounter the shame of Disappointed Expectation or Unwanted Exposure. Ryan immediately accepted this as true.

I wish I could say that this session marked a turning point in his treatment, that Ryan applied for that job and secured a promotion. Contrary to popular conceptions about insight-oriented psychotherapy, insight in and of itself rarely leads to change. Learning something new about yourself is important, but it's how you put that insight to work that matters. Even when Ryan could see that self-hatred protected him from exposure to uncontrollable, unpredictable shame, he found it almost impossible to challenge his jailer. Again and again during the ensuing months, self-hatred shut him down and isolated him.

SMALL STEPS AND LIMITATIONS

Toward the end of our first year of working together, Ryan met Samantha, a young woman he wanted to date. In a rare moment of psychological freedom, he'd agreed to join some old friends from college for drinks, people he hadn't seen in several months. Samantha, a friend of a friend, came along. Ryan immediately found her attractive; in her quiet reserve he also recognized a kindred spirit.

Ryan had known these friends for many years and felt as comfortable with them as he ever felt with anyone. Two drinks and the subdued lighting in the bar helped relax him even more. When asked about his job, he made a few mocking observations about his coworkers, and Samantha laughed at something he said. He could tell that she found him attractive; he instantly began to belittle himself. In that moment it seemed clear to him that this attack of self-hatred had come on as a self-protective measure, to stop him from risking rejection should he do what he wanted to do—ask for her phone number.

He didn't ask for her number. Later that night the experience brought on one of his more severe bouts of self-hatred, with migraine headaches and an entire weekend spent in bed. When the assault at last relented after a few days, he telephoned the friend who'd invited Samantha to join them that night and asked for her phone number. After another two weeks he finally telephoned and invited her (with as much apparent indifference as he could muster) to join him for a movie later that week. She accepted.

The slow, somewhat tortured course of Ryan's relationship with Samantha occupied the final months of our work together. Because the prospect of revealing his body provoked such dread, he almost broke it off several times before they had sex. On the evening of their fifth or sixth date, when going to bed seemed inevitable, he took a Valium before picking her up and had several drinks at dinner. When he told me about it during our next session, he said the sex had gone well and the subsequent attack of self-hatred had not devastated him. He sounded as if he felt relieved to have the experience behind him. He made it seem as if he had taken no joy in the experience, felt no pleasure in having sex.

Samantha struck me as a sensitive and intelligent young woman. From his descriptions it seemed clear to me that she understood his need for reassurance. She frequently praised his looks and said she found him sexy. She also seemed to intuit his need to go slowly, leaving him room to disappear for several days without contact, never pushing too hard or asking for commitment. Although he sounded detached and utterly joyless whenever he mentioned their sex life, he told me that it was getting better. He never made mention of his body hair or Samantha's reaction to it.

Around this time Ryan found an article that I'd posted on my blog, about the healing power of love in the psychotherapy relationship. In that blog post I expressed the view that I've also put forward in this book— that the love between client and therapist, developed over many years, is what most powerfully promotes emotional growth. Ryan had reached out to me because of other articles I'd written on my website; he read this one and felt agitated by it. During our next session he told me that he couldn't ever see making himself vulnerable in the way I had described. He couldn't imagine that he'd ever feel anything like love for me or to accept that I might feel that way about him.

In the weeks that followed, Ryan dropped the subject but I sensed it in the background. I felt him putting distance between us. One day he announced at the beginning of our session that he had decided to discontinue treatment, effective immediately. He told me that the understanding of self-hatred and its protective role in his life had been illuminating; he thanked me for all my help but said he had decided that he now wanted to go it alone.

Lowering his voice and looking away, he almost pleaded, "Please don't make me feel bad about my decision." He sounded shaky and scared as he said it.

I understood what he dreaded, that I would use my position of authority as his therapist to subtly shame him for making what I considered a bad choice. He was afraid that I'd characterize his decision as pure defensiveness and therefore invalid. I felt my own shame at that moment: without quite realizing it, I'd done that very thing to other clients in the past, early in my career when I was building a practice and the loss of a client could have a large financial impact. By interpreting their decision to leave therapy as defensive, I'd tried to shame them into staying.

"Okay," I said.

It was our last session and I never saw him again.

seventeen

MASOCHISM

WHY DO VICTIMS OF RAPE and physical abuse so often feel ashamed about what happened to them? Many women, and sometimes men, spend years burdened by debilitating shame, keeping their awful secret, as if they are somehow to blame for having been raped. The tendency of society to blame women for supposedly leading men on, and for police and criminal defense lawyers to retraumatize assault victims by dredging up their sexual history, surely plays a role, but it doesn't fully account for the need these victims feel to keep the past a secret. Why should deep personal shame be the legacy of violence perpetrated by others against trusting individuals, usually helpless to defend themselves?

Just as a country might feel humiliated during war if invaded and subdued by a foreign power, rape victims suffer enduring shame when they are physically invaded by someone, overpowered, and defiled by his hateful bodily fluids. When the perpetrator is a potential romantic partner (date rape) or a loved one (spousal rape or childhood sexual abuse), such an assault constitutes the most intense form of Unrequited Love imaginable. To seek connection, to feel love and long for it to be returned, only to be sexually exploited or physically brutalized, can instill profound shame.[1] Rather than feeling beautiful and worthy through an experience of reciprocal joy, a rape victim may instead feel ugly and defective—unlovable, as if something is profoundly wrong with them.

We'd been working together by videoconference for several months before James told me his story. He first mentioned it almost in passing, as if it were unimportant, and the full details emerged slowly over several sessions. Bullying in middle school that continued into high school. A locker-room assault. A secret kept for decades. James was in his late forties when we began working together, and he was a wealthy and respected surgeon, a marathon runner, and one of the most eligible bachelors in his community. Attractive, outgoing, and self-confident, at least on the surface, James appeared to have it all. He had many acquaintances, mostly people who idealized him or turned to him for financial help, but no real friends. He'd never been married.

Early in high school James had tried out for the football team but had not made the cut. He'd always been passionate about the game and was crushed by the rejection, although he understood it had to do with physical size and not ability: while he was athletic and fit, James was smaller than the other players. He also felt that the coach didn't like him, for reasons he could not understand. During the practice sessions that were part of the tryouts, the coach regularly mocked him for his size and for the errors he made.

To feel a part of the football team experience, even though he was not a player, James volunteered to be the team's water boy, attending practice every day and of course going to all the games. The team's lead players, probably picking up on the coach's attitude, soon began bullying James. It started with mockery and name-calling, progressed to wet towel slapping in the locker room, and culminated one afternoon when three players physically restrained and sodomized him with a broom handle in the showers. Profoundly humiliated and frightened, James did not report the assault to anyone, especially the coach, who he suspected would deny what had happened to shield his players. When James abandoned his role as water boy, no one (not even his parents) asked him why.

James had never spoken to anyone about what had happened to him in the locker room that day; I was the first person to hear his awful story, recounted with tears and obvious self-loathing. Although he understood that he'd been victimized, he felt deeply ashamed about the assault, almost as if he felt he deserved it—something must obviously be wrong with him for those football players to treat him with such contempt and cruelty. He must be defective in some repulsive way for the coach to dislike him so.

As dramatic and defining as this experience might seem, it did not fully account for James's struggles. Even before the rape, he'd felt unlikable, an outcast with no true friends. He insisted that his parents had loved him deeply and brought him up well, but without quite criticizing them he made clear that parental love had always felt contingent to him. James was the oldest of five children and understood early on that his role in life was to fulfill his father's disappointed dreams—to excel academically and then one day to become a physician. While James's father had been a successful businessman, a pillar of his community, and eventually the mayor of their small midwestern town, he'd always longed to be a doctor. James felt he would be loved only so long as he fulfilled his father's expectations.

There was no evidence that anything of a sexual nature had ever occurred, but James and his father were unusually, even unnaturally, close. It seemed clear that the father suffered from some form of anxiety disorder with occasional panic attacks. When he was riddled with anxiety, he would sleep in James's room on the floor next to his bed, almost as if James had some talismanic ability to keep his father safe. Although the older man was a busy officeholder, he called his son many times each day after James returned home from school and wanted to know exactly what James was doing and where he was going. Even now, as an old man, he continued to call James a dozen times each day. This father struck me less as a controlling parent who wanted to regulate his son's life than as a man who needed constant contact with his idealized child to help manage his own anxiety.

This unusual behavior seemed to continue a family pattern: James's paternal grandmother had also suffered from panic attacks, and after her own husband died, she slept in bed with James's father well into his teens.

I never had the sense of sexual impropriety. Rather, it struck me as a blurring of personal boundaries, a misuse of the parent-child relationship to manage personal difficulties. James's grandmother exploited her son to soothe her own anxieties, and he then made use of his son, James, in the same way.

Not surprisingly, James had no coherent sense of self. Over the years I've heard other clients say they have no idea who they "really are," but other than naming his passion for football and running marathons, James could not identify a single trait that distinguished him from other people. He could not tell me which subjects interested him, the title of a book that he had enjoyed, or even his favorite color. He hated small talk and party conversation, fearing he had nothing of interest to say, and had developed a warm, jokester persona to mask his internal emptiness. Whenever a group gathering was unavoidable, he'd leave at the earliest opportunity.

Although he did not particularly enjoy the experience, James smoked pot compulsively every day—not during his working hours but every night at home. It helped him to cope with the pervasive dread and anxiety that was completely invisible to everyone who knew him. Over the years he'd had several romantic involvements with beautiful women he deemed inappropriate; each relationship had lasted several years and involved intense, almost "pornographic sex," as he described it, as well as the regular use of recreational drugs. When we began working together, he told me he'd never felt emotionally intimate with any of those women. He had not trusted their affection, either, and believed they were only after his money. Not one of them had truly known him.

Then he met Shailene.

AN INEXPLICABLE CHOICE

At twenty-eight Shailene was two decades James's junior, a high school dropout twice married and divorced, with two sons, one from each marriage. Her ex-husbands had primary custody of those boys and she saw them on alternate weekends only. She worked as a fitness instructor at the health club where James trained.

In the relatively small community in which they lived, Shailene had a reputation for promiscuity, drug abuse, and emotional instability. When word spread that they were dating, several acquaintances approached James and warned him off. "She's bad news," he heard more than once. "Stay away." Early on James emailed her picture to me, a photo she no doubt used to advertise her personal training services. With raven hair, flawless skin, and a well-toned body, she was intensively sexy and attractive.

James had always felt the need to have a beautiful woman as his partner in order to prove his worth as a man. Uninteresting to most girls during high school, he'd dated little and felt like a loser. In college he'd had a few sexual experiences fueled by drugs and alcohol, but during his surgical residency life began to change. As a young doctor with a high earning potential, he found himself suddenly attractive to the opposite sex. Beautiful women who once would not have given him the time of day suddenly began to flirt with him outrageously. Attending his ten-year high school reunion with a beauty pageant winner on his arm had felt like redemption: *I'm not the loser you all thought I was.*

His sudden ability to attract women, coinciding as it did with the addition of "Dr." to his name, had left James deeply cynical. No one had ever loved him for himself, he insisted, and no one ever would. The only thing that women cared about was his money. He desired, admired, and hated women. He constantly distrusted their motives; Shailene, he believed, saw him as her meal ticket. She had approached him at the health club and aggressively pursued him. The day after asking for his cell phone number, she sent him a text: Wanna come over and fuck?

They began a torrid physical affair and a turbulent emotional involvement, with frequent fights and breakups, mostly instigated by James when he began to feel trapped. "I'm done with her," he'd insist each time. After a few days Shailene would sext him and soon they'd start up again. It was during this chaotic period that James first reached out to me for treatment. He told me he couldn't stay in the relationship for more than a few weeks without feeling claustrophobic yet couldn't separate from Shailene for more than a few days.

"It's really sick," he told me. "I know it but I can't stop."

From James's descriptions of Shailene, even allowing for his tendency to overemphasize the crazy nature of her assaults, it became clear that she conformed to the clinical picture of borderline personality disorder. Moody and erratic, she idealized him one day—referring to him as her Prince Charming and tucking love notes into his coat so he would find them later—and then devalued him the next as a "fucked-up basket case," weak and whiny. She struggled with substance abuse, above and beyond the pot and alcohol they shared together. She had destroyed both her marriages through infidelity. According to James, she referred to her own family background as trailer trash and told him she'd been sexually molested by both her grandfather and her brother.

When James and Shailene decided to move in together, his friends, pastor, and therapist (me) tried to dissuade him, without success. When they became engaged, his family staged a small intervention and told him he was crazy. James insisted that, despite all the turmoil in their relationship, despite his belief that Shailene viewed him as her meal ticket, he truly cared about her and cherished the time they spent together. He told himself that she actually did care for him, and sometimes he almost believed it. Feeling helpless, and still in the dark about what kept James in that relationship, I watched and waited with a sense of foreboding.

SELF-PITY VERSUS SELF-ESTEEM

James's sessions followed a pattern. He appeared punctually on-screen for our twice-weekly appointments, usually held on days when he wasn't in surgery. He'd look tired and a little unkempt: baggy logo tee shirt, face unshaved, thick brown hair askew and partially hidden by a backward-facing baseball cap. Although he was nearing fifty, he sometimes reminded me of a teenage surfer or skateboarder. In general James came across as much younger, emotionally speaking, than his actual age.

After inquiring after my health—he was unfailingly polite—he'd launch into a long narrative: "So I've been thinking about all the women I never asked out in college, all the times I could have started something and didn't. I don't know why. There was this one girl . . ."

While avoiding eye contact, he'd go on at length about whatever topic had been preoccupying him since our last session, some period in his past he felt compelled to revisit, or another fight with Shailene. He often repeated stories I'd heard before; when I reminded him that he'd already related something to me, he seemed genuinely surprised, with no memory of having done so. But then he would continue with the familiar story anyway, as if compelled to get it all out. I often felt like I was a mere spectator or receptacle, someone whose only role was to bear silent witness to his pain.

Talk therapy means sharing your pain, of course, but the hope is that it involves taking something in, as well—insight, compassion, and guidance from your therapist. Some clients like James relieve themselves in a repetitive, one-sided way and forget the things we tell them. You might have known someone who turns to friends or relatives in a similar way, unloading their pain upon anyone who will listen but ignoring their advice.

While this type of compulsive disclosure does afford a kind of relief, it's only temporary and must be repeated once psychological pain and pressure build up again. Clients who make use of therapy in this way often appear devoted, spending years in treatment without getting any better; they only evacuate and rarely absorb anything useful about themselves.

James treated me like I was a mere function, rather than a caring person with whom he had a relationship. He rarely took in what I had to tell him; although in the moment he always agreed with what I'd said and soon returned to his narrative. It took him a while to understand what I was telling him, about the way he used therapy to unload his pain and how it kept me at a useless distance. Eventually we made some headway in this area. He began to recognize how much he did not want to be truly seen and known. Sometimes it seemed clear that he wanted me to feel sorry for him. At the beginning of a story he often said, "I don't mean to sound pitiful, but . . ." He obviously wanted me to pity him.

James turned to many other people in the same way, a list of interchangeable acquaintances he would telephone for sympathy whenever he and Shailene had another blowout. James had no real friends but he did know a great many people who liked and respected him. Although he didn't smoke cigarettes on a regular basis, from time to time he would buy a pack and drive around town in his car, chain-smoking and making one call after another, repeating exactly the same story to everyone on his list.

"You won't believe what she did this time," he'd begin. "That woman is crazy!"

These stories always exaggerated her bad behavior, made no reference to the subtle ways he provoked her, and painted himself as an innocent victim.

Self-pity is the refuge of people afflicted with core shame, those who lack true self-esteem. Unable to take pride in themselves or their accomplishments, they compensate by feeling sorry for themselves, often seeking to elicit pity from other people as well. Clients may easily feel criticized or humiliated when you draw attention to their feelings of self-pity, so it's crucial to emphasize the core shame that drives it while empathizing with their pain. James resisted at first but eventually accepted what I was telling him. As a result he gradually stopped trying to make me feel sorry for him and began absorbing more insight.

AN IMPORTANT DREAM

During this period in our work James told me about a brief dream. He was living in some kind of compound located at the floor of a deep canyon. With its high windowless walls and remote location, isolated from

life above, it reminded him of a prison. He couldn't recall seeing anyone else living in the compound, but he was vaguely aware of other
faceless people above the edge of the canyon. James and I immediately
agreed that the dream described how he felt about his own existence:
cut off from the mainstream of life, isolated in a state of mind not unlike
a prison.

With more time and work we eventually understood that this prison
dream also described his relationship with Shailene. As many times as he
had told me he was done with her, insisting that he wanted out, he could
never seem to break free. At one point she suffered a brief psychotic break,
probably induced by illicit drugs, and wound up screaming incoherent
abuse outside their house as neighbors walked by. He caught her sexting
with strangers and making plans to hook up while he was away at a medical conference. Nothing seemed to make any difference. Again and again
his resolve would crumble in the face of her tearful pleas for one more
chance.

Was this an addictive relationship? Did he stay with Shailene because,
on a deep level, he felt he deserved no better? Both perspectives seemed
true but not terribly helpful. He had told me in a recent session that when
he contemplated a future without Shailene, one in which he was involved
with someone "more appropriate," it seemed impossible. He could not
imagine dating a peer—another doctor or some other professional with
money and prestige of her own. It finally occurred to me that, as humiliating as he found life with Shailene, it felt better than the prospect of
rejection by someone new. In a strange way life with Shailene felt safe . . .
or at least predictable.

He knew all about her psychological struggles and the ways she regularly humiliated him. In fact it eventually became clear that he intentionally provoked those attacks from time to time. "I decided I'd go home
and start Armageddon," he told me during a session that followed one of
their worst blowouts ever. He told me that he'd deliberately goaded her
until she finally blew up and began to scream familiar insults at the top
of her voice: "Total fucked-up basket case!" "Whiny loser!" "Fucking
wimp!" James stormed out, bought a pack of cigarettes, and spent hours

driving around town, regaling one audience member after another with his pitiful story by cell phone.

I now understand that the ability to provoke shame is a way to control it. To know in advance what will instigate an assault on your character, to skillfully engineer such an assault, holds a kind of comfort. It offers refuge from something far worse: the sudden and unexpected exposure to shame that James encountered years earlier in that locker room or the shame he might feel if he left Shailene and encountered Unrequited Love with someone new. Shame you can predict and control feels less awful than the shame you don't see coming.

Although I didn't treat Shailene, from my experience with other clients like her, I felt sure that profound shame drove much of her behavior too. Both her brother and grandfather had molested her; she thought of herself as trailer trash. But unlike James, she did not try to predict and control her experience of shame; instead, when he goaded her to the breaking point and she temporarily lost her ability to think, she made him feel ashamed. From his descriptions it sounded as if she sometimes took a sadistic kind of pleasure in humiliating him.

The sadist and the masochist unconsciously collaborate on the scenes they write and act out together, finding relief from shame in complementary ways.

IN PROCESS

I have some hope that my interventions will eventually enable James to break free of this destructive relationship, allowing him to form a healthier bond with someone new. As I write these words, we're still meeting twice a week. He still lives with Shailene; from time to time he insists that he wants out, that he's done with her, and neither of us believes he will follow through. It has been a sobering experience and a lesson in the power of sexual abuse to instill tenacious shame.

There's more to work through here than shame alone. When you're a child and your father exploits you to fulfill his own needs, you're prone to develop relationships as an adult that repeat the pattern—all those women who supposedly cared nothing for James and only wanted his money. When you have been bullied during childhood, you develop a set of defenses against shame that do not easily loosen their hold. When you are nearly fifty and feel that you have no real identity, it takes time to build an authentic sense of self.

I imagine that James and I will continue meeting twice weekly for some time to come.

eighteen

CONTROLLING SHAME IN EVERYDAY LIFE

IN THEIR STUDY OF THE differences between guilt and shame, the psychoanalyst Gerhart Piers and the anthropologist Milton B. Singer hold that masochism "prevents the defeat [shame] from being inflicted by others by bringing it about oneself." In other words, as I learned from my work with James (chapter 17), masochism is an attempt to control and predict an encounter with shame rather than meet it suddenly and unexpectedly. In this manner "the real catastrophic shame is prevented."[1]

Nora (chapter 15) and Ryan (chapter 16) likewise attempted to control their experience of shame. In less extreme forms so do all of us. Efforts to predict and control shame, rather than to experience it in sudden and unexpected ways, are commonplace.

I KNEW IT

I attended high school with a brilliant girl named Diana, who eventually graduated as valedictorian of her class. Although she had never earned less than an A on any test, she always appeared distraught after taking one, insisting to her friends that she had failed it. Many of us found this behavior irritating; we assumed that she wanted only to be contradicted and complimented, so we eventually stopped reassuring her. Instead we'd remark, "You always say that and you always get an A."

"No, this time is different," she would insist, with obvious signs of anguish. "I absolutely know that I failed."

"Uh-huh, sure," we'd say and walk away from her.

Diana may have wanted reassurance from her friends, but in retrospect I believe that she could not bear the unexpected (if highly improbable) humiliation she might feel were she to fail a test that she believed she had aced. I imagine that a certain kind of toxic perfectionism ran in her family and that her parents had relied heavily on shame to enforce their standards. Whatever the reason, Diana had evolved her own way of coping with unanticipated shame (Disappointed Expectation or Unwanted Exposure) by predicting it.

In my profiles of Ryan and James I made special mention of the sudden and unexpected nature of the bullying they encountered. They subsequently began to humiliate themselves before anyone else could do it as a way to predict and control that experience. More commonly, believing that you can predict in advance that you'll feel embarrassment offers a harmless sort of consolation, like the pessimist, who always expects adverse outcomes and when something bad finally happens says, "I knew it would turn out this way!" The pessimist cannot bear unexpected disappointment, so he predicts and expects the worst.

Many of us do exactly that same thing in milder forms. Consider the following statements:

"Someone else will probably get the job."
"Nobody is going to come to my party, I just know it."
"I'm sure you've thought of this already, but . . ."
"Dinner probably won't turn out so good."
"This idea will never get off the ground, but . . ."

I hear people say things like this every day. As painful as it might feel to expect disappointment, it apparently feels less painful than to meet with failure, rejection, or mockery when you hadn't anticipated it.

I SAID IT FIRST

Ryan immobilized himself with savage criticism so he wouldn't do any-thing that might empower other people to shame him. But at one time or another most people make self-critical remarks aloud to prevent other people from saying the same thing. Like Diana, they may hope to be con-tradicted, but at the very least they have forestalled an unexpected and hurtful remark. Like prediction, preemption helps us to control the expe-rience of shame: "I know this dress makes me look fat."

Few people, especially friends, are going to respond by saying "You're right, it really does. Go put on something else." Most will insist that the dress is actually quite flattering and compliment you on your taste.

This type of self-deprecating remark is commonplace:

"What a stupid thing to say!"
"God, I'm such a klutz!"
"This is a dumb question, but . . ."
"I'm sorry the cake turned out so bad."
"I'm no expert, but . . ."

As unpleasant as making a disparaging remark about ourselves to other people might seem to be, we apparently find it less painful than hearing the same criticism from someone else. In part we find relief because we have distanced ourselves from the shame experience by identifying with the critic rather than the clueless object of rebuke. It's as if we're saying "Don't imag-ine that I actually think I'm smart, funny, athletic, attractive, a good cook, and so forth. You don't need to point it out because I know it already."

Besides inviting contradiction, self-deprecation often has a disarming effect on other people and inspires friendly feelings. Some websites even offer guidance on the strategic use of self-deprecation to charm and influ-ence people. People who feel friendly toward you are less likely to do or say things in the future that might shame you. Whereas some narcissistic individuals possess a transient ability to charm, most of us find off-putting those people who think too much of themselves. Arrogance inspires a desire to shoot it down, and shaming is the most reliable weapon.

Like Ryan, many people control shame through self-deprecating thoughts that they never voice aloud. The inner critic belittles us, eroding our courage, so we won't risk Unwanted Exposure, Disappointed Expectation, Exclusion, or Unrequited Love.

"You're not smart enough."
"You're not attractive enough."
"You're too fat to pull off that outfit."
"You're too clumsy."
"She's out of your league."
"You're not funny enough to make that joke work."

This list of examples of discouraging self-talk could go on and on. As painful as it might feel to put ourselves down, doing so turns a potentially uncontrolled and humiliating experience into one we regulate within the privacy of our thoughts.

Sometimes the desire to control shame through self-deprecation can inspire observations that are both judgmental and intentionally funny. Nora's talent for making other people laugh was fueled by a fear that someone might unexpectedly ridicule or laugh at her, arousing shame she could neither predict nor control. Her comic gifts empowered her to inspire laughter at her own expense and thereby make her experience of shame a more manageable one. Many people use self-deprecating humor in the same way, although not as constantly as Nora did. They will focus on an area of personal shame—their weight, their love life, their wardrobe—and derive jokes from it.

SHAME AND COMEDY

Shame plays an outsized part in stand-up comedy. Some comics are brilliant physical comedians, others possess an uncanny ability to inspire mirth in an audience simply by laughing, and a great many plumb the shame experience to produce humor. When a stand-up comedian makes jokes about shame and the audience responds with laughter, the comic has controlled the experience of shame in a way that offers a kind of release from it.

Some comics like Don Rickles humiliate other people to arouse laughter. I invite you to visit YouTube, where you can view clips from his appearances on late-night television or at celebrity roasts; you'll see him insult famous people like Johnny Carson, Martin Scorsese, and Robert De Niro—obviously old friends for whom he feels deep affection. He had a knack for building a joke around observable traits in his friends in a way that made them feel loved rather than humiliated.

At a banquet honoring Scorsese with the American Film Institute's Lifetime Achievement Award, Rickles (just off a role in Scorsese's *Casino*) began his tribute by asking someone to get a phone book for the director, who is only five four, to sit on so he could see better. "Forty million jobs in show business, I got a midget to direct me." He went on to tell "Marty" that he was "the most annoying director" Rickles ever met, and the camera shows Scorsese beside himself with laughter. Rickles ended his speech with a heartfelt statement of his love for Scorsese, all the more moving because of what came before.

Of course, the line between affectionate parody and savage mockery is a fine one, and this type of humor can easily become brutally humiliating when affection is absent.

Other comics make themselves the object of ridicule, often by exposing an area of personal shame in a way that makes it both funny and personally resonant for audience members. Being overweight, despite campaigns against fat-shaming, remains one such area of shame for many people. In several of his routines Louis C.K. made fun of himself because of the excess weight he carried, referring to himself as a "piece of shit" and mocking his poor impulse control. "The meal is not over when I'm full," he would declare. "The meal is over when I hate myself. That's when I stop."

As funny as his routines were, you got the sense that self-loathing and lack of self-control were real issues for Louis C.K.; many people in the audience no doubt identified with those struggles and felt relieved by his humor. I can imagine that mining his food/fat issues for comedy and making the audience laugh at his self-deprecating jokes helped the comic to control the experience of shame. People were not making snide comments about his weight behind his back; they were laughing precisely when he wanted them to.

Along with many other comics, Louis C.K. made jokes about getting older. A dwindling sex life, drooping body parts, and the indignities of incontinence provide material for this genre of humor. Middle age invariably involves a kind of narcissistic injury for many men and women, even those who have not relied primarily upon looks to support their self-esteem. Feeling suddenly invisible, no longer a source of interest and sexual attraction to people you find appealing (Unrequited Love), can stir up shame. The press of recent college graduates and newly minted professionals, wearing trendy clothes inappropriate for you and frequenting clubs where you'd feel out of place, can inspire the shame of Exclusion.

In a culture that prizes youth and beauty, an aging body alone represents a kind of Unwanted Exposure, with wrinkles and liver spots visible to all. During the latter part of her career, Joan Rivers explored this terrain to great effect, with hilarious monologues about drooping breasts, vaginas that fall, flatulence, loss of hearing, and graying pubic hair. Given the number of cosmetic surgeries she underwent during her lifetime—liposuction, a neck lift, eye surgery, regular Botox injections, and several face-lifts—Rivers clearly struggled with the shame of aging. In her stand-up routines she found a way to make fun of herself and her body while entertaining her audience. She controlled and made light of her shame experience by ridiculing herself before others could do it, causing them to laugh exactly when she wanted them to. Sadly, her ongoing efforts to control shame by using cosmetic surgery led to her death on the operating table.

From time to time most of us defuse embarrassment by laughing at ourselves and our mistakes. By laughing first, or along with others, we take control of the shame experience and thereby make it less agonizing.

Ellen DeGeneres has a wonderful routine that captures this everyday experience. She begins by asking the audience, "You ever walk into a plate glass window? Two things are happening there: pain and embarrassment. But pain takes a backseat to embarrassment, doesn't it? No matter how much pain you're in, if other people are laughing, you just laugh right along with them." Cupping a hand to one eye, she begins to laugh her infectious laugh, insisting over and over, "Isn't that funny! Am I bleeding? Look, there's blood—isn't that funny!"

Laughing at yourself for clumsiness or for making a faux pas allows you to take control of a shame experience (Unwanted Exposure) and defuse it with humor. We gain distance from our shame through laughter: we're in the audience, poking fun at that awkward person over there, rather than simply being the hapless object of ridicule mired in shame. I consider the ability to laugh at oneself to be a sign of emotional health, proof that you're not so burdened by shame that you must hide or completely deny that you feel it.

When I was twelve or thirteen years old, my brother, Dennis, a recently licensed driver, took me out for dinner at a fast-food restaurant. Our parents must've had other plans that evening. While eating our burgers and fries, Dennis and I sat at a Formica table across from each other. I've always adored french fries, and as a child I usually saved them for last and savored them slowly. My brother downed his meal quickly and impatiently waited for me to finish.

He finally reached across the table and snatched all my remaining fries, cramming them into his mouth and running out of the restaurant to his car. I was outraged.

While disposing of my trash and following him out to the parking lot, I tried to compose my most superior and withering put-down. In my thoughts I vacillated between "You disgust me!" and "I despise you!" As I emerged from the glass doors, I saw Dennis seated behind the wheel of his car with a smirk on his face. I was vaguely aware of another car nearby and a lone man eating his take-out meal in the front seat. Hot with righteous indignation, I filled my voice with all the scorn I could muster.

"I disgust you!"

Dennis and the man in the nearby car both burst into laughter. I felt mortified, my face stinging with heat. I desperately wanted to revoke those words and replay the scene. I wanted to run back into the restaurant.

And then I started to laugh.

From a certain perspective—say, that of the driver in the nearby car—what I had said was truly funny. That precocious boy with his large vocabulary, so eager to sound contemptuous and superior, had inadvertently made himself appear ridiculous.

By laughing along with Dennis and the driver, I distanced myself from humiliation and made it more bearable. It's a device most people use to control an experience of shame.

I will give the final word in this section to Louise, heroine of the classic Broadway musical *Gypsy*. In the final act her mother, Rose, has mocked and humiliated Louise for her pretensions to polite society: "You, the burlesque queen who speaks lousy French, who reads book reviews like they were books! To them, you're this year's novelty act."

Louise savagely turns on her mother and tells her to "turn it off. Nobody laughs at me—because I laugh first!"

SEE EXERCISE 6, PAGES 275-276

Part III

FROM SHAME TO SELF-ESTEEM

The next four chapters describe essential elements involved in the recovery from debilitating shame. Not everyone will pass through a stage of shame defiance, but all of us need to develop shame resilience if we are to grow. As I have shown throughout this book, encountering shame is an inevitable part of daily life; when we avoid, deny, or control our experience of shame to an excessive degree, we remain brittle and defensive, unable to grow, rather than resilient in the face of life's emotional challenges. Successfully weathering our encounters with shame helps us to develop confidence in our future ability to cope; building pride through achievement and then sharing with significant others the joy we feel will consolidate our growing self-esteem.

Part 3 does not describe a step-by-step how-to method for moving from shame to self-esteem (although the sequential exercises compiled in appendix 2 offer guidance to the reader on that journey, and my interactive video series available online goes deeper: www.shametoselfesteem.com/learning-from-shame). Rather, in this section I explain the core elements of authentic self-esteem as I understand them, based on my professional and personal experience and supported by the wisdom of other re-searchers who have written many volumes in their specific area of expertise. Brené Brown's bestselling books include exercises for developing shame resilience; Nathaniel Branden wrote more than a dozen titles on the subject of self-esteem, with extensive exercises that focus on building pride.

nineteen

SHAME DEFIANCE AND NARROW IDENTITY

MANY YEARS AGO, BEFORE THE advent of Internet pornography and webcam girls, I worked with a young woman who earned her living as a pole dancer. Although she aspired to be a veterinarian, Cassie had few college credits and no technical skills at that point. She was attending classes at a community college during the day and worked at several "gentlemen's clubs" in the evening, where she made a good living: after paying all her bills, tuition, and therapy, she still managed to save several hundred dollars each month. Sometimes she worked as a paid escort at a Korean dance club, but she never engaged in sex for money.

When Cassie talked about her line of work during our early sessions, she often stated that she did not feel ashamed; on the contrary, she insisted that she took pride in doing her job well. As a child she had studied gymnastics and dance; as an adult she kept herself in excellent physical shape, carefully choreographed her routines, and made sure to give her customers what they expected from her. She excelled at socializing with the men, putting them at ease, and encouraging them to buy a private lap dance (her primary source of income). As an independent contractor at the clubs where she worked, she always showed up on time and conducted herself in a professional manner with management.

If she happened to be at a party and another guest asked about her line of work, Cassie would quite aggressively announce that she stripped for a living. Although *stripper, exotic dancer,* and *pole dancer* are often used interchangeably, they are not exactly the same thing; she might have been clad in a revealing outfit, usually topless, but Cassie did not remove her clothes onstage while men ogled her. Rather than accurately describing what she did, however, she used an in-your-face expression, hoping to shock the other person.

"I'm a stripper and I'm really good at it." It came across as a challenge: *I dare you to judge me.*

While Cassie was proud to make effective use of her training in dance and gymnastics, she did not, in fact, feel proud of being a pole dancer. On a deeper level she felt it to be a degrading line of work. The customers treated her mostly as a fantasy object rather than a real person; the smoky windowless atmosphere of the clubs made her feel dirty, like the poor hick she unconsciously, and sometimes consciously, felt herself to be. Cassie had grown up in a double-wide trailer with her single mother and a succession of boyfriends, none of whom lasted more than a few months. She suspected that her mother had hired herself out for sex during hard times. While Cassie was growing up, the beauty of dance and the elegance of gymnastics had offered a refuge from the ugliness of life at home.

I would describe Cassie's behavior at parties as one of defying her own feelings of shame; they were not a reflection of true pride. In answer to questions about her work, she replied with a chip-on-her-shoulder attitude, daring her audience to pass judgment. Francis Broucek describes such behavior as a type of reaction formation, in which "exaggerated pride, boastfulness, cultivated vulgarity, and exhibitionistic behavior replace denied shame."[1]

I call it "shame defiance."

I'm not suggesting that Cassie ought to have felt ashamed or that anything about working at a gentlemen's club is inherently shameful. For complicated reasons—some societal, others having to do with her bleak childhood—she did feel ashamed, deeply so, to work as a pole dancer. She might have let that shame shut her down, hiding her line of work in secrecy or avoiding contact with people who might deepen her shame about it. Instead she defied that shame and spoke out.

Because shame defiance does not involve the achievement of actual goals, it does not embody true pride. Think of it as a necessary but insufficient step on the road to recovery: throwing off the yoke of shame before going on to develop sources of authentic pride. Shame defiance is often the first step in recovery for people who have grown up burdened with deep feelings of unworthiness or inferiority because of childhood trauma or for men and women who have been stigmatized, excluded by society, and subjected to lifelong contempt.

PRIDE MOVEMENTS

Coming out is a transformational event for many gays and lesbians that involves a kind of shame defiance similar in some respects to what Cassie displayed. After a lifetime imprisoned by shame and self-loathing, individuals break free of stigma: "I will no longer submit to the shame imposed by society or keep my true nature concealed in darkness. I renounce the burden of shame and publicly proclaim that I feel proud of my sexuality."

Of course, no one has reason to feel proud of being homosexual, just as no one should feel proud of being straight. Homosexual and heterosexual are neutral statements of sexual attraction, neither inherently shameful nor a source of true pride. Joining the Gay Pride movement and adopting its values, in contrast, may promote authentic self-esteem. Because gays pride themselves on their tolerance of diversity and their vigorous support for the civil rights of others who have also been oppressed, identifying with this group may bolster new feelings of self-respect if you happen to cherish those values.

Living up to shared values as a member of a respected community is one way all of us derive feelings of self-esteem. Men and women routinely express pride in belonging to their profession, for example—as teachers, scientists, physicians, and psychotherapists. People often say they are proud to belong to their service branch, their political party, or their church. For most of the clients described in this book, finding membership in, and acceptance by, a new community played a role in their recovery from core shame in much the same way.

Many other groups historically marked by the shame of social stigma have embraced pride movements: Black Pride, Fat Pride (or the fat acceptance movement), Deaf Pride, and so on. Such movements arise in opposition to overly restrictive societal views of what it means to be normal, defying the shame that comes from being an outlier on the human bell curve. Participating in such pride movements often marks a preliminary and essential step in self-acceptance, a means to build self-esteem through the group's shared values and accomplishments.

In contrast, in-your-face expressions of one's deviation from the norm that are intended to shock or offend the values of other people represent a kind of shame defiance that is more defensive in nature. Like Cassie's "I dare you to judge me" statements about her work as a pole dancer, this type of shame defiance does not reflect authentic pride; it depends upon adopting a superior, aggressive, or contemptuous approach to certain other people with the intention of making them feel bad about the intolerant attitudes they supposedly harbor: "You are a small-minded bigot and you ought to feel ashamed of yourself."

Some people remain mired in this type of narrow identity and shame defiance, restricted in their ability to expand their pride and self-respect because they continue to define themselves in defiant opposition to the repressive forces in society. Often this is because of limited resilience in the face of shaming forces in the world at large. Their hard-won self-acceptance cannot withstand challenges from strangers who criticize, exclude, or deliberately humiliate them. In chapter 20, I discuss the role of shame resilience in building additional sources of pride and self-esteem beyond shame defiance.

DISABILITY AND SHAME DEFIANCE

As the great sociologist Erving Goffman describes it, "Society establishes the means of categorizing persons and the complement of attributes felt to be ordinary and natural for members of each of these categories."[2] Those who fail to conform to these normative categories are subject to what he calls stigma, what I would also describe as shame. Stigma has historically attached to nonconforming gender identity or sexual attraction but also to deviations from average physical development in the human body.

Society has historically stigmatized those who are deaf, blind, physically disabled or deformed, missing limbs, extraordinarily tall or short, or who vary from typical in any other way. In this sense stigma reflects a kind of Disappointed Expectation for how the body ought to appear. Both explicitly and subtly society holds a set of expectations for how people ought to behave and what they should look like. Individuals who deviate dramatically from those norms will feel the shame of Exclusion. Whenever their difference draws attention, they will feel the shame of Unwanted Exposure.

Goffman wrote and collected a set of essays focused on how people respond to the shame of stigma. The management of "spoiled identity," as he refers to it, can take various forms. Those who deviate from the norm but accept the validity of society's values may try to pass—to conceal or disguise their stigma and strive for superficial conformity to the norm. Living in the closet exemplifies this strategy. The person who lives in the closet has accepted and internalized shame; the person closeted with homosexual desires sees himself as abnormal and believes that he ought to feel ashamed. To feel damaged in this way, not fully a member of the human race, is a profoundly isolating and painful experience.

Others who suffer from this type of social shame "will have a tendency to come together into small social groups whose members all derive from the [same] category" of stigma, Goffman says.[3] The shame of Exclusion dissipates when you find yourself accepted by a group of people who resemble you; clustering within a group of similar individuals also prevents the shame of Unwanted Exposure that might arise in the presence of people from the wider society. Eventually a person who identifies with a group in this way may come to view it as his "real group, the one to which he *naturally* belongs," as Goffman puts it, and will reject membership in any larger, more encompassing, sense.[4]

NARROW IDENTITY

In *Far from the Tree* Andrew Solomon describes how diverse groups that have historically been stigmatized may find relief from shame through in-group identification, or what he refers to as "horizontal identity." In chapter after moving chapter, he recounts the stories of children born with achondroplasia (dwarfism), Down syndrome or some other physical anomaly, as well as children who were born or become deaf at an early age or developed autism during childhood and who later found feelings of joy, pride, and a sense of belonging with others who shared their so-called disability. I say *so-called* because, for those who have historically been stigmatized, relief from shame often involves learning to view their supposed disability as a form of diversity rather than a defect.

"Most hearing people," Solomon explains, "assume that to be deaf is to lack hearing. Many Deaf people experience deafness not as an absence, but as presence. Deafness is a culture and a life, a language and an aesthetic, a physicality and an intimacy different from all others."[5] As the Deaf activists Carol Padden and Tom Humphries describe it (as quoted in Solomon): Deaf culture "allows them to think of themselves not as unfinished hearing people but as cultural and linguistic beings in a collective world with one another."[6] Deaf culture thus allows its members to develop feelings of pride in values and accomplishments they share with other members.

At the same time such a culture may promote a kind of intolerance that inflicts the shame of Exclusion (countershaming) upon members who do not adhere closely to its values. Solomon describes several instances of young people excluded and even bullied for not being Deaf enough. Deaf people fitted with hearing aids or who have retained some ability to hear from birth are viewed with suspicion, as not truly Deaf. Some Deaf activists compare parents who opt to have their Deaf children surgically fitted with cochlear implants with Nazis practicing genocide. Shame defiance may lead to feelings of pride; it may also reflect a kind of defensiveness that inflicts the shame of Exclusion upon other people who are made to feel that they don't belong.

According to Goffman, some people "who take an in-group standpoint may advocate a militant and chauvinistic line—even to the extent of favoring a secessionist ideology. Taking this tack, the stigmatized individual in mixed contacts will give praise to the assumed special values and contributions of his kind. He may also flaunt some stereotypical attributes which he could easily cover."[7] While those "special values" might include authentic sources of pride (for example, the attitudes of tolerance and inclusiveness that characterize the gay community), the urge to "flaunt some stereotypical attributes" often reflects a wish to shock, offend, and humiliate.

I don't mean to suggest that someone ought to hide those stereotypical attributes to avoid offending other people, but when someone deliberately flaunts certain attributes or behaviors as opposed to their arising spontaneously, the flaunting reflects an effort to defy shame in a defensive way rather than to express authentic pride, not unlike what Cassie did with her aggressive answers to questions about her line of work. This type of shame defiance often includes contempt for the values of other people, whom the flaunter implicitly intends to make feel bad about themselves—for their supposed (and often real) intolerance or narrow-mindedness.

At its most defensive shame defiance often relies on countershaming. On a broader sociological level, our age is characterized by both trends: on the one hand an increasing number of people are defying social shame in all its forms or championing the rights of historically stigmatized groups;

on the other, especially in the social media universe, a vast and vocal co-hort constantly insists that some other intolerant person or group ought to feel deeply ashamed.

COUNTERSHAMING

While I was writing this book, I set up Google Alerts for several search terms relevant to my topic, especially those appearing in newspaper articles online: *shame, ashamed,* and *shameless,* as well as the phrases "I'm not ashamed of" and "ought to be ashamed." I felt curious to see how and when those words appear in the popular media, but the number of hits on those search terms and the way they were used came as something of a surprise. This research formed the basis of an article I eventually wrote entitled "Shame Is for Other People."

Many articles flagged by Google Alerts featured men and women who were proclaiming to the world that they were *not ashamed* about their weight, sexual orientation, gender identity, divorce, having had an abortion, struggle with addiction, having been raped or sexually abused, or suffering from mental illness and a variety of physical disabilities. None of this surprised me. Our age is characterized by an antishame zeitgeist: a great many people of all ages now regard social shame as an oppressive force that must be resisted.

I was unprepared for the larger number of articles insisting that *other people* had something to feel ashamed about. Day after day Google Alerts sent me links to authors pointing an angry finger at bigots, misogynists, xenophobes, doctors who fat-shame their patients, greedy industrialists, shameless tax evaders, uncaring politicians, criminals without remorse, neglectful parents, and so on. By shaming others we often express our support for the values of tolerance, compassion, fairness, and a sense of social responsibility.

In recent years shame has become increasingly weaponized within the realm of politics. On both sides of the divide, politicians denounce their opponents as shameless or insist that they "ought to feel ashamed" of themselves for holding this or that position. Pundits and writers of letters to the editor will insist that members of a certain political party should feel tremendous shame for holding opinions with which the author does not agree. Such accusations implicitly and sometimes explicitly endorse values the writer cherishes. They often have a strident, self-righteous tone. Those who defend oppressed victims of social shame will sometimes express themselves in a similarly self-righteous way.

On the level of individual psychology, when shame defiance goes hand in hand with efforts to inspire shame in other people, it often reflects a kind of false pride: *I feel good about myself because I'm nothing like you.* It resembles the narcissistic strategies used by Caleb (chapter 12), the ambitious therapist who briefly came to me for treatment, or my long-term client Nicole (chapter 13), to offload their shame and force a carrier to feel it instead. At its most defensive, shame defiance substitutes blame and contempt for authentic self-esteem. People who rely too heavily on shame defiance and countershaming may grow increasingly isolated, self-righteous, and judgmental in their efforts to defy the shame they can't bear to feel.

LIZA

Like many of the people I have described in this book, Liza grew up under conditions that fell drastically short of optimal. The details don't matter much; suffice it to say that she came of age burdened with profound feelings of inner ugliness, what I have referred to throughout this book as core shame. In her twenties she went through several medium-term relationships with men who treated her badly. Although they were never physically abusive, these men humiliated her in front of their friends, belittled virtually everything she did, and expected her to service them in bed in ways that can only be considered degrading. In some sense these relationships were sadomasochistic, best understood as attempts to control shame.

During her early thirties the concept of toxic shame entered Liza's awareness. She read books by John Bradshaw and recognized the unhealthy nature of those earlier relationships as well as the role shame played in them. She eventually staged a kind of revolt against shame, vowing never again to let a man humiliate her as the others had. Like Serena, the radical feminist I describe in chapter 1 who bristled at any hint of disrespect, Liza from that point forward insisted she had "too much self-respect" ever to submit to such abuse.

Liza had many talents. A fabulous and inventive cook, a member of a semiprofessional chorus, a potter. She supported herself as a paralegal while pursuing her creative interests on the side. As she approached forty, she appeared to have built a satisfying life for herself, with many good friends, including several married couples, who cared about her. But she never managed to develop a lasting romantic relationship. She never dated a man more than a few times before breaking it off.

Liza had a good reason each time for rejecting her relationship prospects, but they usually came down to some perceived sign of disrespect. He might have neglected to return a phone call in a timely manner or canceled a date for reasons she deemed inadequate. He might have talked too much about himself and asked too few questions when they were at a restaurant. In a way that came across as somewhat self-righteous, she would insist to her friends that self-respect demanded she let him go. Liza did not give second chances or explain to the rejected man her reasons for cutting him off.

Before this revolt against shame, Liza had often come across as self-deprecating: she made light of the beautiful handcrafted gifts she bestowed upon her friends, blamed herself for any misunderstandings she might have had with them, and apologized to an uncomfortable degree if anyone faulted her, no matter how mildly. While she had a lively sense of humor, she tended to make jokes at her own expense.

In the subsequent phase of shame defiance, Liza became angry and accusatory at the least sign of criticism. If one of her girlfriends suggested she might want to give one of those dates a second chance, Liza called her insufficiently supportive and stopped talking to her for weeks. If Liza and a friend had a disagreement, the other person was always to blame. If one of those married couples invited her for dinner but had to cancel because of an unexpected school function for one of their kids, she might tell them to their faces that she of course understood but would then criticize them for rudeness behind their backs.

Liza became increasingly harsh and judgmental. When one of the couples she counted as close friends decided to divorce, she sent the husband a scathing and contemptuous email, essentially calling him a despicable human being, and cut him off—even though the couple's decision to divorce had been mutual and the wife felt no such animosity toward her husband. Liza banished other friends for perceived slights or because she disapproved of their life choices—deciding to stay in a difficult job, for example, when Liza believed they ought to show some self-respect and move on. Over time she eliminated most of her old friends, restricting her social life to a few single women and gay men.

While she had awakened to the role of shame in her life and rebelled against its most debilitating effects, Liza's defiance of shame led to an increasingly narrow life. Rather than expose herself to potential rejection or humiliation by her dates (Unrequited Love), she cut them off first. She gradually reduced, and eventually eliminated, all contact with married couples, who reminded her of the unfulfilled desire for her own spouse and children (Disappointed Expectation). She excluded other people from her life rather than feel excluded.

As she became increasingly harsh and judgmental, Liza also made use of the strategies for denying shame that I describe in earlier chapters. She became righteously indignant at perceived signs of disrespect. She blamed other people if they happened to disagree with her or if they behaved in ways that did not comport with her notions of self-respect, and she often viewed them with superior contempt. Over time she lived in a highly restricted way to minimize contact with potential shame in its various forms.

Like Liza, some people remain mired in shame defiance and never move on. They take refuge in narrow forms of identity that limit exposure to the shame family of emotions, adopting a defensive sort of antishame identity that substitutes for authentic self-esteem. Such narrow identity also prevents these people from developing true intimacy, which by its nature always risks exposure to potential shame (Unrequited Love, Disappointed Expectation). Shame defiance represents a necessary but insufficient step on the road to developing authentic self-esteem.

Because encountering shame is inevitable in a life less restrictive than Liza's, if we are to continue growing we must learn to weather the pain of shame rather than insist we have no reason to feel it (and that others do). The second step in transforming shame into authentic self-esteem involves moving beyond narrow shame defiance and developing what Brené Brown refers to as "shame resilience," the subject of the next chapter.

SEE EXERCISE 7, PAGES 277–278

twenty

SHAME RESILIENCE AND EXPANDING IDENTITY

BECAUSE MY VIEWS ARE INFORMED by my experience as a psychotherapist, much of this book has focused on the clinical manifestations of shame and its roots in early experience. Most of the clients I describe in the middle section of this book suffered from lifelong shame as a result of gross failures in parenting during their earliest years of life—with caregivers whose psychological difficulties rendered them incapable of providing the empathy and shared joy children need to thrive. When the innate human need for love and connection goes unmet, when parenting departs dramatically from Winnicott's blueprint for normality, the result is a profound kind of Disappointed Expectation: core shame takes hold when we do not receive the emotional attunement that our genetic inheritance has led us to expect.

Even those of us who are not afflicted by core shame must confront and learn to cope with the shame family of emotions. When a love object fails to return our interest, we may feel the shame of Unrequited Love. If we find ourselves on the outside of a group to which we'd like to belong, we may feel the shame of Exclusion. Opportunities to feel the shame of Unwanted Exposure abound in daily life, from exposing bodily functions we'd prefer remain private to making an inadvertent faux pas. Whenever we fail to achieve our goals or live up to our own values, we may confront the shame of Disappointed Expectation.

Shame resilience means learning to bear these inevitable experiences without defending heavily against them, that is, by narrowing our lives to avoid encounters with shame, for example, or by insisting we have no reason to feel ashamed (and that other people do).

In addition, social forces in the world at large may deliberately seek to instill feelings of shame. In chapter 2 I discuss the ways that society makes use of the built-in human capacity to experience shame as a way to enforce its values. Sometimes this type of shame helps discourage behavior that would unquestionably harm the social fabric—child sexual abuse, for example, or the ruthless exploitation of the disadvantaged or helplessly dependent. But social shame may also impose an overly narrow set of expectations and inflict feelings of unworthiness whenever we do not meet them.

Thus shame resilience also means learning to recognize and cope with the inevitable influence of social shame—the focus of Brené Brown's work. My views on this subject largely coincide with hers, but because my understanding of shame covers more territory than Brown's, I expand the concept of shame resilience beyond what she so usefully maps out in her several books.

BRENÉ BROWN AND SHAME RESILIENCE

No one has done more than Brown to expose and challenge the oppressive force of social shame, especially its perfectionistic and often conflicting demands for how women ought to look, feel, and behave. She refers to these often-conflicting demands as "social-community expectations" and provides the following description of the impossible bind that such expectations may impose upon women:

- Be thin, but don't be weight-obsessed.
- Be perfect, but don't make a fuss about your looks and don't take time away from anything like your family or your partner or

your work to achieve your perfection. Just quietly make it happen in the background so you look great and we don't have to hear about it.

• Just be yourself—there's nothing sexier than self-confidence (as long as you're young, thin, beautiful . . .).[1]

According to Brown, the inevitable failure to meet those expectations traps women in a "shame web" that leads to isolation and disconnection from other people.

Developing shame resilience begins by identifying a support network of people who will respond with empathy when you describe your experience, who understand what you've been through because they, too, know what it feels like to be shut down by shame. Some of my clients found relief from their shame by connecting with others who shared their experience. Noah (chapter 9) turned a corner when he joined a support group for other sex addicts in flight from shame. Nora (chapter 15) felt better about herself when she made room onstage for the other members of her improvisational company. Rather than allowing shame to isolate us, we become more resilient when we connect with others who validate, accept, and share our experience.

According to the view of shame as an entire family of emotions, shame resilience also means learning to tolerate those emotions rather than simply defying or refusing to feel them, as I describe in chapter 19. Throughout this book I have shown that shame is inevitable, even when other people do not intend for us to feel bad about ourselves, even when perfectionist social-community expectations are not involved. At some point in our lives we probably will encounter the shame of Unrequited Love. Whenever we feel left out or forgotten, we will feel the shame of Exclusion. Unwanted Exposure will always inspire shame. And if we fail to achieve our goals or violate our own system of values, we will feel the shame of Disappointed Expectation.

Developing shame resilience means learning to tolerate such experiences, as painful as they might be, without forcefully defending against them. When we avoid, deny, or control shame in ways that isolate us from other people, we're unable to forge the kind of connection Brown has shown to be crucial.

THE ROLE OF COURAGE

Throughout her work Brown stresses the importance of courage in promoting personal growth—in particular, the courage to make oneself vulnerable to others within a culture that demands perfection and constantly communicates that we are never enough. In *Daring Greatly* she paints a portrait of vulnerability with a list of responses from her research participants, all of whom were asked to complete the following sentence: "Vulnerability is _____." I have made a strategic selection of representative answers from her list and reorganized them here.

Vulnerability is

* the first date after my divorce
* saying "I love you" first and not knowing if I'm going to be loved back
* sharing an unpopular opinion
* presenting my product to the world and getting no response
* exercising in public, especially when I don't know what I'm doing and I'm out of shape
* admitting I'm afraid
* getting promoted and not knowing if I'm going to succeed
* getting fired[2]

The first two items on the list express anxiety about Unrequited Love: Will that first date reciprocate your interest and attraction? Will your loved one say "I love you too" or hang you out to dry? Sharing an unpopular opinion or finding that the world has no value for your product may incite the pain of Exclusion. Exercising in public or openly admitting to fear may lead to Unwanted Exposure. Worrying that you might not succeed after a promotion, or actually getting fired, involves real or potential Disappointed Expectation.

Although Brown doesn't say so directly, what emerges from her research is that to make oneself vulnerable often means risking an encounter with an emotion from the shame family: vulnerability is frightening because it opens us to that painful awareness of self at the heart of embarrassment, shame, and guilt. Daring greatly when faced with the shame family of emotions—rather than shutting down or defending against them—fosters personal growth; it helps us to find connection with other people and to feel that we belong.

For my clients, developing shame resilience also involved the courage to be vulnerable, that is, to be brave when confronting a potential shame experience. Imprisoned by her social anxiety, Lizzie (chapter 7) braved her fears and purchased that single orange from the dour Korean grocer; she eventually went on to join a writers' group in which she could share with and learn from other writers. Dean found the courage to emerge from his shame prison of indifference and reenroll in college with other people his age (chapter 8). At great emotional risk Noah (chapter 9) challenged his shame-based addiction to sex and drugs and found a place within a clinic support group.

During our work together these clients built shame resilience by courageously challenging the shame that had driven them into isolation. In the process they also developed feelings of pride for having been brave. As I discuss in the next two chapters, courage helps us to build pride and enables us to share the joy of achievement with those who matter most to us.

THE VALUE OF HUMOR

Extreme narcissists share many traits, including an inability to laugh at themselves. In flight from unbearable shame, these individuals feel compelled to defend an idealized self-image that disproves their unconscious feelings of defect or unworthiness. On constant guard against any challenge to their inflated self-image, they cannot bear criticism of any kind. If someone makes a joke at their expense or humorously tries to deflate them, they will experience it as an attack and retaliate in kind. And, of course, they never make jokes at their own expense.

In my experience people who lack a sense of humor about themselves are always in flight from shame of an unbearable kind.

In chapter 18 I described self-deprecating humor as a means to control shame. In that sense humor is a defensive maneuver. But the ability to laugh at ourselves may also free us from the prison of shame by connecting us with other people. Instead of hiding the shame of Unwanted Exposure or Disappointed Expectation, we find a way to see the humor in what we do and tell other people about it. Whenever we laugh at ourselves along with people we trust, shame becomes less scary, less isolating. And when others recognize themselves in the behavior or traits we've laughed at or satirized, we connect through humor.

Brown views self-deprecating humor as a purely defensive maneuver, a "kind of painful laughter we sometimes hide behind." She instead advocates "knowing laughter," which is not defensive in nature but "results from recognizing the universality of our shared experiences, both positive and negative."[3] It connects us to others rather than isolating us from them.

But even self-deprecating humor, I believe, can be a kind of knowing laughter that helps us to connect with other people.

My beloved father-in-law, Walter, an articulate man with an impressive breadth of knowledge, had a tendency to pontificate (as we described it in the family); he would often stop at the end of a lengthy monologue, smile, and say, "And now I've told you more than I know." He would sometimes describe himself as "often in error, never in doubt." On those rare occasions when he struck me as self-important or overly opinionated, when I felt relegated to the role of student or silent audience, the way he deflated himself always made me laugh. It brought us back together on a more equal footing.

A self-deprecating comedian like Louis C.K. not only mined his per-

sonal shame for humor but also allowed his audience to recognize themselves in his struggles and to find relief from their own shame. I imagine a
great many people in his audiences secretly felt ashamed of overeating or
some other compulsion, of their ongoing struggle to exert self-control.
When Louis C.K. made a joke at his own expense, he implicitly told us,
"You see—you're not alone." Rather than feeling isolated in our shame, we
laughed together in relief.

Given his close connection to his own shame, it should come as no
surprise that he alone of the men whose behavior came to light during the
#MeToo movement delivered what appeared to be a sincere and shame-
ridden apology.

Although my client Nora at first relied on humorous self-mockery as a
way to control her experience of shame, and sometimes put distance between us when she made jokes during the long middle phase of our work,
she later used knowing laughter in a way that brought us together. With
great insight into her husband's psychological issues, she once dissected
one of their disagreements during a session, reasonably laying responsibility at his feet in a way that did not seem obviously defensive or blaming but
did feel a bit too rational, an overly logical indictment of her husband's
character backed up by fact and insight.

Then she paused and said, in her hilarious singsong way, "Or, on the
other hand, I could be completely lying to myself!" We laughed together,
then went on to discuss her contribution to their fight and what might
lie behind her rationalizations. Although I did not say so during the session, I also recognized the way I, too, sometimes lied to myself with insightful rationalizations, laying blame for my own marital squabbles at
the feet of my then wife. Self-deprecating humor doesn't always deflect
and put distance between the jokester and audience. Sometimes embarrassment or shame that becomes bearable through shared laughter brings
them together.

Donald Nathanson holds that "comedy involves exposure that trig-
gers embarrassment capable of being handled as amusement. Those personal attributes we wish to keep hidden serve as the resource, the reservoir
for shame." Throughout his youth and his subsequent career Nathanson

felt a profound admiration for the stand-up comic Buddy Hackett, who was famous for his bawdy humor, his candor about his internal world, and his tendency to embarrass members of his audience. "His willingness to expose what normally is kept private or secret propels us into a state of mutuality, trust, and openness," Nathanson writes. "We are less likely to worry about our own secrets with such a man—and that, of course, is the major thrust of his art." Nathanson believes that anyone like Hackett "who seeks consciously to reduce the pain of others is a healer, a therapist."[4]

In the later stages of my work with clients, shared laughter often plays an important role as they become more shame resilient. I believe that the ability to laugh at oneself with affection is a sign of emotional health. *There I am, doing that embarrassing or shameful thing I've done so many times before. Admitting it doesn't feel as bad as I thought it would. It's even kind of funny.* Helen Block Lewis holds that "laughter is also a corrective or release for the feeling of shame. When the patient can laugh about [her difficulties], she is free of shame."[5] A therapist with the ability to laugh at himself will also make his clients feel safe, just as Buddy Hackett welcomed his audience into that state of "mutuality, trust, and openness."

While writing this chapter, I happened to observe myself making a joke at my own expense while talking to a dear friend of mine. Kate had come to Colorado for her annual summer visit; one night I was telling her about a heated political discussion with another friend not long before she arrived. I often talk politics with Randy, a longtime lobbyist and Washington insider. Our views mostly align, but occasionally we disagree in respectful ways. Like Randy, I enjoy passionate debate with someone who can argue his points with facts to back them up and listen openly to opposing views.

But as I sometimes do, I became a little too pugnacious, so much so that Randy's wife, Laura, left the table and moved into the other room. Randy never appeared to feel offended, but for days afterward the memory of our disagreement kept coming back to me. When I later described it to Kate, I felt the heat of conviction returning—a renewed sense that I had been right.

Then I stopped myself.

Paraphrasing a line from *Broadcast News*, a favorite film, I said: "You know, it's hard being the smartest person in the room and always knowing better than everyone else."

We laughed together in shared recognition. Kate, too, can express herself in opinionated, sometimes overly assertive, ways. During the more than thirty years of our friendship, we've both made phone calls the morning after a dinner party or other social event to apologize for some perceived misbehavior or to ask for reassurance. I felt safe confiding to her my embarrassment about the way I'd behaved with Randy and Laura. When we laughed together, I felt my love for her and hers for me.

"Laughter itself," notes Michael Lewis, "is likely to be physiologically antagonistic to shame."[6] In other words shame dissipates in the presence of laughter, especially when we share it with people we care about.

LEARNING FROM SHAME

I recount this story not only because it shows how laughing at yourself with a safe person can relieve embarrassment and bring you closer to a friend but also because it illustrates what I consider the most important aspect of shame resilience: the ability to listen to shame and learn from it. When the memory of my debate with Randy kept coming back to me during the next several days, it was a sure sign that I felt uncomfortable with my behavior that night. Call it guilt, remorse, or embarrassment, those recurring memories told me that I was feeling some member of the shame family of emotions.

I finally had to acknowledge that I'd let myself down by arguing more aggressively than I usually do. Because I try to treat other people with respect and not hurt their feelings, my pugnacious attitude toward Randy embarrassed me (Disappointed Expectation). When I could finally acknowledge how I felt, I apologized to Laura for driving her out of the room. I later called Randy to check in; as expected, he hadn't taken offense and had enjoyed our conversation. But I had nonetheless violated my own standards and values.

In chapter 6 I described how nontraumatic encounters with shame during the second year of life help a child's brain to develop as nature intended while allowing the child to continue building self-esteem by meeting parental expectations for how their child ought to be behave and treat other people. In later life shame continues to play a similar role in the building of self-esteem. When we experience an emotion in the shame family, the encounter often tells us something about who we are—our particular foibles as well the values we hold dear, the person we expect ourselves to be. Shame can point toward areas where we need to try harder—in my case, to keep my overly assertive side in check. Shame (in the specific form of guilt) lets us know when an apology is in order, when we need to make amends to a loved one we may have injured.

If we instead defy shame and defend against it, we lose an opportunity to grow.

DISARMING YOUR DEFENSES

Psychological defense mechanisms such as denial, projection, or rationalization are strategies we use to evade pain, and all of us make use of them to one degree or another. Temporarily resorting to denial to cope with unbearable grief is normal and common; it often helps us to weather an emotional crisis until we feel strong enough to confront our pain. In contrast, extensive and continuous denial about a truth we need to face means we're unable to learn from our experience, especially the lessons that shame sometimes has to teach us.

Learning from shame depends on recognizing and disarming our defenses against the painful awareness of self that is inherent in shame. Case studies in the middle section of this book, along with chapters describing the everyday ways all of us try to avoid, deny, and control our encounters with shame, should help you to identify your preferred psychological defense mechanisms (especially if you've engaged in the exercises in appendix 2). Developing shame resilience means facing the truth about yourself, recognizing your defenses at work, and disarming those self-protective measures when they stand in the way of personal growth.

Defending against shame often takes the form of denial, rationalization, and blaming other people while insisting on your own innocence. My client Nicole (chapter 13) began many sessions by recounting an argument with her husband; she indignantly blamed him for their argument, excused her own behavior with rational explanations for why he deserved her abuse, and denied that she had any role in instigating the fight. Earlier in this chapter I described how Nora relied on denial and rationalization in less obvious ways.

In the days after an argument with a friend or loved one, do you find yourself returning again and again to the charged memory of what you both said, reliving the fight in painful detail? If you repeatedly justify yourself in imaginary arguments with the other person, stop and ask yourself what you might have said or done to feel ashamed about. In most arguments both parties bear some responsibility for what happened. If you insist on your own innocence while laying blame entirely at the other person's feet, you may be denying your own shame because you find it intolerable.

Facing shame—that is, listening to and learning from it—can also be a source of pride. I've spent a lifetime in sometimes painful self-examination; for many years I was in denial about my shame, but I'm proud to have since become a person who will face the truth, acknowledge fault, and try to do better. Moving on from shame defiance and developing robust shame resilience is an important stage on the path toward authentic self-esteem; it helps us to build pride by living up to our own standards and by achieving our self-chosen goals. I turn to these issues in the next chapter.

SEE EXERCISE 8, PAGES 279–280

twenty-one

BUILDING PRIDE

IN THE EARLY CHAPTERS OF this book I outline two more or less sequential tasks that parents face in building authentic self-esteem in a child. Their first task, corresponding roughly to the first year of life, is to make the child feel at the center of their emotional universe, beautiful and worthy, a source of immense joy. Unconditional love, as we commonly describe it. When all goes well during the first year of life, besotted parents often feel that no one before them in the history of humankind has experienced such a miracle, that no parent has ever loved a child so much.

Think back to the interactions captured on film at the beginning the Still Face Experiment: mother and baby mutually attuned in a shared experience of joy, locked in eye-to-eye contact that resembles a kind of romantic infatuation—"you are amazing and perfect and I adore everything about you." Occasional misattunement and empathic failures during infancy are inevitable; nontraumatic experiences of pain and frustration help the child's brain to develop as nature intended. On balance, however, the baby grows up in a world that makes her feel good about herself simply because she exists.

During the second year, through the strategic use of nonharsh, manageable shame experiences, parents begin to socialize their child, to communicate their expectations for acceptable behavior and to teach him how to live in a world full of other people whose needs and feelings also matter. Unconditional love, still crucial, must make room for conditional approval: "I love you for who you are, but not everything you do is acceptable. To win my approval, you must learn the rules that help human beings to coexist; you must respect the feelings of members of your family, as well as those of other children and adults you will come to know."

In meeting reasonable expectations the child feels pride in achievement and wins the additional reward of joyful approval and reconnection with his parents.

Building true self-esteem in later life will follow the same pattern. Even if you struggle with the kind of core shame that afflicted my clients, you can still reach a place of self-acceptance and learn to "embrace who you are."[1] You may never feel the sort of supreme self-confidence that comes from having been uncritically adored by devoted parents in early life, but with hard work and honest self-appraisal you may develop feelings of self-compassion and even self-love. By setting realistic goals and meeting your own expectations, you can build pride and share your joy in achievement with the people who matter most to you.

In the last few decades the self-esteem movement has tended to conflate and confuse these two phases in the development of self-esteem. Parenting experts and self-esteem gurus have recommended unstinting praise for everything a child does, based on the belief that any kind of criticism will damage a child's self-esteem. This movement neglects the role of appropriate expectation and how it allows self-esteem to flourish: when children learn the rules of social behavior and meet expectations, they will feel pride in achievement, reinforced by the praise they receive from their parents. When they learn to care about the feelings of other people, children may have to relinquish their spot at the center of the universe, but they earn the reward of *belonging*: they have a place within a family and a larger community that cares about them.

In the realm of popular psychology, many self-help books rely on cognitive techniques that purport to help readers build self-esteem through a kind of unconditional self-love. Positive affirmations and self-talk are their prescription for changing destructive thought patterns boosting self-confidence, and helping readers to succeed. Particularly for those people who struggle with lifelong feelings of shame, such techniques do little to help them build authentic self-esteem for one simple reason: self-esteem grows within an interpersonal context. We feel better about ourselves when we are connected with and loved by others. Our pride in achievement goes deeper when we share our joy with the people who matter most to us.

With the focus on empathy and connection that defines her work, Brown offers a more realistic path to achieving the kind of self-acceptance we normally develop during the first year of life. Although she focuses more on building shame resilience than boosting self-esteem, she outlines a set of practices that readers may follow to cultivate the conditions that will eventually enable them to feel that they are enough. Those of you who are struggling to develop self-acceptance will find a warm heart and a helping hand in Brown's work.

Achieving self-acceptance, the feeling that we are enough, is a necessary but not sufficient step in developing true self-esteem. In addition, we must build pride through setting and reaching goals. We must live up to our own values and standards. When we build pride in this way, we strengthen our self-acceptance in a kind of positive feedback loop, enabling us to face other challenges with confidence and to continue pursuing our goals with courage.

THE ORIGINS OF PRIDE

Francis Broucek describes the earliest form of pride as a kind of efficacy or competence pleasure.[2] Even infants as young as four months old act with intention—by reaching for an object they want, for example, or by trying to roll over. When they succeed, when they achieve their goals, they display obvious signs of pleasure. They smile or make happy sounds. They appear to feel good about themselves.

Competence pleasure sets the pattern for the development of healthy pride throughout life. According to Donald Nathanson, it involves three elements: intentional, goal-directed activity; success in achieving the goal; and pleasure in that achievement. "Throughout life," he explains, "any experience in which personal efficacy is linked with a positive affect will produce healthy pride."[3] While doing our personal best may also contribute to feelings of pride, the pleasure we feel through success-in-achievement is what makes us feel good about ourselves. When you work long and hard for something that matters to you, when you finally achieve your goal, perhaps after enduring frustration and repeated setbacks, the experience of pride and pleasure will lay down memories that last a lifetime.

Think back to your proudest achievements. I imagine your memories are unusually full of detail; you can probably call up the emotions you felt. I was visiting the Cloisters in New York City on the day my literary agent called to let me know that St. Martin's Press had made an offer to acquire and publish this book. After our call I left the museum and found a park bench where I sat, absorbing the impact of this happy news. I can still see the early fall color of leaves in the park, the hazy Hudson and cliffs of New Jersey in the distance. The quality of light and the faint breeze remain vivid to me.

The self-esteem movement has largely neglected the topic of pride-in-achievement. Focused on the delivery of unstinting praise and encouragement, it advocates a kind of unconditional love rather than the contingent approval earned by meeting expectations and living up to standards. In our earliest years our parents, teachers, and other important authority figures lay down those expectations and standards. Under optimal circumstances they encourage us to work hard and convey their belief that we will succeed. When we do, we feel proud when they praise and reward us with approval.

To some degree expectations held by our tribe, especially concerning community standards and values, will continue to play a role throughout our lives. But as adults we must also decide for ourselves what we'd like to accomplish and adopt our own system of values for the person we expect ourselves to be. When we reach those goals and live up to our standards, we feel the joy of achievement. We feel proud of ourselves.

Healthy pride is the antidote to shame, not a complete cure but an essential element in the emotional alchemy that transforms shame into authentic self-esteem. As we build pride over time, shame becomes less important, less pervasive, and less defining. People who have struggled with core shame throughout their lives will always feel its lingering effects to some degree, but they may nonetheless develop authentic self-esteem through achieving their goals and leading lives that embody their standards and values.

Through our work together over many years, most of the clients I describe in this book mustered the courage to face shame rather than defend against it and to pursue their goals. Sometimes, as in the case of the college dropout Dean (chapter 8), this journey meant entertaining the possibility of ambition for the first time, setting goals rather than retreating into apathy, and then working hard to pursue those goals. For others psychotherapy helped them to realize a long-cherished dream—becoming a writer in Lizzie's case. Nora eventually found a way to transform her eccentric, controlling sense of humor into a source of pride through achievement. Along the way I encouraged them if doing so seemed appropriate and shared their joy when they succeeded.

Sharing joy and pride with people who truly care for us will intensify and consolidate our growing self-respect. I turn to that subject in the next chapter.

PERSONAL RESPONSIBILITY

During the 1970s and '80s Nathaniel Branden was the most prominent authority on self-esteem, the author of more than a dozen books during his career. Unlike many other authors in the self-help arena, he emphasizes the role of personal responsibility in building self-esteem. According to Branden, "Every value pertaining to life requires action to be achieved, sustained, or enjoyed. . . . What determines the level of self-esteem is what the individual *does* within the context of his or her knowledge and values."

In short, as I often say to my clients, self-respect (like all forms of respect) must be earned. It is an achievement rather than an entitlement, and it requires careful tending throughout our lives. One fallacy, Branden explains, "is the belief that if we accept who and what we are, we must approve of everything about us."[4]

To earn our self-respect we must define our goals and take responsibility for our actions rather than retreat into blame or victimhood; we must consciously choose the values by which we will live. Our choice of goals and values will vary widely, of course. Some of us want to succeed in our chosen profession and earn the respect of our peers; others with more communitarian values will devote themselves to helping people less fortunate than they are. What you choose will obviously depend on who you are, and building pride begins with knowing yourself well.

THE EXAMINED LIFE

During a recent session my long-term client Rachel described herself as a work in progress. She said this in a somewhat dismissive, contemptuous way, as if she ought to be finished after so many years in therapy. During that session I helped her to accept this work-in-progress status as a source of pride. At considerable expense and inconvenience over many years, Rachel has devoted herself to self-examination. With courage and perseverance she has absorbed the often-painful insights that emerged from our work and eventually put them to good use. She remains open to learning more about herself in the future. I told her how much I respected that commitment, and so should she: "You ought to feel proud of yourself!"

I, too, view myself as a work in progress. My analyst once told me that our sessions together would end once I could carry on the work alone, implying that it would never be finished. Although for years after my analysis ended I was in denial about my shame and took refuge in my superior postanalytic self, I have since come to terms with that shame; I grapple most days with the way it affects me, and I continue to learn more about myself even in my sixties. For me introspection is a way of life.

I respect Rachel for viewing herself as a work in progress; I continue to earn my own self-respect by facing the truth about who I am, even when I find it painful. I'm proud of both of us.

With the exception of Caleb, the competitive therapist in training, all the clients described in this book worked hard to increase their self-awareness. Even though Ryan discontinued his sessions earlier than I would have liked, he had always wanted to learn more about himself; I hope and believe he has followed other self-exploratory paths since our work came to an end. Although many people feel shame about their need for psychotherapy, a commitment to leading the examined life can eventually become a source of pride. Therapy involves hard work and financial sacrifice; it takes courage to face all the painful truths that emerge. Clients who do so can earn their own self-respect along the way.

Many people who can't afford quality psychotherapy nonetheless want to learn more about themselves. Although most self-help books offer shallow and simplistic advice, the works of Brené Brown and Nathaniel Branden can open doors and illuminate their readers' psyches. We have many different ways to increase our self-awareness, but when we commit to leading the examined life, when we face painful truths about ourselves with courage and unflinching honesty, we will build feelings of pride.

THE ROLE OF CHOICE

Self-awareness helps us to make better choices. You can't choose wisely if you don't know who are and what you want from life. In pursuit of an ideal self that would win the approval of her fabulous parents, my client Anna had chosen a career that made her unhappy. As she learned to understand herself better, she eventually abandoned law to become a yoga teacher. Together she and her husband started a successful business that brought them pride and joy.

Sometimes we make poor choices because we lack the information we need, including knowledge about and insight into ourselves. From time to time we also make poor choices despite knowing better. Natalie, the legal assistant I described in chapter 14, wanted to show up for work on time, but rather than go to sleep she chose to watch two episodes of *Homeland* and overslept as a result. She made a poor choice that made her feel bad about herself. From time to time most of us make poor choices despite knowing better. Recognizing that we have chosen badly and learning from that experience, holding ourselves accountable for that choice and choosing better the next time, allows us to build pride. The ability to learn from experience plays a central role in personal growth.

Expecting ourselves to honor our own values and goals does not mean we must be perfect. Both Branden and Brown warn against the dangers of perfectionism, how it shuts us down and leads us to hide in shame or denial. Many people become mired in what my analyst once described as a "cycle of crime and punishment": They make choices that fill them with shame, then beat themselves up for having failed. Within the privacy of their own thoughts, or sometimes aloud to friends, they brutalize themselves for being imperfect. Eventually, once this self-punishment has run its course, memory fades and the person moves on, often to make the same poor choice once again.

Perfectionism prevents us from learning from experience. Admitting that you have room to grow means accepting that you're not perfect, of course. The expectation that you should never make mistakes makes personal growth impossible; holding yourself accountable for the mistakes you make must go hand in hand with self-compassion. All of us make poor choices on occasion, even though we know better: we're only human. The best we can do is acknowledge our mistakes without harshness, learn from that experience, and try to choose better the next time.

THE NEED FOR ACHIEVEMENT

As Nathanson notes, "The self that can do things is my best self simply because it is the 'me' most associated with excitement and joy."[5] From the earliest months of life, human beings are purposeful. Even infants take deliberate action—that is, they want to do things, and they feel pleasure when they succeed at doing them. At every stage of the human life span, a life without intention and purpose feels meaningless. It precludes the possibility of building pride.

Striving to achieve does not mean driving yourself to reach some grandiose goal—to be fabulously wealthy, for example, or to found a company that would rival Google in size (as one of my former clients expected himself to do). The goals we set must be realistic and commensurate with our abilities. At my age, if I aspire to win an Olympic medal, I will certainly fail. Feel-good positive thinking tells us to reach for the stars, to "dream big" and have faith in our abilities. But if you expect too much of yourself, you will deprive yourself of the chance to achieve more appropriate goals.

A culture that worships celebrity, bombarding us with images of impossibly beautiful people who lead glamorous lives of immense wealth and privilege, makes it difficult to value a life of everyday ambition and achievement. Brown describes the widespread fear of, and shame about, being ordinary that characterizes our age, a result of those images of perfection that surround us.[6] She believes we must find ways to reject those images and celebrate the ordinary if we are ever to feel that we are enough.

That does not mean accepting a life without intention or purpose. To build pride we must set goals, even small ones, and work to achieve them. If Natalie had succeeded in getting to the office on time as she intended, she would have felt better about herself. If she had fulfilled her shared responsibility to clean their apartment, as she had committed to her roommate, Selena, Natalie would have earned some small measure of self-respect.

The need to achieve does not mean setting grandiose goals that we can't achieve. It involves humble self-awareness and knowing who we are—our strengths as well as our limitations—and then defining goals and expectations we can realistically meet. When we achieve our goals and live up to our self-chosen values, we feel better about ourselves. If we expect little of ourselves, leading a life without intention or purpose, we lose the opportunity to build pride.

NARCISSISM VERSUS AUTHENTIC PRIDE

Extreme narcissists divide human beings into two mutually exclusive and interconnected categories, the winners and the losers, and they have a fixed-pie view of self-esteem: there's a limited amount available, and I can feel good about myself only if I make you feel bad about yourself. Self-esteem, for extreme narcissists, is thus a kind of zero-sum game, and they are constantly on guard against the competitor whom they believe wants to win at their expense. When ruthless competition takes hold, when winning involves a gloating contempt for the rival who goes down to defeat, this type of narcissistic drive always plays a role.

Authentic pride makes room for other people to feel good about themselves too. I can achieve what I want and build pride without diminishing your self-respect. In other words authentic pride has an expanding-pie view of self-esteem: there's room for everyone to set and achieve goals, live up to their own values, and thereby increase the amount of self-esteem in the world. In fact because we are "wired for connection," as Brown continually emphasizes, we will feel even better about ourselves when we commune with people who support our efforts to achieve and whose efforts we in turn encourage—that is, when we succeed together.

Sharing the joy of achievement with people you care about will consolidate your feelings of self-respect. Sharing joy is the final step in building authentic self-esteem, the subject of the next chapter.

SEE EXERCISE 9, PAGES 281–283

twenty-two

SHARING JOY

IN THE FALL OF 2016, I sublet an apartment on West 80th Street in New York City for two months. At the end of my workday, weather permitting, I would usually walk to nearby Central Park and often across it to the Metropolitan Museum of Art. On my longer weekend walks through the park, I'd venture farther north into the Ravine and the North Woods, then come down through the Conservatory Garden near Fifth Avenue.

On Sunday, November 6, the unexpected sound of cheering grew steadily louder as I approached the Upper East Side. It didn't take me long to realize what it meant. That fall even someone with no interest in distance running couldn't help but notice all the announcements in storefront windows and pasted to plywood walls around construction sites: the New York Marathon was under way. I found a bench on Fifth Avenue where I could watch.

Smiling faces lined both sides of the streets. Many spectators held placards they had obviously made themselves, and groups of people were waving banners: FRIENDS OF TOM. GO, ALLISON! WE'RE HERE FOR YOU, SARAH! YOU CAN GO THE DISTANCE, BILL! As runners passed—some jogging slowly at this late stage of the race, others walking or limping in twos and threes, one man with massive arms powering his wheelchair— the bystanders would cheer and call out their support. Volunteers handed out bottles of water and offered support to runners they didn't know: "Good job! You're almost there! You can do it!"

A feeling of joy radiated from the crowd. As I sat on my bench, I felt happy too; I found myself smiling.

Until that day I'd never understood the appeal of marathon running. Why subject yourself to such a grueling ordeal that inevitably involves pain and exhaustion? What's the point? Sitting there on my Fifth Avenue bench, glad to share in this New York experience, I finally understood that to train for and run a marathon, often with friends, to have family members and supporters cheering you along, embodies everything I have come to believe about the role of building pride and sharing joy in the development of true self-esteem.

Entrants in the New York Marathon must have run previous marathons and met time standards to qualify. They typically train for months before the actual day. Readiness for such a race depends on hard work over time to develop the necessary strength and stamina. Runners know the race date months in advance and prepare for it with progressively longer runs. Sometimes they increase their endurance capacity with long-distance bike rides or strength training at the gym. Unless you plan to walk the entire route, you can't show up on the day of the marathon and hope to complete it.

When runners cross the finish line, their pride is obvious, despite their feelings of exhaustion. Hard work toward a goal and the pride you feel in achieving it will make you feel good about yourself. This pride runs deeper when you share it with caring friends and family, when you rejoice together in your achievement. Later in the afternoon, when I returned to the Upper West Side, groups of friends and families, many of them still in their running clothes, filled the sidewalk tables in front of restaurants along Columbus Avenue, all celebrating together.

Building pride, sharing joy—this is how we grow to feel good about ourselves.

I also thought about James, discussed in chapter 17, that day, my client who vigorously trained for and ran marathons. James found it difficult to acknowledge his feelings of pride in achievement when he completed a race. He also finished in solitude, despite all the other entrants around him. Without stopping to acknowledge the moment, he would pack up at the end of each race and go home alone. Shailene once trained for and ran a marathon with James, but she envied his much better race time. She resented him for being in better shape, for having worked harder and longer than she had. They shared no joy together.

Only one person wins a division of the New York Marathon, of course, and only an elite cadre of world-class runners aspires to do so. The rest of the entrants don't feel like losers because they didn't cross the finish line first. On the contrary, they feel good about themselves. They had set a goal, worked hard to prepare themselves, and then achieved what they had set out to do. Competence pleasure, if you will. They also shared their joy in achievement with loved ones who had come that day to support and cheer them on.

When they crossed the finish line, those runners embraced and slapped the backs of other runners who had also finished. They opened bottles of water and poured them on each other's head. They laughed and sometimes cried together. Authentic self-esteem wants other people to feel good about themselves too.

ENVY, SHAME, AND RIVALRY

Finding others to share your joy in achievement isn't always so easy. Intensely competitive people may feel threatened by your success, as if your winning means that they are losing. Men and women who struggle with core shame, who have not yet found a way to build their own pride, may hear about your happiness in a narrowly personal way: *You've achieved something I want but don't have.* As a result they may envy you.

When my client Lizzie received word that another of her short stories had been accepted by a literary journal for publication, she shared the joyful news with her writers' group. While most of the other writers applauded her achievement, one of the more competitive members said, "Well, it may not be *The New York Times* but at least it's something." This particular comment, rather than the joyful congratulations she had received, stuck with her for days after that meeting. This envious writer had spoiled Lizzie's pleasure, at least temporarily.

Even when you don't intend your joy in achievement to make other people feel bad, they may nonetheless envy you when you speak of pride. Envious and competitive feelings are part of human nature, an unavoidable fact of social life. Sometimes envy can show us what we would like to have for ourselves and help us to work for it. Sometimes it makes us want to tear other people down, as Lizzie learned. Speaking pride can be dangerous. It sometimes makes other people feel bad about themselves even if you don't gloat or describe your achievement in a narcissistic way.

Humility and tact help us to speak pride in ways that will minimize the risk. This doesn't mean we must downplay our achievements, or express them in a self-deprecating manner, but humility will prevent us from overstating or going on too long about them. Tact, which Léon Wurmser describes as the ability to understand the other person's nearness to shame, will also help.[1] Tactful awareness of how listeners could feel diminished enables us to avoid unintentionally shaming them when we would like to speak pride. Sometimes that means keeping our achievements to ourselves. Feeling pride and joy in achievement can sometimes be a lonely experience.

Belonging to a group of individuals not too dissimilar from you—who will support your efforts to build pride and share your joy in achievement—may relieve that loneliness.

BELONGING

Nora's controlling sense of humor isolated her onstage, despite her success in making people laugh; she felt better about herself when she made room for the other members of her company to excel. Belonging to a group of actors with shared goals and with whom she could rejoice in success built deeper self-esteem. Although the writers' group to which Lizzie belonged had one or two competitive members, it gave her a sense of connection with like-minded people who honored her achievements and shared her joy.

Andrew Solomon describes parents who challenge the isolation of social stigma on behalf of their children with such disabilities as autism or Down syndrome. Sometimes these parents work to mainstream their children in school classrooms so they may take part in a larger world that includes typicals, or typical students; these parents also make sure their sons and daughters find community with others who share their disability. While mainstreaming removes children from segregated classrooms, which by nature stigmatize and isolate them, finding community with people who share their experience is even more crucial for building self-esteem.

As one mother advises, "Invest in inclusion, but keep one foot firmly planted in the Down syndrome community. This is where your kid's ultimate friendships are going to come from."[2] Especially during adolescence, when their differences become more apparent, exposure to typicals can make children with Down syndrome painfully aware of abilities they do not possess and accomplishments they cannot hope to achieve—the shame of Disappointed Expectation, as it were, where the typicals around children with Down syndrome define expectation. Socializing within the Down syndrome community redefines that expectation, thereby affording far greater opportunities to build pride. People who share a disability can empathize more fully with each other's goals and rejoice when someone achieves them.

As Brené Brown often states, human beings are "wired for connection." Everyone needs to belong. Because we build identity and define ourselves to a significant degree through our interpersonal relationships, we need to find groups whose members empathize with our experience, understand the challenges we face as we work toward our goals, and will rejoice in our achievements when we succeed. Taking part in the Down syndrome community or participating in a writers' group are but two of many options.

Belonging to a cohesive and productive team at work, playing league volleyball, or acting in community theater affords other opportunities to build pride and share joy. Many more options are available, depending upon your particular goals and interests. And not all social relationships revolve around building pride and sharing joy, of course. Finding unconditional love with romantic partners and close friends also makes us feel good about ourselves. Building pride and sharing joy makes self-esteem go deeper.

SHAME, PRIDE, AND JOY

The short essay "Welcome to Holland," by Emily Perl Kingsley, the mother of a child with Down syndrome, has been shared and published thousands of time across the Internet. It has become a painful allegory for the experience of giving birth to and rearing a child with a disability when you had hoped to have a typical one.

I reproduce it here in full because it might also serve as allegory for the enduring pain of core shame and how it can coexist with pride and joy.

I am often asked to describe the experience of raising a child with a disability—to try to help people who have not shared that unique experience to understand it, to imagine how it would feel. It's like this . . .

When you're going to have a baby, it's like planning a fabulous vacation trip—to Italy. You buy a bunch of guide books and make your wonderful plans. The Coliseum. Michelangelo's David. The gondolas in Venice. You may learn some handy phrases in Italian. It's all very exciting.

After months of eager anticipation, the day finally arrives. You pack your bags and off you go. Several hours later, the plane lands. The flight attendant comes in and says, "Welcome to Holland."

"*Holland?!?*" you say. "What do you mean Holland?? I signed up for Italy! I'm supposed to be in Italy. All my life I've dreamed of going to Italy."

But there's been a change in the flight plan. They've landed in Holland and there you must stay.

The important thing is that they haven't taken you to a horrible, disgusting, filthy place, full of pestilence, famine and disease. It's just a different place.

So you must go out and buy new guide books. And you must learn a whole new language. And you will meet a whole new group of people you would never have met.

It's just a *different* place. It's slower-paced than Italy, less flashy than Italy. But after you've been there for a while and you catch your breath, you look around . . . and you begin to notice that Holland has windmills . . . and Holland has tulips. Holland even has Rembrandts.

But everyone you know is busy coming and going from Italy . . . and they're all bragging about what a wonderful time they had there. And for the rest of your life, you will say "Yes, that's where I was supposed to go. That's what I had planned."

And the pain of that will never, ever, ever, ever go away . . . because the loss of that dream is a very very significant loss. [italics added]

But . . . if you spend your life mourning the fact that you didn't get to Italy, you may never be free to enjoy the very special, the very lovely things . . . about Holland.

I italicized the second-to-the-last sentence to stress that some kinds of pain—the pain of having parents who did not love you, for example—will last a lifetime. When core shame takes root during the first months and years of life, or even later because of an unforeseen and unexpected trauma, it will mark you for life.

I believe that developing shame resilience, building pride, and sharing joy will help us to heal, but it will never be a complete cure. In Allan Schore's MRI studies of neonatal brain maturation (see chapter 5), he describes critical periods for development during the first months and years of life; if infants fail to receive the emotional attunement and shared joy they need, their brains will show the effects and they will feel the pain of that loss for life.

I don't mean to suggest such early deficits prevent us from growing and thriving in important ways. Neuroplasticity has received much attention in recent years; almost every day scientists are discovering ways that the brain can rewire itself. But neuroplasticity has its limits. If the brain were infinitely plastic, brain damage would be an insignificant event, a physical injury that might heal itself like any other wound. As with many new discoveries hyped by the media, news coverage of neuroplasticity has exaggerated its potential as a kind of miracle cure.

I believe psychological and emotional growth is possible throughout the human life span; I believe it sometimes has limits, especially when core shame takes hold during childhood. With courage and hard work a meaningful life full of pride and shared joy is possible, provided we do not deny or lose sight of shame and the important lessons it often has to teach us—in part about our values and standards for the person we expect ourselves to be but also about our limitations.

In her moving account of daughters brought up by mothers who did not love them—who belittled and humiliated them, usually because of their own envy and narcissism—Peg Streep advises readers to stop asking themselves who they might have been if only they'd had a different mother, to stop hoping for a complete cure. "I think that the way we think and talk about healing isn't productive; we expect our recovery to render us as 'whole' as someone who was well-loved and tended to, which, frankly, isn't possible. This kind of expectation fuels our impatience with ourselves when our wounds are reopened by an event or experience, or when we disappoint ourselves and act out in those old, familiar patterns. It encourages us to stay self-critical."[3]

Streep believes meaningful growth is possible, even for women who grew up with "mean mothers," provided they don't have idealized expectations for a complete cure.[4] I share her views.

Readers sometimes object when I liken core shame to a physical handicap. If you are a paraplegic with high aspirations, you might enter the

New York Marathon in your wheelchair, but you wouldn't expect your-self to run it. Physical handicaps and disabilities place limits on what we can achieve in certain ways, but they don't prevent us from setting and achieving goals within those limitations. We can still share our joy in achievement with others. The same kind of limitations and possibilities pertain to core shame. We may bear the scars of a traumatic childhood for life, but that doesn't mean we can't experience profound pride and joy.

Let me be clear: I do not mean that I think those individuals ought to feel shame; I am saying that they inevitably will.

Solomon recounts the story of a boy with Down syndrome whose par-ents made heroic efforts to shield him from stigma: they provided him with an environment full of nonstop stimulation, taught him the things typical children his age would learn, and helped him to build self-esteem through achievement and shared joy. He cowrote a book about his expe-rience, discussed it in lectures and on national television, and had a re-curring role on *Sesame Street*.

One night when his mother was tucking him into bed, he said, "I hate this face. Can you find a store where we can get me a new face, a normal face?" On another occasion he told her, "I'm so sick and tired of this Down syndrome business. When is it going to go away?"[5] Surrounded by typicals who vastly outnumbered him, he had fallen prey to a remorseless kind of expectation that they embodied. Although he was loved, admired, and respected by millions of people, he felt the shame of differing from all those people with a typical face. That shame of Disappointed Expec-tation didn't ruin his life, however; despite his disability he continued to lead an existence that filled him and his parents with pride and joy.

My self-injuring client Nicole was a troubled young woman when she sought therapy; without treatment her life might have ended badly. After many years of hard work she grew enormously and managed to marry, build a career, and have children. To prevent herself from destroying her marriage, she learned to stop denying her own shame and accept that Bor-derline Nicole had not been supplanted by an entirely new and superior self. She needed to recognize that, while she was quite capable in many respects, she tended to deteriorate when she overcommitted herself, reverting to blame and accusation as she fell apart, hallucinating spiders or feeling persecuted by endless song loops in her head.

When she stayed in close touch with her shame, when she worked hard without pretending to be Superwoman, Nicole could manage to balance career and marriage while being a good-enough mother to her children. Provided she respected her limitations and didn't defy shame, she continued to build feelings of pride and share them with family, friends, and other musicians. As Emily Perl Kingsley tells us, it's possible to appreciate and enjoy the many lovely aspects of life in Holland, provided your longing to be in Italy doesn't get in the way.

In short, shame and self-esteem are not opposites. For some of us realistic growth toward pride depends upon respecting the limitations imposed by core shame; for *everyone* it means listening to and learning from shame when it says we have disappointed our healthy expectations for the person we'd like to be.

The road to authentic self-esteem, as I stated at the beginning of this book, inevitably passes through the land of shame and never entirely leaves it.

SEE EXERCISE 10, PAGES 284–286

APPENDIX I

SURVEY SCORING AND DISCUSSION

For each of your "Never" answers, give yourself 0 points. For each of your "Rarely" answers, give yourself 1 point, then 2 points for "Occasionally," and so on until you have sixteen numbers. Total them for your score.

In the survey sample I conducted after first developing this test, the average respondent score was about 27, and approximately 68 percent of respondents scored between 11 and 42. If your score lies within that range, your encounters with the shame family of emotions resemble what most other people experience in their everyday lives. Bear in mind that we are talking about *shame* and not SHAME. This test focuses on the familiar opportunities afforded by social life to feel embarrassment, self-consciousness, guilt, shame, and other emotions in the shame family, not pathology.

As a whole the answers provided by survey takers clustered in the categories of Rarely (36 percent) or Occasionally (34 percent). At first this might seem to mean that encounters with shame are not common. But when you consider that, on average, 34 percent of respondents occasionally encountered *each* of the experiences described in the sixteen statements, shame begins to seem more commonplace. If I *occasionally* find I've been the subject of unkind gossip, and I *occasionally* feel alone with my opinions in a group, and so on for the fourteen remaining statements, then I must be feeling some member of the shame family of emotions on a regular basis.

It should come as no surprise that 36 percent of respondents said they frequently fail to keep New Year's resolutions. Twenty-seven percent said they frequently feel alone in their opinions in a group context. Fewer—11 percent—said they frequently do something clumsy in public, and nearly as many (13 percent) acknowledged that they frequently drink more than they had intended at a social event, although I had expected that percentage would be higher. In my experience these are fairly commonplace experiences.

What if your score is outside the average range of my sample? The test is not designed to explore the reasons, and I can only offer some possibilities. If your score is lower than average, you might have led a fortunate (or overly sheltered) life that shielded you from these common experiences. You might have led a solitary existence without much contact with other people. On the other hand you might be heavily defended against encounters with shame because you find them difficult to acknowledge and tolerate. In part 2 I discuss the typical defensive strategies people use to avoid, deny, or control their encounters with shame. You might recognize yourself in those pages.

If your score is higher than average, then shame plays a larger role in your life than it does for most people who took the survey. You probably are quite sensitive to shame for various reasons—parents who made excessive use of shame to correct you, for example. Or because your childhood was marred by trauma or extreme parenting failures. Throughout the book I discuss the role of such early childhood events and how they instill a core sense of defect and unworthiness that makes the child more than usually sensitive to everyday encounters with shame.

The sixteen statements in this survey address the four Shame Paradigms that I discuss in chapters 3 and 4. For a closer look at the statistics and the role each paradigm plays in the survey sample, please visit www .shametoselfesteem.com. You might also take another survey on that site designed to identify your particular defensive strategies for coping with shame. The survey is scored automatically; individualized results include recommendations for how to decide whether your defenses are maladaptive, with guidance for developing better coping techniques.

APPENDIX 2

THE EXERCISES

Before you begin these exercises, I suggest you take some time to bring your intentions into focus. Because we build pride through achieving our goals, and feel shame when we fall short, it's important to know exactly what you expect of yourself. It might help to read through all the exercises first so you'll know what lies ahead before committing to do them. Especially in the later exercises, I recommend taking actions that are likely to arouse anxiety and call for courage to complete.

The size of your goals doesn't matter as much as defining them carefully and then achieving them.

You might commit to reading and thinking about the exercises but no more.

You might go further and decide to write in a journal or notebook as you undertake the exercises, which I recommend. (The results of numerous studies show that writing your journal entries by hand, as opposed to typing them on your screen, leads to deeper and more lasting benefits from self-help exercises.)

You might decide to take the exercises one at a time, committing to complete only one before deciding whether you will continue to the next.

You might limit your goals to completing the journal entries without committing to the active steps I recommend.

Know what you expect of yourself and define it clearly.

Here at the outset I'd like to offer some guidance that will make it more likely for you to complete what you set out to do and build pride as a result. Because the headings that follow identify crucial issues in the development of self-esteem, these headings will reappear in the exercises that follow.

AVOID PERFECTIONISM

If you have read other self-help books without using their exercises, do not commit to completing all the exercises in this book without good reasons for believing that this time will be different. If you define an expectation that you are unlikely to fulfill, you set yourself up for a shame experience. Take your other commitments into account: How much time can you realistically devote to these exercises? Do not set an ambitious goal for yourself if you are already stressed by the demands of your life.

If you start a given exercise, do not savage yourself if you find it too difficult to complete. Instead use it as an opportunity for self-exploration. What emotional issues stood in the way of completion? Were you avoiding a potential encounter with shame because it frightened you? How might you do better next time?

Building self-esteem is not about achieving perfection but instead involves a process of growth and self-exploration that will, it is hoped, last a lifetime.

HOLD YOURSELF ACCOUNTABLE

If you commit to doing these exercises, hold yourself accountable for following through to whatever degree you used to define your commitment. If you do not, you will only feel worse about yourself unless you learn something useful from the experience.

Holding yourself accountable does not mean you must complete every exercise perfectly, but if you do struggle to fulfill what you set out to do, try to understand what stood in your way. Do not rationalize or make excuses for yourself. Do not avert your gaze, gloss over it, and move on to the next one. If an exercise presents an obstacle, it probably focuses on an area in which you are especially sensitive to shame. What can you learn from the experience? You might set the exercise aside and try again at some later point when you feel more confident of success.

INCLUDE OTHERS

Because developing self-esteem is an interpersonal experience, you will derive the most benefit from these exercises if you find a way to connect with other people as you go along. One early exercise involves an imaginative effort to understand how shame might influence your friends and members of your family and to empathize with their experience. Later exercises ask you to reach out and share your experience with carefully chosen others.

As you build pride through accomplishment, sharing your joy with the people who matter most to you is important. Authentic self-esteem also means honoring their achievements. It's not all about you.

In addition, the video lecture series I offer at www.shametoselfesteem.com/learning-from-shame includes a discussion forum that allows participants to share their experience (anonymously, if they prefer) with others taking the course.

AUTHOR'S ACCOUNT

Because facing shame and building pride can be a difficult, sometimes lonely, experience, it helps to know that other people have grappled with the same issues. From time to time throughout these exercises, I'll share some of my own struggles; I hope this will make you feel that you're not alone, that I'm not a distant expert and a finished product but someone who, like you, must deal with the inevitable shame in his life.

I like to think that I'd do a little better today, but for most of my life, if I had read the advice about how to approach these exercises, I would have promptly ignored it. I would have rushed out to buy myself a fresh new journal—my favorite kind, the lined theme books we used in college—and immediately undertaken the first two exercises. Feeling excited and enthusiastic, I would have thrown myself into the project with muddy expectations for myself but full of confidence that I would benefit and grow from the experience.

I might have completed the third exercise but probably would have discontinued the fourth one midway through it. After a few days of ignoring my journal, I would have tucked it away on a shelf in my bookcase. Months later, when I came upon the abandoned journal, I would have dealt with the shame of Disappointed Expectation by throwing it away.

Don't follow my bad example!

EXERCISE 1—THE SHAME FAMILY OF EMOTIONS

Recall a moment when you felt each of the following emotions. Try not to focus on situations in which another person clearly intended to hurt or embarrass you. Push yourself to provide as much detail as possible.

To the extent you can, try to describe in each instance: (a) the physical sensations or other feelings you noticed (e.g., a flush of heat, stinging sensations in your face, a longing to disappear); (b) the cause or reason why you felt that way (had you made a mistake or did you feel painfully exposed to scrutiny?); and (c) how long the feeling lasted or what you did next to find relief.

Describe an occasion when you felt

- embarrassed in public
- self-conscious about how you appeared
- guilty about something you had said or done
- left out or excluded
- disappointed in your performance

Include Others

Think of an occasion when someone you know appeared to feel embarrassed in public, self-conscious, guilty, left out, or disappointed about falling short of achievement. Make use of what you noticed in the first part of this exercise to imagine how the other person felt. Put yourself in that person's shoes and try to empathize with the painful feelings that must have come up.

EXERCISE 2—THE SHAME PARADIGMS

After reminders about what to avoid and what to do, this exercise lists the Shame Paradigms, followed by the shame vocabulary words that conclude the discussion of each paradigm in chapters 3 and 4. Memorizing these words is not important, but use this exercise to expand your concept of shame beyond the narrow way we usually define it. Descriptions of typical shame situations from those chapters no doubt stirred memories, many of them painful. Go deeper into those memories and explore the role of these feelings in your past.

Don't worry if you find that some of the words in one section also apply to another of the paradigms. The point of chapters 3 and 4 is not to define clear-cut categories but rather to use these paradigms to shed light on when and why each of us is likely to experience a member of the shame family of emotions.

Avoid Perfectionism

Answering the questions that follow might stir up some harsh feelings about yourself. Focusing intently on past shame experiences might intensify your self-criticism; bear in mind that these are universal experiences that everyone confronts on a daily basis. Feeling shame does not mean that you're defective and unworthy. It means you're human.

Include Others

After you go through this exercise, revisit the shame vocabulary, and try to recall occasions when other people you know appeared to feel rejected, left out, foolish, inadequate, and the like. The more people and situations you can recall, the less alone you will feel. Everyone feels shame on a regular basis.

Shame as Unrequited Love

Try to remember a time when you felt one or more of the following:

- hurt, rejected, or spurned
- unlovable or unworthy of love
- ugly (not attractive or fit enough)
- not masculine (or feminine) enough
- humiliated
- unwanted (not valued or uncared for)
- ignored or slighted
- unimportant, overlooked, or forgotten

Shame as Exclusion

In relation to a group, did you ever feel

- like an outsider or a loner?
- lonely and misunderstood?
- like you didn't belong?
- unpopular, uncool, or unwelcome?
- left out, shunned, or excluded?
- weird or strange?
- second tier, less important?
- that people were avoiding you?
- overlooked, forgotten, or invisible?

Shame as Unwanted Exposure

When you were out in public or at a social event, did you ever do something that made you feel

- embarrassed, shy, or bashful?
- vulnerable and exposed?

- foolish, ridiculous?
- like an idiot, a dope, or a jerk?
- mortified?
- as if you were a laughingstock?
- stupid or uninformed?
- awkward, inept, or clumsy?

Shame as Disappointed Expectation

Think of a time when you wanted to do or achieve something and fell short of your goal; did you feel

- let down, sad, or disappointed?
- defeated or discouraged?
- frustrated with yourself?
- that you couldn't make the grade?
- like a wimp or a dud?
- inept, feeble, or ineffective?
- inadequate or incompetent?
- like a failure or a loser?
- weak, undisciplined, or lacking in resolve?
- crestfallen, despondent?

EXERCISE 3—FACES FROM CHILDHOOD

Chapters 5 and 6 probably stirred up memories from your own child-hood and your relationship with your parents. The questions that follow will help you to explore those memories and understand the role of joy and shame in your upbringing. Focus on facial expressions rather than what might have been said or done.

1. What is your earliest memory from childhood? How old were you? Do you remember how you were feeling at the time? Can you recall the facial expressions of other people in your memory?

2. Did you feel that you were a source of joy to either of your parents? In retrospect is it easy or difficult to imagine them smiling at you? Do you recall whether their faces usually lit up when they saw you—when you came home from school, for example, or they returned from work? If you do have such memories, how does it make you feel today to recall your parents' joyful faces?

3. Can you recall seeing expressions of anger, disgust, or contempt on their faces, especially in response to something you may have said or done? Were those expressions mild or intense? Can you remember whether their facial expressions made you feel bad about your-self at the time? If you do have such memories, how does it make you feel today to recall your parents' faces?

4. If you have a collection of photos from your childhood, take some time to look through them. Because they're often posed and arti-ficial ("Everybody smile!"), old photos don't necessarily capture the emotional truth, but you might find some candid or spontaneous shots. Pay attention to the facial expressions. Who is smiling? Does anyone look sad or left out? Who looks displeased or angry? Do the facial expressions in those posed photos feel true, even if they're somewhat artificial?

5. Were you a source of joy to any other important figures from your childhood? Maybe you had a favorite teacher who smiled at you

when you came to class or grandparents who doted on you. Identify the person who took the most joy in your existence and try to recall how he or she made you feel.

Include Others

Whenever it feels safe and appropriate, ask the same questions of someone you trust and who might be open to a conversation on this topic. It might be a sibling or a close friend. Ask about the role of parental joy and shame in the other person's childhood; focus on facial expressions. What did you learn from completing this exercise that you might safely share with the other person? Do you have a photo you might show to your friend or relative, one that captures some emotional truth?

Author's Account

My own first memory is probably an imaginary recollection that nonetheless captures a truth. I would have been less than a year old at the time, not yet able to move on my own, resting in an infant seat placed on the kitchen counter. I am gazing up at the cabinets and ceiling, which are a pale green. I am alone.

My mother probably suffered from postpartum depression after I was born. I was the third child, the result of an unplanned pregnancy, and she was already overburdened by motherhood. When I try to imagine her smiling, I can call up only an image of her smirk, gaze averted, usually accompanied by one of her supposedly funny jibes delivered in a blunt sarcastic tone.

EXERCISE 4—WHAT ARE YOU AVOIDING?

From time to time most of us avoid situations that make us feel overly self-conscious. We may decline an invitation to a party where we don't know anyone. We will pick up fast food rather than dine alone in a restaurant. We might keep quiet amid a group of strangers.

Identify one such situation that you regularly avoid. Choose something that clearly involves one of the Shame Paradigms.

Now imagine yourself in that situation. Describe in as much detail as possible how you would feel. Do you fear that something unflattering would be revealed about you? Try to be specific. What would onlookers think if they observed you in that situation?

Does merely imagining this scenario stir up discomfort or anxiety? Does this exercise make you want to stop writing in your journal or pick up your cell phone to check the latest posts on Facebook? Try not to jump away.

Avoid Perfectionism

Be on the lookout for any harshness in your self-evaluation. Contempt might color your fantasy—either in your own thoughts or what you imagine other people would think about you. One way to counter such harsh and perfectionistic thoughts is to ask other people about their experiences.

Include Others

Choose a trusted friend or other safe person and ask whether she or he avoids the same situation. Many (if not most) people prefer not to eat alone in restaurants, for example; most of us do not like going to parties where we don't know anyone. Try to *normalize* the experience by connecting to other people who may feel the same way.

Author's Account

As an experiment a couple of years ago, I ate dinner alone at a restaurant, something I've always dreaded. I automatically avoided looking at the other diners because expressing interest in contact with them would expose me to potential shame. I tried to keep a neutral gaze as I looked ahead, without focusing on anyone else, or glancing from object to object. After a few minutes of discomfort I reached for my cell phone and felt much better.

I feel no need to become more shame resilient in this situation; my feelings seem perfectly reasonable and even normal. I prefer not to dine alone in restaurants and I don't have to if I don't want to!

Hold Yourself Accountable

Perhaps your tendency to avoid a potential shame experience prevents you from achieving important goals. You might not speak up at work, for example, and as a result your colleagues do not recognize that you are a creative thinker. If you are unhappy about the potentially self-defeating way you avoid certain situations, it might be better not to let yourself off the hook, as I have done with dining out alone. If so, make a note in your journal. In later exercises you will address goal setting and how to take gradual steps toward shame resilience and achieving your goals.

EXERCISE 5—THE ART OF THE APOLOGY

From time to time each of us does or says something for which we need to apologize, and an inability to do so reflects a denial of shame. We often rationalize our behavior, making excuses for ourselves, or blame the other person for our own insensitivity. We may insist it's no big deal and that we needn't apologize. The more we defend against shame in this way, the more we isolate ourselves from other people. Whenever we refuse to acknowledge our mistakes, we are unable to learn from our experience.

Hold Yourself Accountable

Identify a person whose feelings you may have hurt. It might be something small, like having forgotten a birthday; it might be something big, like having been unfaithful in a romantic relationship. You might have done something long ago that has bothered you for years, but don't let yourself off the hook by pretending that so much time has passed that the other person must have forgotten all about it.

Be specific:

- What, exactly, did you say or do and how do you imagine it affected the other person?
- Do you understand what motivated you at the time? Be honest about your reasons and frame your answer as accurately as you can.
- Did the act or omission violate your expectations for yourself? How do you think you ought to have behaved?

It's likely that your act or omission exposed the other person to some member of the shame family of emotions. Try to imagine how you might have felt if the positions were reversed. Try to recall another situation in which you felt that same emotion and what happened to make you feel that way.

Now write out an apology. Do *not* use the words *if* or *but*, as in "I'm sorry if I hurt your feelings," or "I know I stood you up for lunch but . . ." Take full responsibility for your own act or omission; don't make excuses or assign blame to anyone else. Allow yourself to feel guilty.

Avoid Perfectionism

All of us make mistakes and behave in insensitive ways from time to time, despite meaning well. Don't beat yourself up for having treated someone in an insensitive way. Instead consider what you can learn from this experience. How might you avoid making a similar mistake in the future?

Include Other People

Deliver the apology in person. It helps to have written it out in advance so you'll be clear on what you need to say. Focus on how the injured person probably felt and try not to become defensive if that person expresses hurt or anger after you apologize. Say you are sorry but do *not* ask for immediate forgiveness. Leaving room for the other person to forgive you in his own time and way demonstrates true remorse.

Notice whether you become defensive. If the other person acknowledges feeling angry, do you feel the urge to become indignant, insisting that she's making too big a deal about something petty?

"Look, I already said I'm sorry, okay?"

Do you want to blame the other person for something *they* may have done?

"I said I was sorry, but *you* always . . ."

Do you feel contempt rising in your throat?

"Now I wish I'd never brought it up. You're so touchy about everything!"

If you are like most people, including me, you may find that admitting fault and feeling the shame of Disappointed Expectation will activate your defenses. On the other hand, if you successfully complete the exercise, apologize in full, and keep your defensiveness in check, you will feel proud of yourself for being courageous and taking responsibility.

EXERCISE 6—WHEN WE DON'T WANT OTHER PEOPLE TO SAY IT

This exercise requires self-observation over time. To begin with, you will need to listen for any self-deprecating remarks you make to friends and colleagues—not the blatantly harsh or judgmental ones but the subtle kind that often go unnoticed because they're so common.

For example, to preempt a response that might shame them, many people preface voicing an opinion by saying something along the lines of "This is probably a bad idea, but . . ." They don't want to be told that their idea isn't a good one (Disappointed Expectation, Unwanted Exposure). Behind such preemption usually lies an area of insecurity or self-doubt:

> *Am I smart enough?*
> *Am I a creative person with interesting ideas?*
> *Do other people value my opinions?*

If you notice yourself making this type of self-deprecating remark, use it as an opportunity to explore what might be an area of special shame sensitivity for you. Typical areas of concern include one's physical appearance, intelligence, education level or general knowledge, and sexual attractiveness.

Avoid Perfectionism

As you tune in to such self-deprecating remarks, you might also begin to notice some extremely harsh thoughts, those with the potential to make you feel even worse about yourself. As a result you might want to shut down or disappear. Instead try to talk to other people whom you have noticed making similar remarks about themselves.

Include Others

While undertaking this exercise, you probably realized that other people qualify their opinions and suggestions in the same way. It's common. Think about which specific anxiety the other person's comment revealed. Was he afraid of rejection? Did she fear that her recommendation was half baked or not fully worked out? Did they worry that they weren't attractive? If you find that you share an area of concern and you feel safe enough, try having a conversation with the other person. You might find it a relief to learn you are not alone in your concerns. If you choose well, the other person might be fascinated to hear about the ways all of us try to control our experience of shame.

Author's Account

As I was finishing the last draft of this book, I watched a movie with my partner. As a young man Michael was an actor, and to this day he usually knows the names of most cast members in a stage play or movie.

"Who's that actor?" he asked, referring to the man appearing at that moment on the TV screen.

Billy Crudup, I thought, but I wasn't sure. Without even noticing what I was saying, I said, "It's not Billy Crudup."

"Yeah, that's who it is," Michael replied.

It took me a few minutes to realize what I had done: to prevent Michael from telling me that I was wrong, I disqualified my answer in advance.

It's a small thing; you might believe that I'm making a mountain out of a molehill, and I agree that my preemptive remark does not reflect an area of extreme shame sensitivity. But knowing the right answer has always been extremely important to me. As a child I compensated for profound feelings of shame by excelling academically, which meant always raising my hand in class to answer the teacher's question or acing a test because I'd studied hard and knew most of the answers or even all of them.

Knowing has always been part of my antidote to shame.

EXERCISE 7—DAILY FOCUS

The preceding six exercises should have raised your awareness of the shame family of emotions in your daily life and alerted you to the ways you might try to avoid, deny, or control your experience of shame. This exercise, and the ones that follow, will help you to develop the mind-set necessary for building self-esteem. Unlike the earlier exercises, these final four are not to be completed once and then put behind you. Each requires ongoing effort; together they will help you develop mental habits conducive to ongoing growth.

Building and maintaining self-esteem is a continuous process; we're never done with it—it's something like a garden that must be tended on a daily basis. You don't need to pay nonstop attention to your garden, but at some point each day it must become the object of your focus. In our age of nonstop distraction (Facebook, texting, your iPod, television, and social life, in addition to the demands of work and family), it's easy to lose sight of your expectations, to get so caught up in your day that you forget what you intended to do and remember it days later. This exercise asks you to clear a space *each day* and develop a regular practice for bringing yourself into focus.

Set aside a specific amount of time (as little as five minutes) and commit to keeping it free from distraction. Leave your cell phone in another room. Find a place to be alone, with the TV off and no music playing. In the three exercises that follow, you will expand your daily focus to include specific goals and expectations, but begin by asking yourself a few simple questions:

- *Is there something specific I would like to accomplish today? Given my other commitments, how much can I realistically expect to get done?*
- *Was there anything I meant to do yesterday that I didn't complete? Can I continue pursuing it today?*
- *Do I need to reach out to any of my friends or family members, to nurture my important relationships and let them know they matter to me?*

These daily questions will bring your intentions and expectations into focus. They'll also remind you of the significant others who influence how you feel about yourself. Building self-esteem is an interpersonal experience; it's important to maintain connection with the people who matter most to you, because achievement without connection means little.

These questions are only suggestions (they're the ones I ask myself), but I believe them to be crucial. Add or substitute others, as you see fit, provided you develop an ongoing daily practice.

Hold Yourself Accountable

Try to ask yourself these questions every day. No matter how busy you are, you can always set aside five minutes during each twenty-four-hour period to check in with yourself, even though you will inevitably forget from time to time. If you intend to undertake the remaining exercises, you will need to make this commitment.

Avoid Perfectionism

Do not expect too much of yourself and do not beat yourself up for not doing what you intended. The goal of this exercise is to help you develop an awareness of yourself as a person with ongoing intentions and expectations, not to set up an exacting set of standards you can't meet. If you forget to check in with yourself one day, don't view it as failure. Simply resolve to remember your intention the next day. Perhaps you might put a note on the refrigerator, or a Post-it on the bathroom mirror, as a reminder.

Author's Account

I'm an early riser and usually wake up long before anyone else in the house. I usually check my emails and read the news on my cell phone with my first cup of coffee; I set my phone aside for my second cup as I think ahead to my day.

EXERCISE 8—LEARNING FROM SHAME

When shame is not a toxic experience or based on internal or external demands for perfection, it often has something important to teach us about our standards and values—the person we expect ourselves to be. This exercise will help you to develop a core habit of mind essential for developing true self-esteem—the ability to listen to and sometimes learn from your encounters with the shame family of emotions.

In chapter 20, I described one such experience. In the days after a heated debate with my friend Randy, the memory of ways I had expressed myself kept surfacing. When I finally stopped mentally defending myself and examined how I felt, I realized I had violated my own standards for behavior (Disappointed Expectation). That realization prompted me to apologize and to try harder next time not to be so combative.

Perhaps you have uncomfortable memories like mine. From time to time you might recollect something you said or did that you can't quite let go of. Whenever you remember it, you might feel the need to justify yourself in your thoughts.

Focus on one such memory. Based on what you have learned about the ways all of us try to avoid, deny, or control our encounters with shame, search for signs of defensiveness. Do you repeatedly justify your actions, perhaps in the form of an internal argument? Do you blame someone else for your behavior or instead make light of it? Do you beat yourself up by calling yourself names, as if you have committed a crime for which you must be punished? All these defensive reactions to shame will prevent you from learning something from that experience.

What might that feeling of shame teach you about yourself? Not all encounters with shame contain lessons, but many of them reflect an appropriate and understandable feeling of disappointment in ourselves. Can you connect that memory with other instances when you might have behaved in similar ways? Try to discern a pattern. Be humble: all of us have shortcomings, foibles, or areas that need improvement. How might you use what you've learned to earn your self-respect next time?

Avoid Perfectionism

The purpose of this exercise is not to make you feel bad about yourself. Everyone makes mistakes; from time to time we behave in ways we don't respect or that violate our core values. If you harshly berate yourself, or punish yourself for having erred, you'll be unable to learn from the experience. Don't make unrealistic vows to never again make the same mistake. Recognize trends or tendencies in your personality (they won't go away) and commit to doing a little better the next time.

Hold Yourself Accountable

Earlier exercises will have sensitized you to the shame family of emotions. Going forward, be on the lookout for the shame experience that contains a lesson. They occur more often than you might think. When we disappoint ourselves or fall short of nonharsh expectation, we will experience shame; if we can listen to that shame rather than defend against it, we may learn something about our own standards and values. Shame sometimes brings intention into focus and may help us to do better in achieving our goals.

The ability to learn from shame is an essential skill in building self-esteem.

EXERCISE 9—BUILDING PRIDE

Setting and achieving goals allows us to build pride, a core element in authentic self-esteem. This exercise will help you to define and reach realistic goals that will contribute to your feelings of self-respect.

Avoid Perfectionism

If you have set goals for yourself in the past but failed to reach them, you might have set the bar too high and held perfectionistic expectations. Look back on your past disappointments and ask yourself whether your goals were unrealistic or too exacting. Without being overly critical, make an assessment of your strengths and limitations before setting a goal.

Start Small

Because these exercises are designed to help you develop habits of mind that will promote self-esteem, begin with goals you can easily achieve and then build on them. If you have longer-term goals, break them down into smaller steps that you can achieve one by one. Completing each step can be a source of pride that gives you the confidence to try for a little bit more the next time. People who want to take part in a marathon don't try to run twenty-six miles on the first day of their training program. Runners typically develop a plan that spans months and begins with a brief and achievable goal.

Expect Setbacks

If you find yourself unable to complete a goal, you will inevitably encounter the shame of Disappointed Expectation; rather than beating yourself up as a failure, however, use it as an opportunity for self-exploration. Was the goal unrealistic? What emotional or psychological issues might have stood in the way of success? Perhaps you need to take a step back and break down your goal into smaller stages.

While many boosters in the realm of self-esteem encourage you to dream big and aim high, I suggest you find ways to take pride in smaller achievements. I don't mean you should always settle for less or think small, but starting with grandiose plans for your future will ensure that you don't complete them.

Hold Yourself Accountable

We often fail to achieve our goals because we begin with muddy expectations or fail to specify what we want to achieve. Be clear about your goals; it will probably help to write them down in your notebook and refer to them regularly. If you have identified a longer-term goal and broken it down into stages, define a realistic time line for each one. Be clear on your intentions and what you'd like to achieve.

As part of achievement, you will need to develop habits of self-discipline and reflection. Becoming more self-disciplined and focused is a primary goal that everyone should try to achieve; it, too, begins by starting small. All the opportunities for distraction available today erode our ability to focus on other important issues, so you may need to limit your exposure to them, but don't decide to go cold turkey on Facebook and Twitter.

Here's an achievable goal you might consider: *I will not open up Facebook or check my email until I've undertaken my daily focus* (exercise 7). Expect to feel the pull of habit—your former routine of picking up your smartphone first thing each morning. Listen for the inevitable excuses— not to follow through or to put off starting until tomorrow—that you will make for yourself. You might instead decide, *I will allow myself only ten minutes on the Internet each morning before I begin my daily focus.*

Include Others

Sometimes we do better when we share a goal with someone who aspires to achieve the same thing. You can support each other as you strive toward your goals, sharing your feelings of frustration and disappointment along the way while offering encouragement to try harder. Like those runners in the New York Marathon, you may find you can go a greater distance alongside someone who cheers you on. You probably have friends who have complained about how much time their social media habit consumes; you might do better at curtailing that habit if you work together.

You will need to choose carefully, of course. Do not align yourself with someone unlikely to work diligently toward your shared goal or who will use your inevitable setbacks as an opportunity to feel superior to you.

Author's Account

Because I have found I am unable to write a personal narrative in a journal, I instead keep a notebook with a numbered list of things I'd like to accomplish. Sometimes an item is as simple as "Call Kate"—a reminder of my desire to nurture close friendships rather than lose touch because I'm so caught up in my work. Goals and intentions don't need to be major ones to merit your ongoing attention.

I look at the list in my notebook every week or so. I'm often surprised by how much on that list I've forgotten.

EXERCISE 10—SHARING JOY

When we share pride in achievement with supportive people in our lives, it consolidates and strengthens our feelings of self-respect. Because self-esteem grows within an interpersonal context, this exercise asks you to speak pride and share your joy with carefully chosen friends, family members, or romantic partners. Focus on small achievements, the ones you undertook and completed in exercise 9. You do not need to disclose every step of your journey, but when you feel proud of reaching a goal, find ways to share your pride with someone else.

Include Others

Choose carefully. In earlier exercises you probably identified a few individuals whom you found were open to and interested in discussing what you have learned from this book and, in particular, your growing awareness of the role played by the shame family of emotions in everyday life. These individuals are most likely psychologically minded people, perhaps invested in their own personal development goals and not trying too hard to make their life look perfect from the outside.

When considering a candidate, ask yourself this question: *Does this person's face light up at the sight of me?* I don't mean in an overblown or idealized way, but are they obviously happy to see you? It's important to choose someone who takes joy in their relationship with you and who has demonstrated an ongoing interest in your life. In my experience such friends are few and far between; everyone else is an acquaintance. I have also learned that people who feel reasonably content with their lives and have enjoyed some degree of success in achieving their own goals are better able to honor the achievements of others.

As part of this exercise pay attention to the other people you value and what they are striving to achieve. A friend may be taking night classes for career advancement, trying to develop a gym habit and get in better shape, or pursuing a hobby as a creative outlet. How might you honor their achievements? Some people find it hard to speak pride, but they usually take great pleasure when a friend notices and acknowledges their achievements.

Avoid Perfectionism

Don't expect too much . . . from other people. When I speak pride to friends I trust, they usually smile and say something supportive like "That's great! I'm so happy for you." I hope your friends will do the same, and that may be the end of it. They may also ask questions that reflect a deeper interest in what you're doing, which is the most gratifying way they may share your joy in achievement. You might model the sort of response you'd like to receive by drawing out your friends when they speak pride, probing more deeply into their goals.

As adults we can't expect other people to feel about us the way besotted parents optimally feel about their babies, but the most nurturing confidants are those who are proud to number us among their friends. You'll feel more gratified when you receive support from someone you respect and whose achievements you also honor. Don't look to them to validate what you've accomplished, however; when we locate our self-worth in the opinions of others, we undermine our hard-won feelings of pride by making them contingent on approval.

Hold Yourself Accountable

In part because of societal injunctions against it ("Pride goeth before a fall"), speaking pride is not always easy. Be cautious but brave. Be humble, too, and avoid bragging. Bear in mind that other people, despite what you intend, may feel shamed when you speak pride. It would be ill-advised to describe your pride to someone struggling unsuccessfully in a similar area. Tact, as Wurmser said, means understanding another person's proximity to shame.

Honor the achievements of others whenever you can. Make a habit of it. When I see pleasure on the face of someone I've praised, it also makes me feel good about myself. Having a generous spirit contributes to our feelings of self-respect. Because building true self-esteem takes place within an interpersonal context, sharing joy must be mutual. Unlike narcissistic striving, true self-esteem wants other people to feel good about themselves too.

ACKNOWLEDGMENTS

The hour completes the day, the writer completes his work.
(Terminat hora diem; terminat auctor opus.)
—CHRISTOPHER MARLOWE, *THE TRAGICAL HISTORY OF DOCTOR FAUSTUS*

I first read the Marlowe epigraph when I was eighteen years old, in a class on Renaissance drama with the eminent Shakespearean scholar A. R. "Al" Braunmuller, then at the beginning of his career. The quotation comes at the end of *Doctor Faustus* as a coda to the play. One day Al began class by reading it aloud.

"Why is this here?" he asked. "What is the author saying to us?"

Al's somewhat impatient brilliance could be intimidating; most of my classmates looked down at their open notebooks. Mustering my courage, I finally raised my hand and said, "It almost feels like he's surprised by the play he wrote, like it turned out better than he expected."

Al gave me an ironic smile. "While I don't like to encourage such interpretations of a writer's psyche, I think you may be on to something there, Joe."

I hadn't thought about Marlowe's coda to *Doctor Faustus* in decades, but as I neared the end of this book it resurfaced in memory. *Shame* has surprised me. As I conducted my research and formulated my ideas, the subject matter kept growing in scope until I found myself writing a book that seemed richer and more meaningful than I had originally envisioned. At the end of this long day I feel it has turned out better than I imagined and hoped it would be. In the language I've used to describe shame and the development of pride, my book has met and exceeded my expectations.

When I originally envisioned the client stories at the core of this book, I intended them to rise above the usual dry case study—I wanted them to be longer, more vivid accounts that would read like compelling fiction. These case studies surprised me too. While drafting them, I allowed myself the freedom to describe my own experience—my thoughts and feelings while in the room with my clients, insights I've gleaned during the past thirty-five years. In the process *Shame* has turned out to be a kind of memoir of my career as a psychotherapist. I'm proud of my work and grateful to the many clients who have trusted me to help them.

Even when we belong to a writers' group, writing can be a lonely experience because we usually write in solitude. Like most writers, I enjoy such solitude, but I once complained to my friend Rochelle Gurstein, then a graduate student in history, about the loneliness of writing. In reply she described the sense of communion she felt with intellectuals whose work she respected, most of whom she'd never met, some of whom, like Hannah Arendt, were dead. Writing history might be a lonely experience, she told me, but if you work hard and achieve something you respect, you can count yourself as part of a tradition. You can feel that you belong to a line of thinkers spanning centuries.

The research I conducted as background for *Shame*, the profound books I read, brought me into contact with many fine minds. I never met Silvan Tomkins (who is deceased), Donald Nathanson, and Allan Schore, although I've developed an important internal relationship with each of them and their work. While formulating my ideas on the inevitability of shame and how it may coexist with pride, Andrew Solomon, who has written extensively about shame and stigma, was never far from my thoughts. I've spent years thinking about the same subjects that other researchers have passionately pursued for decades, and I'm proud to belong to their tradition.

I'm also proud to be a member of Laurel Goldman's Thursday afternoon writing class in Chapel Hill, to which I've belonged for the last eighteen years. When I moved away from North Carolina in 2015, I installed a videoconference system so I could continue to connect by Skype for our weekly meetings. As I was drafting this book, I read every word of the manuscript to Laurel and my classmates, the most sensitive and insightful critics I've ever known. Christina Askounis, Angela Davis-Gardner, Peter Filene, and Peggy Payne all helped me to hone my message and polish my prose. I'm deeply grateful for their advice and encouragement.

Along the way, friends and family members also read this manuscript and cheered me on. Sam Bradbury, William Burgo, Carolyn Fisher, Anastasia Piatakhina Giré, Peg Streep, and Cathryn Taylor offered their support and suggested ways to improve the book. My partner, Michael Eha, read each chapter as I completed it. The challenge of being married to a writer and reading his work calls for enthusiastic and heartfelt support more than critical insight. Michael excels at the job.

A special thanks to my colleague Susan Tesch, who introduced me to the work of Allan Schore and urged me to root my book in hard science.

I would also like to thank Karen Wolny, executive editor at St. Martin's Press, for believing in me and my book, and for her suggestions for improving the manuscript. Thanks also to Joel Fotinos, who stepped into Karen's shoes when she left St. Martin's Press. My longtime agent, Gillian MacKenzie, is that rare combination of good taste, strong writing skills, business acumen, and insight into what sells in the publishing world. She helped me refine the book proposal with her acute insights and marketing savvy.

Midway through the drafting of this book, as I began to feel confident I would fulfill my expectations for it, my old friends Sue Jarrell and Sherry Kinlaw came to dinner one night. Because I'd been thinking all day about the importance of sharing joy, I decided to put belief into practice. Somewhat awkwardly, because speaking pride in this way was new territory, I announced: "I'm really happy because I know I'm writing a good book." To see the joy break out upon their dear faces, to hear the genuine interest in the questions that followed, deepened my feelings of pride.

As the manuscript was nearing completion, my friend Kate came to visit. Not long after I told her the embarrassing story about my argument with Randy, I also shared my feelings of pride in this book and the pride I feel in achieving a gratifying level of professional and financial success. As I talked, I could see the play of mixed emotions across her face. Because Kate has spent many years in therapy, with a man to whom I referred her long ago, we speak to each other with a level of depth and candor I share with few people.

"When I tell you that I feel envious," she told me, "I know you'll understand it's the good kind of envy. I'm truly happy for you, Joe. I also want the same things for myself." At that time Kate was facing some now-or-never decisions in her life; she wanted to make good choices and find herself in a place similar to mine several years in the future. It's a rare friend who knows herself well enough to make such a nuanced disclosure about her emotions. I've known Kate for more than thirty years; the history of our friendship tracks our respective weddings, the births of our children, divorce, and life thereafter. A friendship of such depth and duration is a source of both pride and joy.

In my middle age I have found that marriage to a man I love and admire, who loves and respects me in return, allows me to share my joy in achievement in the deepest way possible. Michael never competes with me, or feels threatened by my accomplishments, in part because he has led such an enormously rich and successful life himself—as a young actor on Broadway and London's West End; as an accomplished horseman who trained horses for the U.S. Equestrian Team and took his own horse to the Olympic trials; as a producer of ad campaigns and TV commercials that have won Palme d'Or awards at Cannes; and as an independent rep for film directors, with a sterling reputation in his field.

When we first moved in together, Michael wholeheartedly embraced the role of third parent to three young children. The improbability of our finding each other in Chapel Hill after both our first marriages collapsed—the Broadway actor–ad exec from New York, the psychoanalyst from Los Angeles—is the greatest piece of luck to befall me in my life. Our marriage fills me with pride, joy, and gratitude.

NOTES

INTRODUCTION
1. Nathanson, *Shame and Pride*, 21.
2. Bradshaw, *Healing the Shame That Binds You*, 30.
3. M. Lewis, *Shame, the Exposed Self*, 124.
4. Broucek, *Shame and the Self*, 7.

ONE: THE SHAME FAMILY OF EMOTIONS
1. M. Lewis, *Shame, the Exposed Self*, 83.
2. Tangney and Fischer, *Self-Conscious Emotions*.
3. H. Lewis, *Shame and Guilt in Neurosis*, 30.
4. Tomkins, *Affect Imagery Consciousness*, 351.

TWO: THE VALUE OF SHAME
1. Izard, *Psychology of Emotions*, 17.
2. In *Affect Imagery Consciousness* Tomkins holds that affects occur along a spectrum of intensity; he usually identifies them with a pair of names, one from each end of the spectrum—for example, shame-humiliation.
3. Tomkins, *Affect Imagery Consciousness*, 5.
4. Shields, "There's an Evolutionary Reason Humans Developed the Ability to Feel Shame." See also Sznycer et al., "Shame Closely Tracks the Threat of Devaluation by Others, Even Across Cultures."
5. Elias, *Civilizing Process*.
6. I have borrowed and simplified this analogy from Donald Nathanson, who uses it in *Shame and Pride*, pp. 26–29, to explain how the affect system operates.

7. Burgo, "Shame Has Fallen Out of Fashion but It Can Be a Force for Good."

8. Jacquet, *Is Shame Necessary?*, 26.

9. Cillizza, "Donald Trump Keeps Getting Things Wrong."

10. Lynd, *On Shame and the Search for Identity*, 20.

11. Twenge and Campbell, *Narcissism Epidemic*.

12. See, for example, Tangney and Fischer, *Self-Conscious Emotions*.

THREE: UNLOVED AND LEFT OUT

1. Winnicott, "Basis for Self in Body."

2. H. Lewis, *Shame and Guilt in Neurosis*, 16.

3. See, for example, McClellan, *Human Motivation*.

4. Nathanson, *Shame and Pride*, 220.

FOUR: EXPOSED AND DISAPPOINTED

1. Broucek, *Shame and the Self*, 6.

2. Gurstein, *Repeal of Reticence*.

3. Lynd, *On Shame and the Search for Identity*, 31.

4. Ibid., 43–44.

5. M. Lewis, *Shame, the Exposed Self*, 29.

6. Brown, *I Thought It Was Just Me (but It Isn't)*, xxiii.

FIVE: JOY AND THE BIRTH OF SELF-ESTEEM

1. Schore, *Affect Regulation and the Origin of the Self*, 98.

2. White, *New First Three Years of Life*, 263.

3. Gianino and Tronick, "Mutual Regulation Model."

4. Schore, *Affect Regulation and the Origin of the Self*, 143.

5. Tronick, *Neurobehavioral and Social-Emotional Development of Infants and Children*, 173.

6. James Grotstein, foreword to Schore, *Affect Regulation and the Origin of the Self*, xxv.

7. Tronick, *Neurobehavioral and Social-Emotional Development of Infants and Children*, 173, 174.

8. Kaufman, *Psychology of Shame*, 79.

SIX: SHAME AND THE GROWTH OF SELF-ESTEEM

1. Power and Chapieski, "Childrearing and Impulse Control in Toddlers," 272.

2. Izard, *Psychology of Emotions*, 349.

3. M. Lewis, *Shame, the Exposed Self*, 110–11.

4. Schore, *Affect Regulation and the Origin of the Self*, 230.

NINE: PROMISCUITY AND ADDICTION

1. Herek et al., "Correlates of Internalized Homophobia in a Community Sample of Lesbians and Gay Men."

TEN: AVOIDING SHAME IN EVERYDAY LIFE

1. Wurmser, *Mask of Shame*, 49, 82–83.
2. Broucek, *Shame and the Self*, 70.
3. Goffman, *Presentation of Self in Everyday Life*, 1–2.
4. Moran, *Shrinking Violets*, 41.
5. Ibid.
6. Wurmser, *Mask of Shame*, 50.
7. Moran, *Shrinking Violets*, 116, 133.
8. Nathanson, *Shame and Pride*, 356.
9. Wurmser, *Mask of Shame*, 29.

FOURTEEN: DENYING SHAME IN EVERYDAY LIFE

1. Broucek, *Shame and the Self*, 59.
2. Carnegie, *How to Win Friends and Influence People*, 5.
3. Malkin, *Rethinking Narcissism*.

SEVENTEEN: MASOCHISM

1. As Broucek explains, "It is when one is trying to relate to the other as a subject but feels objectified that one is apt to experience shame." Broucek, *Shame and the Self*, 47.

EIGHTEEN: CONTROLLING SHAME IN EVERYDAY LIFE

1. Piers and Singer, *Shame and Guilt*, 26.

NINETEEN: SHAME DEFIANCE AND NARROW IDENTITY

1. Broucek, *Shame and the Self*, 81.
2. Goffman, *Stigma*, 2.
3. Ibid., 23.
4. Ibid., 112.
5. Solomon, *Far from the Tree*, 62.
6. Ibid., 56, quoting *Inside Deaf Culture* (2005).
7. Goffman, *Stigma*, 113.

TWENTY: SHAME RESILIENCE AND EXPANDING IDENTITY

1. Brown, *I Thought It Was Just Me (but It Isn't)*, 22, 23.
2. Brown, *Daring Greatly*, 35–37.

3. Brown, *I Thought It Was Just Me (but It Isn't)*, 130.

4. Nathanson, *Shame and Pride*, 20–21, 391, 394.

5. H. Lewis, *Shame and Guilt in Neurosis*, 203.

6. M. Lewis, *Shame, the Exposed Self*, 131.

TWENTY-ONE: BUILDING PRIDE

1. This quotation comes from the subtitle of Brené Brown's book *Gifts of Imperfection*.

2. Broucek, "Efficacy in Infancy."

3. Nathanson, *Shame and Pride*, 83, 84.

4. Branden, *Six Pillars of Self-Esteem*, 60, 100.

5. Nathanson, *Shame and Pride*, 84.

6. Brown, *I Thought It Was Just Me (but It Isn't)*, 204.

TWENTY-TWO: SHARING JOY

1. Wurmser, *Mask of Shame*, 285–286.

2. Quoted in Solomon, *Far from the Tree*, 175.

3. Streep, *Daughter Detox*, 212.

4. Streep, *Mean Mothers*.

5. Quoted in Solomon, *Far from the Tree*, 174.

BIBLIOGRAPHY

Bradshaw, John. *Healing the Shame That Binds You.* Deerfield Beach, FL: Health Communications, 1988.

Branden, Nathaniel. *The Six Pillars of Self-Esteem: The Definitive Work on Self-Esteem by the Leading Pioneer in the Field.* New York: Bantam, 1994.

Broucek, Francis J. "Efficacy in Infancy," *International Journal of Psychoanalysis* 60 (1979): 311–16.

———. *Shame and the Self.* New York: Guilford, 1991.

Brown, Brené. *Daring Greatly: How the Courage to Be Vulnerable Transforms the Way We Live, Love, Parent, and Lead.* New York: Avery, 2012.

———. *The Gifts of Imperfection: Let Go of Who You Think You're Supposed to Be and Embrace Who You Are.* Center City, MN: Hazelden, 2010.

———. *I Thought It Was Just Me (but It Isn't): Making the Journey from "What Will People Think?" to "I Am Enough."* New York: Avery, 2008.

Burgo, Joseph. "Shame Has Fallen Out of Fashion, but It Can Be a Force for Good," op-ed, *The Washington Post,* November 17, 2017.

Cain, Susan. *Quiet: The Power of Introverts in a World That Can't Stop Talking.* New York: Broadway, 2013.

Carnegie, Dale. *How to Win Friends and Influence People.* 1936. New York: Simon & Schuster, 2009.

Cillizza, Chris. "Donald Trump Keeps Getting Things Wrong. And There's Not Much We Can Do About It," *The Washington Post,* March 21, 2017, https://www .washingtonpost.com/news/the-fix/wp/2017/03/21/donald-trump-keeps -getting-things-wrong-and-theres-not-much-we-can-do-about-it/?noredirect =on&utm_term=.572550750478.

Elias, Norbert. *The Civilizing Process*. 1994. Malden, MA: Blackwell, 2000.

Erikson, Erik H. *Identity: Youth and Crisis*. New York: W. W. Norton, 1968.

Gianino, Andrew and Ed Tronick. "The Mutual Regulation Model: The Infant's Self and Interactive Regulation, Coping, and Defensive Capacities," in T. Field, P. McCabe. & N. Schneiderman, eds., *Stress and Coping Across Development*. Hillsdale, NJ: Erlbaum, 1988.

Goffman, Ervin. *The Presentation of Self in Everyday Life*. New York: Anchor, 1959.

———. *Stigma: Notes on the Management of Spoiled Identity*. New York: Simon & Schuster, 1963.

Goldberg, Carl. *Understanding Shame*. Northvale, NJ: Jason Aronson, 1991.

Gurstein, Rochelle. *The Repeal of Reticence: A History of America's Cultural and Legal Struggles over Free Speech, Obscenity, Sexual Liberation, and Modern Art*. New York: Hill & Wang, 1996.

Herek, G. M. et al. "Correlates of Internalized Homophobia in a Community Sample of Lesbians and Gay Men," *Journal of the Gay and Lesbian Medical Association* 2 (1998): 17–25, as quoted in the abstract of this article: http://psychology.ucdavis .edu/rainbow/html/ihpitems.html.

Izard, Carroll E. *The Psychology of Emotions*. New York: Plenum, 1991.

Jacquet, Jennifer. *Is Shame Necessary? New Uses for an Old Tool*. New York: Vintage, 2016.

Kaufman, Gershen. *The Psychology of Shame: Theory and Treatment of Shame-Based Syndromes*. New York: Springer, 1989.

Lewis, Helen Block. *Shame and Guilt in Neurosis*. New York: International Universities Press, 1971.

Lewis, Michael. *Shame, the Exposed Self*. New York: Free Press, 1992.

Lynd, Helen Merrell. *On Shame and the Search for Identity*. New York: Harvest Books, 1958.

Malkin, Craig. *Rethinking Narcissism: The Bad—and Surprising Good—About Feeling Special*. New York: Harper Wave, 2015.

McClellan, David. *Human Motivation*. Glenview, IL: Scott Foresman, 1983.

Moran, Joe. *Shrinking Violets: The Secret Life of Shyness*. New Haven, CT: Yale University Press, 2017.

Nathanson, Donald. *Shame and Pride: Affect, Sex, and the Birth of the Self*. New York: W. W. Norton, 1992.

Piers, Gerhart and Milton B. Singer. *Shame and Guilt: A Psychoanalytic and a Cultural Study*. Mansfield Centre, CT: Martino, 2015.

Power, T. G. and M. L. Chapieski. "Childrearing and Impulse Control in Toddlers: A Naturalistic Investigation," *Developmental Psychology* 22 (1986): 271–75.

Ronson, Jon. *So You've Been Publicly Shamed*. New York: Riverhead, 2015.

Schore, Allan. *Affect Regulation and the Origin of the Self: The Neurobiology of Emotional Development*. Hillsdale, NJ: Lawrence Erlbaum, 1994.

Shields, Jesslyn. "There's an Evolutionary Reason Humans Developed the Ability to Feel Shame," How Stuff Works, March 25, 2016, https://health.howstuffworks.com/mental-health/human-nature/why-humans-evolved-feel-shame.htm.

Solomon, Andrew. *Far from the Tree: Parents, Children, and the Search for Identity.* New York: Scribner, 2012.

Streep, Peg. *Daughter Detox: Recovering from an Unloving Mother and Reclaiming Your Life.* New York: Ile d'Espoir, 2017.

———. *Mean Mothers: Overcoming the Legacy of Hurt.* New York: William Morrow, 2009.

Sznycer, Daniel et al. "Shame Closely Tracks the Threat of Devaluation by Others, Even Across Cultures," *Proceedings of the National Academy of Sciences of the United States of America* 113, no. 10 (March 8, 2016): 2625–30.

Tangney, June Price and Kurt W. Fischer. *Self-Conscious Emotions: The Psychology of Shame, Guilt, Embarrassment, and Pride.* New York: Guilford, 1995.

Tomkins, Silvan S. *Affect Imagery Consciousness, the Complete Edition.* New York: Springer, 2008.

Tronick, Edward. *The Neurobehavioral and Social-Emotional Development of Infants and Children.* New York: W. W. Norton, 2007.

Twenge, Jean M. and W. Keith Campbell. *The Narcissism Epidemic: Living in the Age of Entitlement.* New York: Atria, 2009.

White, Burton L. *The New First Three Years of Life: The Completely Revised and Updated Edition of the Parenting Classic.* New York: Fireside, 1995.

Winnicott, D. W. "Basis for Self in Body," *International Journal of Child Psychotherapy* 1, no. 1 (1972): 7–16.

Wurmser, Léon. *The Mask of Shame.* Baltimore: Johns Hopkins University Press, 1981.